The Boxing Film

Screening Sports

*Series Editors: Lester D. Friedman, Emeritus
Professor of Media and Society, Hobart and William Smith Colleges,
and Aaron Baker, Professor of Film and Media Studies,
Arizona State University*

Sports and media have had a long and productive relationship. Media have transformed sports into a global obsession, while sports in turn have provided a constant flow of events to cover and stories to tell. This symbiosis with media has both sold sports as entertainment and enabled them to comment on issues and identities in contemporary culture. Movies tell some of the most insightful stories about sports, which have also been defined throughout their history by a convergent media landscape that includes print, radio, television, and digital technologies. Books in the Screening Sports series will focus on the relationship between sports, film, and other media forms and the social and culture issues raised by that complex collaboration.

The Boxing Film

A Cultural and Transmedia History

TRAVIS VOGAN

Rutgers University Press
New Brunswick, Camden, and Newark, New Jersey, and London

Library of Congress Cataloging-in-Publication Data

Names: Vogan, Travis, author.
Title: The boxing film : a cultural and transmedia history / Travis Vogan.
Description: First edition. | New Brunswick ; Camden ; Newark, New Jersey ; London :
    Rutgers University Press, 2020. | Series: Screening sports | Includes bibliographical
    references, filmography, and index.
Identifiers: LCCN 2020004920 | ISBN 9781978801356 (paperback) |
    ISBN 9781978801363 (cloth) | ISBN 9781978801370 (epub) |
    ISBN 9781978801387 (mobi) | ISBN 9781978801394 (pdf)
Subjects: LCSH: Boxing films—United States—History and criticism.
Classification: LCC PN1995.9.B69 V64 2020 | DDC 791.43/6579—dc23
LC record available at https://lccn.loc.gov/2020004920

A British Cataloging-in-Publication record for this book is available from the British Library.

Copyright © 2021 by Travis Vogan

All rights reserved

No part of this book may be reproduced or utilized in any form or by any means, electronic or
mechanical, or by any information storage and retrieval system, without written permission
from the publisher. Please contact Rutgers University Press, 106 Somerset Street, New Brunswick,
NJ 08901. The only exception to this prohibition is "fair use" as defined by U.S. copyright law.

♾ The paper used in this publication meets the requirements of the American National
Standard for Information Sciences—Permanence of Paper for Printed Library Materials,
ANSI Z39.48-1992.

www.rutgersuniversitypress.org

Manufactured in the United States of America

For Ozzie.
Please don't box.

Contents

	Introduction: The Boxing Film over Time and across Media	I
1	The Boxing Film through the Golden Age of Sports Media	9
2	St. Joe Louis, Surrounded by Films	33
3	TV Fighting and Fighting TV in the 1950s	59
4	Muhammad Ali, *The Super Fight*, and Closed-Circuit Exhibition	75
5	The 1970s, *Rocky*, and the Shadow of Ali	91
6	HBO Sports: Docu-Branding Boxing	III
7	Protecting Boxing with the Boxing Film	129
	Conclusion: Handling the Rules	147
	Filmography	159
	Acknowledgments	163
	Notes	165
	Index	181

The Boxing Film

Introduction

The Boxing Film over Time and across Media

> There's more boxing movies than all
> other sports films put together. I've got a
> list I could read to you, but I've got to be
> someplace by 5 p.m. next Friday.
> —Bert Sugar, boxing historian

As one of popular culture's most popular arenas, sports are often the subject of cinematic storytelling—from Hollywood blockbusters to independent documentaries. People like sports. People like movies. People will pay to watch movies about sports—*Pride of the Yankees* (Sam Wood, 1942), *Hoosiers* (David Anspaugh, 1986), *Any Given Sunday* (Oliver Stone, 1999), *Bend It Like Beckham* (Gurinder Chadha, 2002), and so on. But boxing films are special. There are more movies about boxing, by a healthy margin, than about any other sport, and boxing accompanied and aided the medium's late nineteenth-century emergence as a popular mass entertainment. Many of cinema's most celebrated directors—a group that includes Busby Berkeley, Tod Browning, Michael Curtiz, Alfred Hitchcock, John Huston, Stanley Kubrick, Oscar Micheaux, Martin Scorsese, and King Vidor—have made boxing films. And while the production of other types of sports movies generally corresponds with the current popularity of their subject, boxing films continue to be made regularly even after the sport has wilted from its once prominent position in the sports hierarchy of the United States. This book explores why boxing has so consistently

1

fascinated cinema, and popular media culture more generally, by tracing how boxing movies inform the sport's meanings and uses from the late nineteenth century to the early twenty-first century.

Boxing uniquely lends itself to enduring myths about identity, achievement, and violence. "What could be more basic than making a living by hitting another person on the head until one of you falls or stops?" asks *Raging Bull* (1980) director Martin Scorsese. "I've always had a feeling for boxing," echoes *Rocky* (1976) creator and star Sylvester Stallone. "It's barbaric but it's basic, it's pure, it's the natural man and it lends itself to film."[1] Boxing is certainly basic— far more so than increasingly technologized team sports like football and baseball—but it is not natural. Prizefighting is carefully staged to maximize the drama and gore that will drive fans to see live competitions as well as the stories Scorsese and Stallone use the sport to create. While representations of boxing span media, film scholar Leger Grindon maintains that "no art has shaped our perception of the boxer as motion pictures."[2] These films do not simply depict boxing, of course, but also manufacture versions of it that color how the sport is understood. *Rocky* protagonist Rocky Balboa is as well known as any actual prizefighter and is deployed just as often to make sense of the sport and those who practice it. Stallone and his character are even in the International Boxing Hall of Fame alongside Jack Dempsey, Joe Louis, and Muhammad Ali.[3]

Boxing is commonly depicted as an activity that allows the disadvantaged, even when faced with unfair and corrupt circumstances, to improve their social station. If fighters are on the wrong end of the crooked fight game—a scenario that occurs more often than not in boxing films—they can prove their moral and physical mettle in the singularly meritocratic space the boxing ring provides. This physical and spiritual valor—or body and soul, to use boxing film argot—is deeply gendered. The boxing movie had thrived for over a century before Karyn Kusama's *Girlfight* (2000) offered the first serious production about women in the sport. "Boxing is for men, and is about men, and *is* men," writes cultural critic and novelist Joyce Carol Oates, "a celebration of the lost religion of masculinity all the more trenchant for being lost."[4] This nostalgic, and decidedly toxic, masculinity is baked into professional prizefighting—the brand of boxing most films depict. Pro fighters, for instance, compete without shirts or headgear. Boxers, however, do not sweat any more than basketball or soccer players, who wear shirts despite the pools of perspiration their sports generate. And headgear protects against cuts, not knockouts or even concussions. These conventions are in place, then, to emphasize boxing's gladiatorial and sexualized hypermasculinity by transforming fights into seminude and bloody spectacles.

Extending boxing's stereotypical machismo, the writer Norman Mailer likened the heavyweight champion—traditionally the sport's most visible figure—to "the big toe of God. You have nothing to measure yourself by."[5] Mailer was referring here to Muhammad Ali, the outspoken Black Muslim champion whose achievement toppled a host of ideologies regarding which types of bodies ought to be able to serve as emblems of masculinity's peak. Given the heavyweight champion's symbolic import, various efforts—some more deliberate and pernicious than others—have been levied to make it more difficult for non-Whites to occupy this vaunted role. These gender and racial politics bleed into the sport's less prominent corners and weight classes.

Boxing films, through both their representations and how they circulate, participate in creating the sport as a site of cultural production. When Jack Johnson became the first Black heavyweight champion in 1908—after years of being denied a title opportunity because of his race—efforts to subdue the recalcitrant fighter centered on controlling the distribution of films that showed him easily thumping White challengers. In 1912 the U.S. Congress passed legislation directed explicitly at Johnson that barred the interstate transportation of all fight films—an overtly bigoted law that was in place for twenty-eight years. The Hollywood boxing films that emerged shortly after Johnson lost the title in 1915 seldom depicted non-White protagonists regardless of boxing's racial composition—a tradition that has continued ever since and that inaccurately imagines the sport as one that White American fighters dominate. But boxing films also offer occasional challenges to the status quo. These alternatives, however, typically come in the form of less visible independent productions and documentaries.

Adding to its cultural import, boxing sits at the foundation of not only cinema but also radio, network and cable television, and, more recently, live digital streaming. Boxing films helped to establish and maintain the sport's status as a commercial attraction that budding media platforms could reliably employ to gather an audience. The Radio Corporation of America (RCA) used Jack Dempsey and Georges Carpentier's 1921 heavyweight championship bout to debut the first commercial radio broadcast. Five years later, RCA employed Dempsey's match against Gene Tunney to launch its National Broadcasting Company (NBC), the first U.S. radio network. NBC built an audience with *Gillette Cavalcade of Sports*, a series of prime-time sports radio programming focused on boxing, and the network used these fight broadcasts to broker its expansion into television. When NBC canceled *Gillette Cavalcade* in 1959, the sponsor gave the American Broadcasting Company (ABC) its sports advertising budget on the condition that it continue producing a regular prime-time boxing show. The Gillette investment composed the seed money upon which ABC built ABC Sports, the network division that codified modern sports television's main formal practices. When cable TV outlets like HBO and ESPN launched in the 1970s, they looked to boxing to forge market share—a strategy that live sports streaming companies have adopted more recently. These varied media sell the sport by building on the narratives boxing movies craft and, in doing so, share in creating its meanings and uses.

4 • The Boxing Film

Scholars including Grindon, Aaron Baker, Seán Crosson, Lester D. Friedman, and Tony Williams have expertly identified and critiqued the boxing film's generic properties. In particular, Grindon's *Knockout: The Boxer and Boxing in American Cinema* (2011) offers meticulous textual analyses of how the genre engages topics that include race, class, gender, assimilation, and violence. Adopting a different approach, Dan Streible's *Fight Pictures: A History of Boxing and Early Cinema* (2008) focuses on the boxing film's place in cinema culture as the medium took root in fin de siècle America. Streible is less interested in the boxing film's formal dynamics—which were decidedly stripped-down in the pre-Hollywood context on which he focuses—than in how it helps to explain early cinema's development, practices, and politics.[6]

This book, subtitled *A Cultural and Transmedia History*, combines these critical and historical approaches to explore how, over time and across media, boxing films shape and confront the sport they take as their topic. To piece together this history it is necessary to consider many films. For the sake of manageability, I limit this book almost entirely to movies made in the United States that focus on the sport in America, although dozens of international productions merit scholarly consideration. I liberally define the boxing movie as any production in which the sport of boxing—whether officially sanctioned or not—plays a significant role. As a result, both *Champion* (Mark Robson, 1949), which is squarely about professional boxing, and *Hard Times* (Walter Hill, 1975), which focuses on illicit bareknuckle fights, are boxing films as far as I'm concerned. I also consider films that stretch beyond mainstream cinema, such as indie productions, documentaries, made-for-TV movies, teleplays, and even one-off experiments like Woroner Productions' 1970 *Super Fight* film that pitted a suspended Muhammad Ali against a retired Rocky Marciano and was exhibited in the style of a closed-circuit TV broadcast. These eclectic films all participate in composing boxing's presence on screen and, as such, build the sport's cultural significance. But they do so in tellingly different ways depending on their production, distribution, and consumption. Charting this long history and the broad collection of films that make it up—rather than focusing on a handful of "greatest hits"—reveals some instructive patterns that illuminate boxing, film, and their intersections. In particular, it shows how the racial controversies surrounding films of Jack Johnson lingered and evolved to inform productions made during the ascendance of Jack Dempsey, Joe Louis, Rocky Marciano, Muhammad Ali, Mike Tyson, and Floyd Mayweather. This historical and transmedia approach also makes clear the varied roles boxing has consistently played across media over time—and how the politics of boxing films shape mediations of the sport that might otherwise seem to be motivated by purely economic or technological ends.

The first chapter outlines boxing's important roles in early cinema's aesthetic techniques, industrial norms, and politics leading to the emergence of the

Classical Hollywood studio era. It explains how the racism surrounding Jack Johnson provoked the federal restriction of fight films and how, by stark contrast, the White heavyweight champion Jack Dempsey triggered an explosion of commercial sports media after he won the title in 1919. While films of actual fights remained banned through Dempsey's professional career, fictional films, print journalism, and radio broadcasts voraciously capitalized on his image through the 1920s. Beyond exploiting Dempsey's celebrity, boxing movies stressed the increasingly spectacular status the sport achieved during this time by dramatizing prizefighting's relationship to the media it attracted and supported. These films also perpetuated efforts to remove Johnson from public view by building worlds that excluded Black fighters. Chapter 1 shows how early boxing movies, through both their representations and their regulation, turned Johnson into an outcast and made Dempsey the wealthiest and one of the most famous athletes of his era.

Boxing briefly lulled after Dempsey's 1927 retirement. Joe Louis rejuvenated the sport when he became the first Black champion since Johnson in 1937—albeit a very different kind of African American celebrity whose success depended on his willingness to eschew Johnson's defiance. Louis's impact extended into boxing movies, which similarly sagged after Dempsey's career ended. The champ acted in and inspired various Black-cast and independently produced "race" films targeted to African American moviegoers. Beyond these niche productions, Louis catalyzed Hollywood's most vigorous era of boxing films. These studio movies benefitted from the Black champion's renown but did not feature a Black protagonist until *The Joe Louis Story* in 1953—a work that was released after Louis retired and the White fighter Rocky Marciano had secured the heavyweight title. As Streible claims, "The role that films played in [Louis's] career merits further study."[7] Chapter 2 takes up this call by discussing how the mainstream boxing films made during Louis's career exploited the interest in prizefighting that the Black champion generated while imagining a sport that omitted the racial difference he embodied.

Louis's popular matches aided television's rise—through both closed-circuit public exhibitions and domestic broadcasts. But much like Dempsey prompted a surge in sports media during the 1920s, Marciano amplified interest in the new medium when he became champ. Television boosted Marciano's stardom and reinforced the racial politics that constituted it. The medium, for instance, offered disproportionate opportunities to White fighters who would more effectively draw viewers and sell advertisements. TV also ushered potentially corrupting shifts in the sport. Chapter 3 considers how boxing films of the 1950s confronted television's impact on the culture and business of prizefighting.

Echoing the circumstances surrounding Jack Dempsey's retirement, Hollywood boxing films receded after the immensely popular Marciano left the sport in 1956. Prizefighting, however, remained a fixture of theatrical spaces and exhibition. In particular, live closed-circuit TV broadcasts were the sport's biggest revenue source and the main way marquee fights were consumed through the middle 1970s. Muhammad Ali fueled closed-circuit's rise. But Ali's controversial image turned closed-circuit exhibitions of his matches into public spaces where debates about the divisive champ occurred prior to and amid his 1967 suspension from professional boxing for refusing military induction. Ali's expulsion inspired efforts to cash in on the banished fighter—many of which took the form of documentaries and fictional films that appeared in the theatrical spaces from which his lucrative fights had abruptly vanished. Chapter 4 focuses on Woroner Productions' 1970 *Super Fight*, a film exhibited in the style of a live closed-circuit broadcast that was based on a computer-simulated match between Ali and Marciano. It explains how the *Super Fight* worked around Ali's suspension and controversies surrounding closed-circuit broadcasts of his bouts while reasserting the racial norms the suspended prizefighter upset and easing his reinstatement into pro boxing.

The momentarily hibernating Hollywood boxing film resurged with *Rocky*, which took inspiration from both the *Super Fight* and closed-circuit exhibitions to tell the story of a White long shot modeled partly on Marciano who challenges a flamboyant Black champion based on Ali. *Rocky* became the most popular boxing film ever and spawned a decades-long franchise. The film's reactionary racial politics complemented conservative responses to Ali and celebrated a return to traditional social mores through Balboa's success. The surprise hit propelled a wave of boxing movies that engaged Ali and the customs he disrupted. While Hollywood productions tended to reinforce *Rocky* with tales of White achievement, a collection of blaxploitation and independent films countered the critically acclaimed blockbuster with stories of Black triumph that took Ali as their muse and even subject. Chapter 5 examines how the 1970s revival of boxing films that *Rocky* stimulated was driven by efforts to capitalize on Ali's polarizing image and negotiate the cultural hierarchies he dismantled.

As with radio and network television, cable TV used boxing to establish itself during the 1970s. In particular, HBO—the focal point of chapter 6—relied on boxing to build its subscribership by carrying matches on its main channel and distributing them via pay-per-view feeds, which steadily overtook closed-circuit as the main way big fights were consumed. HBO, through the subsidiary HBO Sports, accompanied its boxing coverage with documentaries that promoted the fights it carried and stressed the media outlet's importance to the sport. Beyond these documentaries, HBO participated in a range of practices that similarly mediate boxing's reality and emphasize the premium cable outlet's centrality to prizefighting. These docu-branding activities—which include original docudramas, brand placements in films and video games, and reality TV programs—craft versions of boxing's past and present that reinforce HBO's status as home to the sport's most significant events.

Prophesies of boxing's demise followed prizefighting throughout its history, with reasons that included its notorious corruption, the debilitating injuries prizefighters suffer, and the introduction of new media technologies. These grim projections gained extraordinary momentum in the 1990s and 2000s. Boxing had few major stars, and mixed martial arts (MMA) emerged with an exciting and cannily marketed sport that siphoned prizefighting's already shrinking fan base. As a result, some filmmakers began using MMA as the backdrop for the types of tales boxing films traditionally offered. Amid this crisis, boxing films argued for the struggling sport's continued relevance and worked to delegitimize MMA. Many of these productions made the case for boxing's sustained cultural import by appealing not simply to the sport but to the heritage that boxing films created for it. Chapter 7 explores these filmic efforts to protect boxing.

The book concludes by explaining how the boxing film has at once shifted and maintained consistency in the twenty-first century with productions like Antoine Fuqua's *Southpaw* (2015) and the *Rocky* reboots *Creed* (Ryan Coogler, 2015) and *Creed 2* (Steven Caple Jr., 2018). These films all feature Black directors—a rarity in the Hollywood boxing film—and the *Creed* films have a Black protagonist. As such, they mark an important transition in the historically White-dominated genre. However, they also continue to buttress the boxing movie's traditional conventions with varying degrees of subtlety. The conclusion probes these recent boxing films' ambivalent cultural politics and outlines how the long-standing genre continues to resonate in sport and media culture over a century after it began appearing on screen.

Sports sit at the center of popular media culture, but they occupy the margins of media scholarship. Boxing helps to explain the many roles sports play in shaping media's cultural, political, and industrial contours since the late nineteenth century. Boxing films play an outsize role in building the meanings that have driven boxing's consistent presence in popular culture over time and across media—even after the sport has dwindled in popularity. As such, their long history adds to the still nascent discussion about sport and media's interdependence and the thorny politics that mark this commercialized symbiosis.

1

The Boxing Film through the Golden Age of Sports Media

●●●●●●●●●●●●●●●●●●●●●●●

Although illegal in most states as the twentieth century dawned, prizefighting composed an alluring and provocative spectacle that gathered a nationwide audience through coverage in publications like the *National Police Gazette*, *Spirit of the Times*, and *New York Clipper*. The sport also conveniently suited nascent cinema technologies. Early cameras, as film historian Terry Ramsaye comments, "had about the same pictorial availability as a knothole in a ballfield fence." Luckily, little more was needed to capture boxing matches. "The ropes of the prize fight film automatically limited the radius of action," Ramsaye writes. "It was simple to set the ponderous camera to cover the ring. The cameraman could then grind away, secure in the certainty that the picture was not getting away from him, unless indeed the combatants jumped the ropes and ran away."[1] The boxing film established itself as cinema's first and most popular genre, with more than two hundred fight films made by 1915. "It was boxing," glibly asserts film historian Luke McKernan, "that created cinema."[2] Boxing films offered early glimpses of the stylistic, economic, and cultural practices that came to characterize the Classical Hollywood studio era. They also hastened boxing's growth into a national spectacle.

But boxing and cinema's union was not simply borne out of technological convenience. The sport and medium occupied a common "sporting and theatrical community" that served overlapping—and mostly male—consumers.[3]

10 • The Boxing Film

Their symbiosis also shaped sport and media's mutual development. The popular boxing film was at the center of debates regarding which types of activities and people should be celebrated, marginalized, and even suppressed. These attitudes carried over into the explosion of commercial mass media that undergirded the so-called Golden Age of Sports during the 1920s. The boxing film propelled this convergent sports media environment and the attendant assumptions about which sorts of bodies were best fit for public exhibition.

Early Fight Films

In an 1891 interview with the *New York Sun*, Thomas Edison predicted that prizefights would compose an ideal complement to the kinetoscope moving picture machine that he was fine-tuning.[4] Three years later, the Edison Studio's first major film project showcased a fight between journeyman lightweights Mike Leonard and Jack Cushing at Edison's Black Maria production facility in West Orange, New Jersey. The match was staged to complement Edison's myriad technological limitations, which required natural light and necessitated a smaller ring than was standard for competitions at the time. Leonard and Cushing sparred for ten single-minute rounds in front of extras posing as trainers and fans cheering from ringside. The fighters rested for seven minutes instead of the typical one minute between the truncated rounds so that technicians could reload and adjust the cameras.[5] While only six of the ten rounds turned out, Edison's *Leonard-Cushing Fight* composed the longest motion picture created to date. It was distributed by the Kinetoscope Exhibition Company in August 1894 as six separate minute-long films—one for each round. The sixth film conveniently finished with Leonard knocking Cushing to the ground. Edison, in an effort to maximize patronage, did not announce the fight's result. But many customers simply skipped to the final film to see the match's outcome. Leonard claimed he could have felled Cushing far earlier but was protecting Edison's financial interests. "Mr. Edison treated me right," Cushing said, "and I didn't want to be too quick for his machine." The carefully orchestrated competition offers an early illustration of how media's intersecting technological horizons and commercial imperatives shape sporting contests. It also composed one of the medium's first hits that "drew almost riotous crowds for many days on end" to kinetoscope parlors and established the fight film's viability. It remained in the Edison Company's film catalogue well into the twentieth century.[6]

Edison's *Corbett and Courtney Before a Kinetograph* (1894) adopted the same six-round format as *Leonard-Cushing* but with higher profile participants and more deliberate orchestration. "Gentleman" Jim Corbett was heavyweight champion at the time and Peter Courtney was a top contender. The film's title suggests the display of a boxing match on film was as interesting as the match itself—a reflection of the technological novelty that film scholar Tom Gunning identifies as characteristic of early cinematic attractions before narrative storytelling became the norm.[7] The producers decided that "the fight should be precisely six rounds of one-minute each and that the sixth should be concluded by a handsome knockout delivered by the star, James Corbett," who was instructed to turn his face toward the camera during the filming so that audiences could get a better look at the handsome fighter as he doled out punishment. Ramsaye locates *Corbett and Courtney* as "the ancestor of dramatic construction for the motion picture. Here was the first glimmering of creative motion picture effort, the first step toward having things happen for the camera rather than merely photographing events ordained by other forces."[8] Adding to its aesthetic significance, the film occasioned the industry's first "star" contract when Corbett agreed to perform exclusively for the Kinetoscope Exhibition Company. Corbett became so identified with the company that it eventually pasted his coiffed profile on its official letterhead.[9]

Leonard-Cushing and *Corbett and Courtney* established boxing as early cinema's most popular subject. The sport became a backdrop for productions that spanned beyond fights, such as Edison's *The Boxing Cats* (1894)—the ancestor of the ubiquitous modern-day cat video—and *The Gordon Sisters Boxing* (1901). Whether representing legitimate bouts or feline gags, the boxing film was as invested in staging entertaining spectacles as it was in documenting events. Filmed reproductions of fights—such as re-creations based on newspaper reports and illicit adaptations of extant films—were commonplace. Streible explains that fake fight films actually outnumbered those shot at the ringside of sanctioned bouts until 1910. These fake films, as historian Charles Musser adds, came in handy and were gratefully accepted by audiences when no documentation of the actual bout was available.[10] Early fight films, then, are as indebted to fiction as to fact—a fluidity that illustrates boxing and theater's entanglement. Fighters were athletes as well as actors, and these complementary roles intersected. Most popular boxers appeared on the vaudeville circuit and made more money on stage than in the ring. Corbett, for instance, starred in plays that included *A Naval Cadet* in 1896 and 1906's *Cashel Byron's Profession*, an adaptation of George Bernard Shaw's novel of the same title. Many boxers, then, transitioned with relative ease into film roles once narrative cinema took hold and began casting fighters to add star power and realism.

The transition from single-use kinetoscopes to public exhibitions that more closely approximated the communal experience of attending a fight amplified the boxing film's popularity. The Veriscope Company's production of Corbett's 1897 match against Bob Fitzsimmons in Carson City, Nevada, composed what Streible identifies as the "most important product of the early marriage of film and fights" and was cinema's most lucrative ever property—within or beyond boxing. Moreover, *Corbett-Fitzsimmons Fight* changed the economy of sports by making films more profitable than ticket sales to bouts.[11] Aggressive promotional efforts accompanied this business to ensure nationwide audiences would be aware of the fight that would eventually appear on film in theaters. The marketing blitz made Corbett-Fitzsimmons such a spectacle that people gathered at public places throughout the country to hear announcements of telegraphed round-by-round updates from Carson City. Veriscope's Enoch Rector used three cameras to document the match and protected the property against copies by painting a trademark on ringside—"Copyright The Veriscope Company"—to designate his film as the genuine article.[12]

Although fakes routinely circulated, fight films of unstaged bouts like *Corbett-Fitzsimmons* helped to inaugurate cinema's capacity to offer reliable documentary evidence. While Fitzsimmons won the fight and the heavyweight title that came along with it, reports indicated that he may have committed a disqualifying foul toward the end of the match. Anticipating current replay technologies, the films furnished a way to investigate this alleged offense. The *New York World* reported that *Corbett-Fitzsimmons* "marked a triumph of science over the poor imperfect instrument, the human eye, and proves that the veriscope camera is far superior."[13] The film offered evidence of intricacies beyond even the referee's reach. Musser cites *Corbett-Fitzsimmons* as propelling documentary cinema's function as an arbiter of truth about the world it indexes. "Promoters and spectators recognized the possibility of and the demand for, what is now called 'observational cinema.' The filmmaker's role was to record an event and then re-present it with as little intervention as possible, so that the audience was in the position to judge the outcome for themselves."[14] The boxing film thus stood at the root of both narrative and documentary cinema.

Although popular, profitable, and instructive, fight films traded in controversial subject matter. New York State did not legalize prizefighting until 1920. And the *New York Times* lamented *Corbett-Fitzsimmons'* popularity. "It is not very creditable to our civilization," the paper remarked, "that an achievement of what is now called the veriscope that has attracted and will attract the widest attention should be the representation of a prizefight."[15] Alabama congressperson William F. Aldrick submitted an unsuccessful bill that proposed "no pictures or description of any prize fight or encounter of pugilists or any proposal or record of betting on the same shall be transmitted by the mails of the United States or by inter-state commerce, whether in a newspaper or telegram." But Musser points out that *Corbett-Fitzsimmons'* status as "an 'illustration' of a fight rather than a fight itself made the attraction not only legally but socially acceptable viewing material." Prizefighting films broadened boxing's audience beyond the comparatively few who could witness matches in person. They also helped to legitimize the consumption of boxing by allowing spectators, especially women, to view matches without entering the vice-laden settings where bouts took place.[16] Some exhibitors actively marketed fight films toward women to broaden their audience and give their screenings a sense of respectability that would insulate their establishments from critics like Aldrick. These gendered efforts to legitimize fight films also, and unintentionally, offered women patrons rare and even transgressive glimpses of seminude male bodies that constitute early reversals of cinema's endemic and objectifying "male gaze." Corbett seemed to realize and take advantage of this by wearing shorts that rode halfway up his buttocks. While fight films offered some permissible titillation, these sexualized spectacles sparked increased outrage when they featured Black men, particularly Black men who beat White opponents.

"Mixed-race fight pictures were deemed among the lowest grades of screen entertainment," Streible explains.[17] The heavyweight Jack Johnson brought these attitudes into focus. Beyond his skill in the ring, Johnson was dissident and outspoken. "Jack Johnson was his own man when it was not economically or physically advisable for blacks to be 'men,'" explains biographer Al-Tony Gilmore. "He refused to let anyone—white or black—or any laws or customs—to dictate his place in society or the manner in which he should live."[18] Johnson flaunted his wealth, married White women, and, building on Corbett, paraded his sexuality by packing his shorts with gauze to make his penis look larger while competing. Most important, he dominated the White heavyweights he encountered in the ring.

More than other weight classes, the heavyweight champion—Norman Mailer's big toe of God—symbolized manhood's summit. To preserve this myth, White heavyweight champions instituted de facto color lines restricting Black competitors from even having the chance to compete for the title. Johnson repeatedly and unsuccessfully tried to convince champion Jim Jeffries to grant him a title shot. "Jack Johnson is a fair fighter," Jeffries said in 1904, "but he is black, and for that reason I will never fight him. If I were not champion I would as soon meet a negro as any other man, but the title will never go to a negro if

FIG. 1 Jack Johnson and Tommy Burns fight for the heavyweight title on December 26, 1908. Johnson's victory made him the first Black heavyweight champion. (Wikimedia Commons)

I can help it."[19] Jeffries retired as champ in 1905 and handed the title over to the relatively undistinguished Marvin Hart, who was deposed by the Canadian Tommy Burns seven months later.

After over two years of Johnson's goading and an offer that escalated to thirty thousand dollars, Burns finally granted the Black challenger a title match in Sydney, Australia, on December 26, 1908. Promoter Hugh D. "Huge Deal" McIntosh marketed the fight and its films through emphasizing the racial tensions they would put on display. One advertisement for the films promised that "the Champion Representatives of White and Black races" would meet "for Racial and Individual Supremacy" in the biggest fight "since Cinematographic pictures have become a fine art."[20] Johnson easily controlled the match and even jeered Burns throughout it until police stopped the competition in the fourteenth round. Some reports indicated that authorities cut out the cameras prior to ending the match. Others said the films were later edited to excise Burns's humiliating final moments.[21] Either way, the fight was terminated before cameras could document Johnson overcoming the White champion. Johnson was well aware of the cameras' placement and, reflecting the stage directions Edison gave to Corbett a decade earlier, he made sure they would clearly showcase the ease with which he dispatched Burns—and the great pleasure he took in doing so. According to ringside reporter Jack London, Johnson "cuffed and smiled, and in the clinches whirled his opponent around so as to be able to assume beatific and angelic facial expressions for the cinematograph machines."[22] McIntosh, who refereed the fight, said the films "did not half tell how badly [Burns] was punished." Johnson's "best punches," McIntosh claimed, were delivered while Burns had his back to the cameras and the challenger was posing for them.[23] The films, however, were persuasive enough to convince the *New York Times* that the best man prevailed. "To those who saw the pictures there is no mystery why Johnson won," the newspaper reported. "There was not a single minute from the tap of the first gong to the time when the Police Inspector stopped the contest in the fourteenth round that Johnson was not clearly the master of Burns."[24] The films proved that Johnson did not simply win the match but was Burns's "master"—a loaded term to apply to a Black man beating a White champion that was certainly not lost on the publication's editors. Johnson's victory, exhibited repeatedly on film around the world, made him the first ever Black heavyweight champ and fractured the white supremacist ideology that previous champions safeguarded by ducking Black opponents.

Films of Johnson's October 1909 title defense against Stanley Ketchel even more convincingly verified the new champion's prowess. Rumors swirled that Johnson agreed to carry Ketchel long enough to ensure film profits. Unlike the Burns fight, authorities did not stop the Ketchel match and the cameras captured Johnson knocking out his White opponent in the twelfth round. Streible claims the films established Johnson as the first Black movie star and constitute the earliest instances of African American cinema given their immense popularity at Black theaters.[25] The productions also elicited ravenous calls for Johnson to be ousted by a White contender—a White Hope—who would restore the racial order he so brazenly shattered. Embittered critics charged that Johnson's championship was illegitimate since Burns never beat Jim Jeffries—claims that cascaded into an effort to coax Jeffries out of retirement.

Even though he had not competed or trained in five years, Jeffries agreed to fight Johnson in San Francisco on July 4, 1910. He claimed to be motivated principally by "that portion of the white race that has been looking to me to defend its athletic superiority" and said he was fighting "for the sole purpose of proving that a white man is better than a negro."[26] Media coverage similarly framed the fight as a proving ground for racial superiority—an effective strategy for selling papers to a readership that stretched beyond the typical sports fan. But Jeffries was at least as driven by the unprecedented financial rewards the "Fight of the Century" promised. Most of this money would come from Vitagraph's film proceeds, two thirds of which he and Johnson agreed to split.

The Johnson-Jeffries fight relocated to Reno after San Francisco mayor P. H. McCarthy withdrew his city from hosting the controversial match. The Nevada city became the "center of the universe" leading up to the bout, which drew six hundred reporters from around the globe. "It is no exaggeration," reported the trade publication *Moving Picture World*, "to say that the entire world will await pictorial representation of the fight." Vitagraph's *Johnson-Jeffries Fight* "became more widely discussed than any motion picture of its era." The production company used nine cameras in relays of three to ensure nothing was missed and to cover enough angles so that editors could patch together a dramatic final product.[27] *Johnson-Jeffries* also included introductory material of the fighters readying for the event and unsurprisingly presented Jeffries as the more sympathetic protagonist. Despite the film's stylistic innovations, *Moving Picture World* speculated that Vitagraph's production would underperform financially unless Jeffries won. The observation elicited speculation that Johnson—who was always more of an opportunist than an activist—might throw the fight to cash in on his share of the film proceeds.[28]

But Johnson cruised to a fifteenth-round technical knockout, taunting Jeffries and his corner (which included Jim Corbett) as he punished the out-of-shape former champ. Gilmore says the victory "had the effect of a second emancipation" for African Americans. "Never before had they witnessed at once such collective celebrating and race pride manifested toward a single event." The fight's result provoked widespread hate crimes that included the murder of eighteen African American men. One Black man in New Orleans was reportedly shot for entering a local diner and gleefully crowing, "Gimme eggs, beat and scrambled, like Jim Jeffries." The fight films—as testaments to

16 • The Boxing Film

Johnson's inciting achievement—were immediately identified as dangerous items that necessitated containment. One postfight report indicated that spectators during the Reno match entreated cameramen to "cut out the pictures" as it became evident that Johnson would win—requests that suggest film records of the defeat were as threatening as the event itself.[29]

As the *San Francisco Examiner* reported, "within twenty-four hours" of Johnson's victory demands to suppress the films "assumed the proportions of a national crusade." The Society for Christian Endeavor "telegraphed every governor and big city mayor in the country advocating for the film's prohibition," and former president Theodore Roosevelt published a denunciation of fight films in *Outlook* magazine.[30] The Johnson-Jeffries film was banned throughout the southern United States, and the mayors of Baltimore, Boston, Buffalo, Cincinnati, and Toledo issued executive orders barring screenings in their cities. England and South Africa followed suit.

"There was never a time when the general interests of the moving picture business were more at stake than during the period immediately following the Johnson-Jeffries fight," *Moving Picture World* commented. "For years and years fights have been reproduced in moving pictures, and it was not until the Reno fight that the guardians of public morals discovered that such pictures were beyond the pale of public policy." Vitagraph's film of a Black champion reducing a symbol of White virility to a bruised and pitiful lump sent the entire film industry into crisis. Creative entrepreneurs devised a collection of efforts to get around bans of the *Johnson-Jeffries Fight* that included lantern slide exhibitions, parodies, and re-creations featuring actors as the fighters. The American Cinephone Company's *Jack Johnson's Own Story of the Big Fight* filmed Johnson narrating his experience in the fight while wearing a tuxedo. Exhibitors would play the audio and film components in tandem. An advertisement for the production in *Moving Picture World* stressed that "these pictures can be shown anywhere" and that they offered a substitute for those locations where films of the fight were banned.[31] While *Johnson-Jeffries* was widely prohibited, fight films continued to circulate legally until Congress passed the 1912 Sims Act immediately after Johnson's July 4, 1912, title defense against "Fireman" Jim Flynn, another undistinguished White Hope he defeated without much trouble.

The ban, led by Tennessee's Thetus Sims and Georgia's Seaborn A. Roddenbery, was modeled after restrictions on obscene publications. The congressmen originally wanted the prohibition to encompass "any record or account of betting" on prizefights, but it was amended to targeting only films. The Sims Act restricted the interstate transportation of all fight films, but it was designed to stop depictions of Johnson, whose Blackness ensured the overtly racist legislation's successful passage. Roddenbery called Johnson's victory over Flynn "the grossest instance of base fraud and bogus effort at a fair fight between a

Caucasian brute and an African biped beast that has ever taken place. It was repulsive. This bill is designed to prevent the display to morbid-minded adults and susceptible youth all over the country of representation of such a disgusting spectacle." Roddenbery made even more explicit the racism driving the legislation by claiming that "no man descended from the Old Saxon race can look upon that kind of contest without abhorrence and disgust."[32] The Sims Act sequestered legal fight films to the state where their featured match took place and, as a result, rendered the thriving genre unprofitable. It also quarantined Johnson's image and limited his ability to earn. Shortly after the legislation passed, Johnson was charged under the Mann Act for taking his White girlfriend Lucille Cameron (whom he eventually married) across state lines for what prosecutors deemed "immoral purposes." He was convicted on the trumped-up charges the following year but fled to Europe before entering prison. Although Johnson took his title with him across the Atlantic, these racist legal conspiracies largely removed the boxer and his publicly projected image from American life.

Johnson returned to North America in April 1915 to defend his title against Jess Willard in Havana. The enormous White Kansan, known as the Pottawatomie Giant, knocked Johnson out in the twenty-sixth round. Films of the match were produced despite the ban, with speculators assuming the prohibition would not be enforced since the White fighter triumphed. But the ban was upheld despite ravenous demand for films of Johnson's long-awaited defeat. The restrictions prompted one entrepreneur to project the film across the Canadian border and rerecord it in New York State to claim it was technically produced in that location—an inventive gambit that was nevertheless quashed.[33]

Jess Willard rarely defended his title. He preferred to capitalize on his exalted status by appearing on the vaudeville stage, and even in a circus act briefly.[34] To be sure, many would rather have an idle White champ than an active Johnson, and Willard reinstituted the color line. Black contenders were again unofficially barred from opportunities to compete for the title, and those films of Johnson that circulated did so only illegally. But boxing expanded and gained legitimacy amid Willard's mostly inactive reign.

While films of actual prizefights were forced underground, the budding Hollywood industry routinely used the sport as the backdrop for fictional productions that spanned genres. Boxing offered a stage for the physical action and humor commonplace in silent cinema and proved able to lure both men and women to the theater by combining sports and drama. Keystone Studios' *The Knockout* (1914) starred Fatty Arbuckle as the down-and-out drifter Pug and included Charlie Chaplin in a supporting role as a bumbling referee. Pug changes his destitute fortune by posing as the boxing champion Cyclone Flynn. His ruse works until the real Cyclone (Edgar Kennedy) appears and challenges him to a fight, which Pug has no chance of winning. Their match quickly

18 • The Boxing Film

devolves into a series of pratfalls highlighted by Chaplin bouncing around the ring while unsuccessfully attempting to officiate the chaotic contest. Other boxing films built on the sport's association with gambling and vice. Chaplin's *The Champion* (1915), Jerome Storm's *The Egg Crate Wallop* (1919), and Bray Productions' Krazy Kat cartoon *The Best Mouse Loses* (1920) all center on fighters tempted to throw bouts—a theme that became a staple of the genre.

Despite their prohibition, fight films resurfaced as illicit political weapons used to combat a spread of racist productions that were emboldened by the Sims Act, most infamously D. W. Griffith's *The Birth of a Nation* (1915). Cultural critic Gerald Early speculates that Griffith had Johnson in mind when he made his film, which offers a retelling of the Civil War that depicts Black men as savages, condemns miscegenation, and glorifies the Ku Klux Klan. Griffith's film, in fact, was the first motion picture screened in the White House and gathered rave reviews from President Woodrow Wilson, who enthusiastically likened it to "writing history with lightning." Black newspaper editors, however, pointed out the hypocrisy that allowed *Birth of a Nation* to circulate freely—even in the White House—while films of Johnson's conquests were suppressed. Some Black theaters staged defiant screenings of *Johnson-Jeffries Fight* to protest *Birth of a Nation*.[35]

The Golden Age of Sports Media

The military began teaching soldiers to box during World War I, and these GIs returned home with an interest in the sport that a growing mass media industry identified and served. Guided by manager Jack "Doc" Kearns and promoter Tex Rickard, Jack Dempsey emerged out of Manassa, Colorado, to give this swelling sports media market one of the biggest stars of the 1920s. Kearns viewed sports as another facet of entertainment that merited the same type of ballyhoo that moves Hollywood properties. "Like a strip tease, I always figured you couldn't get anywhere without exposure," he explained.[36] While Dempsey's ring record did not obviously warrant a title shot, Kearns transformed him into a self-made Western tough guy and stoked a rivalry with Willard by harnessing a happily obliging press. Kearns delivered newspaper clippings on Dempsey to sportswriters, whose coverage created enough buzz for Rickard to book a title match on July 4, 1919, in Toledo. Kearns billed the smaller challenger as Jack the Giant Killer, who would endeavor to slay the lumbering and comparatively uncharismatic Willard. He also created the *Jack Dempsey Revue* vaudeville show to generate interest prior to the match.[37] Willard capitalized on the fight buildup by starring in the feature melodrama *The Challenge of Chance* (1919). He played a virtuous ranch foreman who buys horses for a crooked El Paso trader (Harry von Meter). But once he learns of his boss's plans to rob an innocent maiden

(Fay Calvert), he elects to protect the young woman through a series of gallant acts that make frequent use of his famed punching ability. *Billboard* remarked on *The Challenge of Chance*'s potential to attract women through its romantic themes and speculated that the film would perform particularly well if Willard remained champion.[38]

But Dempsey knocked Willard out in the third round to fulfill the heroic image Kearns manufactured and to establish himself as the Manassa Mauler. Though films of the fight were prohibited, newspapers more than compensated and made Dempsey "the greatest boon to circulation in twenty years." The new champ's ascendance coincided with sports media's proliferation across print, film, and radio. This expanding media infrastructure, much like the emergent Hollywood studio system, needed stars around whom to focus its efforts. Kearns and Dempsey collaborated with media practitioners to give, in media historian Bruce J. Evensen's words, "the public the Dempsey it wanted."[39] Sport historian Benjamin G. Rader suggests Dempsey embodied commercial entertainment's role as a salve for the alienation that accompanied modernity: "As the society became more complicated and systematized and as success had to be won increasingly in bureaucracies, the need for heroes who leaped to fame and fortune outside the rules of the system needed to grow. No longer were the heroes the lone business tycoon or the statesmen, but the 'stars'—from movies and sports."[40] Dempsey fused these two varieties of idols to establish a new brand of hypermediated sports celebrity. Five boxing matches gathered million-dollar gates during the 1920s. Dempsey was the featured attraction in all of them.

Kearns reminded Dempsey that his livelihood depended on the media coverage he attracted. "It's important, Champ," the manager told Dempsey, "to keep the sportswriters on your side."[41] The boxing magazine *Ring* launched in 1920, and newspaper sports sections became commonplace by the middle of the decade, with nationally syndicated scribes like Grantland Rice, Damon Runyon, Paul Gallico, Ring Lardner, and W. O. McGeehan serving as Dempsey's key chroniclers. These writers built and sustained their readerships by prioritizing vivid yarn spinning over neutral, fact-based reportage. As Grantland Rice—the most famous of the bunch—asserted with characteristic grandness, "When a sportswriter stops making heroes out of athletes, it's time to get out of the business."[42] Though Rice took Dempsey to task for never serving in World War I, a critique that dogged the boxer throughout his career, he also routinely deified the Manassa Mauler. After Dempsey beat Willard, Rice described the new champion as "the greatest fighting tornado, in a boxing way, the game has ever known" who "must be able to hit harder than any man that ever lived." Matching his colleague's flowery prose, Runyon likened Dempsey to a "young mountain lion in human form, from the Sangre de Christo Hills of Colorado."[43]

By the mid-1920s, one in every four readers purchased newspapers for the sports pages that featured such overblown writing. Publications allowed their profitable sports divisions greater editorial leeway than other pages, an affordance that precipitated sports reporting's marginalized reputation as journalism's frivolous "toy department."[44] Rickard admitted that paying sportswriters became "a routine business expense" well worth the investment because of the exposure it yielded. These journalists were hired expressly to imbue their sporting subjects with drama and romance that resonated with the Hollywood tales that had also begun to sell so well. The sportswriter Robert Lipsyte suggests the 1920s Golden Age of Sports would be better described as the Golden Age of Sports Writing given the influence these journalists had on public understandings of figures like Dempsey.[45] While centrally important, sportswriters were joined by Hollywood films, newsreels, radio, and the intersections across these media. The 1920s Golden Age of Sports Writing, then, may be even more accurately labeled the Golden Age of Sports Media.

Shortly after winning the championship, Dempsey appeared in a comic newsreel with Chaplin and the actor Douglas Fairbanks. The newsreel exhibited sport and Hollywood's increased intermingling along with Dempsey's ascension. Unable to make significant money off films of his matches, Dempsey began appearing in scripted dramas. The champion, in fact, worked far more in film than in boxing through the 1920s. With a face caked in stage makeup to soften his harsh mug, Dempsey first played Jack Derry in Pathé's 1920 serial *Daredevil Jack*. The serial begins with Jack's family being swindled out of their Nevada gold mine. Derry perseveres amid the adversity. He enrolls in college, becomes a star football player, and falls in love with a popular coed (Josie Sedgwick). But Derry quickly discovers that his beloved's father (Herschel Mayall) is the very crook who cheated his family out of their mine. He eventually wins her love as well as her father's begrudging respect by beating up a gang of thugs and earning enough money to go into business for himself. *Daredevil Jack*'s plot is borderline nonsensical; but the film was little more than an excuse to "show Jess Willard's conqueror to the film fans." A Pathé advertisement plugged the production by stressing Dempsey's status as "the best known man in the world" and reassuring exhibitors that *Daredevil Jack* was "not a prize-fight serial" that would be hindered by the film ban.[46]

Jack Johnson returned to the United States in 1920 and was incarcerated in the Leavenworth Penitentiary until July 1921 for his Mann Act conviction. But the former champion still inspired various race films during the early 1920s. Oscar Micheaux's *The Brute* (1920), for instance, evokes the Johnson mystique and features the Black fighter Sam Langford. Other race films cast the divisive former champion after his release from Leavenworth. *As the World Rolls In* (1921) stars Johnson as a trainer who helps a young man (Reed Thomas) learn how to protect himself and win a girl's (Blanche Thompson) heart; the fantastical melodrama *Black Thunderbolt* (1921) features Johnson as a gallant strongman; and Johnson plays a fighter who flees to Mexico after taking the blame for a crime his brother (Andrian Joyce) committed in *For His Mother's Sake* (1922). The films were carefully marketed as noncontroversial. A trade publication report on *Black Thunderbolt* assured exhibitors that the production "is said to contain nothing that would be offensive to any." But the Ohio State Bureau of Motion Pictures banned *For His Mother's Sake* from exhibition in the state because of Johnson's criminal past.[47] Johnson's image remained polarizing—even when he played fictional and seemingly sympathetic roles. Meanwhile, violent productions like *The Challenge of Chance* and *Daredevil Jack* circulated without incident.

Already a star in print and on film, Dempsey's media-driven image helped to stimulate commercial radio's emergence with his July 1921 title defense against Georges Carpentier in Jersey City. Rickard promoted the fight by billing Carpentier as a war hero and emphasizing Dempsey's reputation as a slacker. Upon the urging of Madison Square Garden promoter Julius Hopp, media executive David Sarnoff decided that broadcasting Dempsey-Carpentier via wireless radio would publicize his fledgling RCA and help it to compete with Westinghouse for market share of the new medium. Sarnoff secured Rickard's permission and arranged to relay the match from ringside via a direct wire to a transmitter two miles away in Hoboken, which broadcast the signal, according to *Wireless Age*, "more than 125,000 square miles."[48] Sarnoff established goodwill for RCA's experiment by attaching it to war relief charities. He collaborated with philanthropist Anne Morgan (the daughter of J. P. Morgan) and assistant secretary of the Navy, and eventual president, Franklin Delano Roosevelt to donate portions of the broadcast's proceeds to the Committee for Devastated France and the Navy Club.

Sarnoff conscripted RCA employee J. Andrew White, a well-known figure in radio who served as the acting president of the National Amateur Wireless Association and editor of *Wireless Age*, to handle the ringside fight call. White's blow-by-blow, however, went only as far as the Hoboken transmitter, where RCA technician J. O. Smith relayed White's account for the thousands listening to the wireless broadcast. Rickard worked with Sarnoff to equip auditoriums, town halls, movie theaters, Elks clubs, and other communal spaces throughout the East Coast with the receivers and amplifiers necessary to exhibit the match. *Wireless Age* estimated that about three hundred thousand heard the fight—the largest radio audience ever to that point.[49] While Dempsey knocked out Carpentier in the third round, the quick fight turned out to be a blessing for RCA, whose transmitter likely would have melted down had the bout lasted much longer. Aided by the radio exposure, Dempsey-Carpentier generated boxing's first million-dollar gate. Reuters dubbed RCA's transmission "the world's first real broadcast," and *Wireless Age* praised it as "the ushering in of a new era" of commercial radio.[50]

Rickard sold Fred Quimby the rights to film Dempsey-Carpentier on the condition that the filmmaker emphasize the fight's status as a legitimate undertaking. Accordingly, Quimby's production opens with shots of Rickard joining New Jersey's governor for an inspection of the Jersey City arena prior to the match. Although still officially banned, the Dempsey-Carpentier films managed to circulate widely and turn a profit.[51] But the fight established radio broadcasts—many of which were consumed in the same theatrical spaces that exhibited fight films—as the preferred way to experience big matches for those who could not attend them in person.

Evensen describes the flood of media coverage surrounding Jack Dempsey as "Dempseymania"—an obsession with the celebrity that helped him to earn more money than any athlete of the 1920s, a decade that included the likes of Babe Ruth and Bobby Jones. "We are all part of the Dempsey cult," admitted Paul Gallico, "and we were blinded by our own ballyhoo." Dempseymania maintained its economic value in part by reinforcing the white supremacist attitudes Johnson threatened; in fact one could convincingly argue that Dempsey's star value was negligible without his Whiteness. Rickard, for instance, would not let Dempsey, who said he was game to compete against anyone, fight the Black contender Harry Wills. "If a nigger wins the championship, then the championship ain't worth a nickel," Rickard said. "That's what Johnson taught us."[52] Dempsey did not defend his title between 1923 and 1926. Like Willard, he cashed in on his status through acting, public appearances, and occasional exhibitions that did not risk the championship. In 1924, Universal Pictures' president, Carl Laemmle, signed Dempsey to a million-dollar contract to appear in a string of adventure-themed serials titled *Fight and Win*. Dempsey played the gallant Tiger Jack O'Day, and the installments boasted titles that include *Winning His Way*, *The Title Holder*, and *K.O. for Cupid*. As part of the contract, Laemmle stipulated that Dempsey would train at a facility on the Universal lot.[53]

In 1925, Dempsey married the film star Estelle Taylor, whom he met while hobnobbing with the Hollywood set. Upon his new bride's urging, the champ underwent plastic surgery to make his mangled nose resemble more closely those of his statuesque movie star peers. Dempsey and Taylor then costarred in the feature *Manhattan Madness* (1925). Dempsey plays Steve O'Dare, a transplanted western cowhand who returns east to collect money he is owed. O'Dare's college friends prank him by staging the kidnapping of Taylor's character, known only as "the girl." O'Dare takes courageous measures to rescue the beautiful ingénue—and turns on his pals when they reveal the mean-spirited hoax. In the process, he and the girl fall in love. Like *Daredevil Jack*, the unexceptional film drew interest primarily because of Dempsey's involvement. The

FIG. 2 Jack Dempsey and his wife, Estelle Taylor, star in *Manhattan Madness* (1925). Promotion for the film billed Taylor as "Mrs. Jack Dempsey" to enhance the production's appeal. (Wikimedia Commons)

stars were marketed as "Mr. and Mrs. Jack Dempsey" to emphasize the champion's presence in the film. As *Variety* sarcastically put it, "Mrs. Jack Dempsey is more widely heralded than Estelle Taylor."[54]

Dempsey finally defended his title against Gene Tunney in September 1926. Rickard plugged the Philadelphia fight in ways that reflected his promotion of Dempsey-Carpentier.[55] He marketed Gene "The Fighting Marine" Tunney as a brave combat veteran and billed Dempsey as an antiheroic draft dodger. Pathé hired Tunney to star in *The Fighting Marine* (1926), a serial it released just prior to the fight to exploit the interest surrounding it. Like Dempsey, Tunney understood that he needed media attention, and he invested 5 percent of his income into publicity. But—and despite his distinguished military service—Tunney lacked Dempsey's populist charisma. The educated pugilist was widely viewed as pretentious and wooden. He also fought with a cautious and defensive style that bored fans and contrasted Dempsey's more dramatic tendency to take big hits and swing freely in pursuit of explosive knockouts.[56]

Anticipation for the fight, according to Evensen, was so great that the Associated Press established a twelve-person sports department to cover it. Grantland Rice, in a rare moment of cynicism, called Dempsey-Tunney "the golden

24 • The Boxing Film

fleece"—a match overshadowed by the hype surrounding it.[57] Philadelphia's Sesquicentennial Stadium attracted 130,000 spectators for the fight. RCA built on its experimental 1921 Dempsey-Carpentier broadcast by using Dempsey-Tunney to publicize the launch of its National Broadcast Company—the United States' first major network. RCA reasoned that the big-ticket fight would accelerate radio's growth into a medium that would eventually deliver "every event of national importance to every home in America."[58] The NBC broadcast—hosted by Graham McNamee and relayed via a thirty-one-station network—reached thirty-nine million listeners. It was again exhibited in movie theaters and other public places. Most of the showings were sponsored by newspapers that owned radio stations and used the broadcast to promote their content across platforms. An advertisement in Dayton, Ohio's, *Dayton Evening Herald* stressed that all fight fans—"Men, Women, Children"—were invited to hear the match at the city's Memorial Hall, which held three thousand and would feature "4 RCA Loudspeakers Placed So That All May Hear Every Word."[59] The fight, which the calculating and methodical Tunney won by a unanimous decision, generated nearly two million dollars—unprecedented and radio-driven profits that made a rematch imminent.

Staged at Chicago's Soldier Field almost exactly one year after their first encounter, Dempsey and Tunney's rematch was an even grander spectacle than the Philadelphia tilt. A smattering of Hollywood celebrities including Chaplin, Arbuckle, Fairbanks, and Buster Keaton—a group as interested in the publicity their presence at the match would generate as in viewing the bout—purchased ringside seats. Death row inmates used their last requests to hear NBC's broadcast, which McNamee announced to fifty million listeners through a fifty-eight-station hookup. Tunney again won the fight by a unanimous decision, but this time under suspicious circumstances. New rules instituted before the match required fighters to retire to a neutral corner after knocking opponents down. When Dempsey did not immediately comply with the new regulation after flooring Tunney in the seventh, referee Dave Barry delayed his count by several seconds. Many claimed Tunney was down longer than ten seconds and that Dempsey should have regained the title.

The legendary status Dempsey and Tunney's rematch has acquired in U.S. sport history is a testament more to the proliferation of convergent mass media during the 1920s than to the fight itself. The "long count" became the rematch's key storyline. Ten fight fans reportedly died of heart attacks while listening to McNamee narrate Tunney's knockdown. The controversy also increased demands for films of the fight, which would allow audiences to judge what happened for themselves. In this case, the ban could not quell interest in Goodart Pictures' film of the bout, which ran nationwide. Rickard stoked the controversy further by manipulating films to make it seem Tunney was down longer than the original recordings showed. Streible explains that thirty-five New York

City theaters openly screened the *Tunney-Dempsey Fight*, including some family movie houses.[60] The popular film rendered the fight picture ban an outmoded and largely unenforceable restriction akin to the prohibition of alcohol. Dempsey retired after the rematch and turned his full attention to acting. Expanding on *Fight and Win*, he starred as Tiger Jack Dillon in the 1928 Broadway play *The Big Fight*.

Aided by Dempseymania, boxing remained a consistent topic for fictional films into the sound era—from comedies like Laurel and Hardy's *Battle of the Century* (1927) to melodramas like *Iron Man* (1931) and *The Champ* (1931) to the musical *Young Man of Manhattan* (1930). These productions often evoked the identifiable Dempsey archetype. For example, Buster Keaton's *Battling Butler* (1926) centers on the pampered Alfred Butler, who is sent on a hunting and fishing trip to become a man. Butler encounters and falls in love with a hard-scrabble mountain girl (Sally O'Neil) during the masculine rite of passage. To win her love, and gain the respect of her similarly hardy family, Butler poses as a fighter with the same surname—Battling Butler. His comic effort to prove his manly vigor works through masquerading as the sort of frontier tough guy Dempsey represents and reinforcing the Western fighter's position as a virile ideal.

The Champ, *The Life of Jimmy Dolan* (1933), and *Winner Take All* (1932) similarly situate the American West that Dempsey signified as a haven of masculine vitality. *Winner Take All* references Dempsey's enchantment by the comparatively soft culture Hollywood represents. It focuses on the fast-living boxer Jimmy Kane (James Cagney), who leaves New York City for New Mexico's Rosario Ranch to take a break from "booze and dames."[61] While regaining his bearings, he falls for Peggy (Marian Nixon), a widow whose son is recovering from an illness. At one point Kane takes a fight in Tijuana to help the struggling Peggy pay her son's (Dickie Moore) medical bills. He eventually returns to New York and promises eventually to send for Peggy. But Kane soon falls into the same decadent scene that he originally fled. In particular, he becomes infatuated with the superficial socialite Joan (Virginia Bruce), who finds Kane's rowdy profession thrilling but is embarrassed by his coarseness. Desperate to win Joan's love, Kane turns down a title shot in favor of undergoing plastic surgery to fix his battered nose and cauliflower ear. He also enrolls in etiquette courses to fit in with Joan's haughty clique. At one point Kane's etiquette teacher suggests he recite Shakespeare to work on his diction. "I don't want any of that Shakespeare guy," Kane retorts. "He's the one that ruined Tunney." Kane's misguided and ultimately ineffective efforts to impress Joan work through evoking Dempsey's story and commenting on the intellectualism that tarnished Tunney's image. Less directly, Laurel and Hardy's *Battle of the Century* lampooned overblown sporting events like Dempsey and Tunney's fights. The main characters begin a slapstick scuffle that degenerates into a town-wide pie fight. A send-up of so many bouts promoted as the "Fight of the Century," Laurel and Hardy's romp comments on the frivolity underlying the excessive spectacles that captivated millions and nourished a growing sports media industry. These boxing films also contributed to the racial politics Dempsey enforced during his championship reign by depicting a sport populated entirely by White heroes.

Boxing Films in Transmedia Sports Culture

Boxing films stressed the sport's increasingly spectacular status by dramatizing its relationship to the media it attracted and supported. Melodramas like *Iron Man*, *Winner Take All*, and *The Big Chance* (1933) integrate newspaper headlines to emphasize protagonists' celebrity and convey their transformation into stars. *The Big Chance* uses a montage of newspaper reports to show main character Frankie Morgan's (John Darrow) ascendance into a promising fighter that gangsters unsuccessfully attempt to bribe. *Winner Take All* employs a similar montage of sports pages to convey Kane's successes upon his initial return to New York City. Such newspaper-themed transitional devices are not exclusive to boxing films, of course, but they demonstrate prizefighting's intimate alliance with print during the Golden Age of Sports Media. More specifically, they highlight newspapers' role in granting celebrity boxers their status, which often composes the centerpiece of the films' dramatic conflict. Along these lines, *Winner Take All* includes a sequence in which a tabloid publication criticizes Kane for his plastic surgery and suggests he has become soft. The headline reads, "Fighter Becomes Social Lap Dog. How the Two-Fisted Champion of the Prize Ring Became a 'Powder Puff' Boxer by Having His Nose and Ears Made over by a Plastic Surgeon to Please the Whims of a Pretty Society Girl." The sports page includes a cartoon of a cowardly Kane fleeing his opponent in an effort to protect his expensive new features.

Other boxing films more directly integrated print media into their plots. In *Night Parade* (1929), the sportswriter Sid Durham (Lee Shumway) helps to dissuade middleweight champion Bobby Martin (Hugh Trevor) from throwing a fight. And *Young Man of Manhattan* opens at Dempsey and Tunney's first encounter in Philadelphia. The sportswriter Toby McLean (Norman Foster) meets the entertainment columnist Ann Vaughn (Claudette Colbert) at the big fight, and they form the relationship that makes up the musical's key narrative thread. *Young Man of Manhattan* comments on Dempsey-Tunney's status as a mega event that preoccupied the entire media industry and was newsworthy enough to attract entertainment writers as well as sports journalists. *The Great White Way* (1924), a production of William Randolph Hearst's Cosmopolitan Pictures that Warner Brothers later remade as *Cain and Mabel* (1936), explores the blurry lines separating news from publicity in the 1920s.

The silent comedy centers on welterweight champion Joe Cain (Oscar Shaw), who has become so dominant in the ring that fans will no longer pay to see him compete. On the recommendation of Tex Rickard, who plays himself, Cain hires Jack Murray (T. Roy Barnes) to be his press agent. Murray also represents the dancer Mabel Vandergrift (Anita Stewart) and devises a plan to gin up publicity by saying the famous dancer and boxer are engaged. Like so many romcom duos, the celebrities initially dislike each other but eventually fall in love. Beyond *The Great White Way*'s promotional plotline, the Hearst film glorifies the intersecting newspaper and publicity industries and features prominently the media mogul's properties as product placements. "Part of the film might easily be mistaken for an educational reel entitled 'The Making of a Newspaper,'" commented the *Washington Post* given the blatant marketing the production gives to Hearst's properties. Other film producers complained that *The Great White Way* enjoyed an unfair advantage because of the promotion it received in Hearst newspapers.[62]

Iron Man, The Big Chance, Night Parade, and *They Never Come Back* (1932) display nascent radio broadcasts alongside the newspaper coverage. Like the coverage in newspapers, the depictions of ringside radio broadcasts and postfight interviews stress boxing's growth into a popular and commodified media spectacle. After the fight that composes *The Big Chance*'s climax, a radio reporter (George Morrell) rushes into the ring to interview the triumphant Frankie Morgan. "There's twenty million people out there just waiting to hear the words of the champion," the sportscaster says, emphasizing the immense audience to which the broadcast makes the fight available. *The Life of Jimmy Dolan* (1933), a melodrama Busby Berkeley remade as *They Made Me a Criminal* in 1939, depicts the combined and increasingly symbiotic importance of print and radio to prizefighting. It begins with boxer Jimmy Dolan (Douglas Fairbanks) winning a championship fight. In a postfight radio interview, the boxer presents himself as a gracious and abstemious young man who loves his mother above all. He even uses the interview to convey a message to his mom, who is listening at home. "I'm coming home! I got the money, and you can get that house in Yonkers," he proudly announces. Dolan's pious image, constructed through radio, has made him a popular sensation—a family-friendly breath of fresh air among the sport's stereotypically rowdy and inarticulate bruisers. The radio report sums up the fight broadcast's glowing depiction of Dolan: "'No booze, no women,' said the new champion. America can be well proud of Jimmy tonight, who by his victory vindicates the sponsors of this program, the Health Biscuit Corporation of America."

But the film transitions to shots of a disheveled hotel room littered with empty bottles and cigarette butts as the broadcast extols Dolan's virtue. Dolan is drunk and lounging with the dissolute vixen Goldie West (Shirley Grey). His pristine image is a cynical ruse he concocted with the scheming manager Doc

Woods (Lyle Talbot)—a reference to Doc Kearns—to garner positive attention and the economic rewards that accompany it. Woods and some friends join Dolan and Goldie for a postfight celebration. One of the guests, unbeknownst to Dolan and Woods, is the journalist Charles Magee (George Meeker). The reporter quietly observes Dolan joking about his sham and the gullible public that falls for it. "I haven't got a mother," Dolan divulges with an inebriated snicker. "That's just a line for suckers." Shortly thereafter, Magee reveals that he is a journalist and that he intends to expose Dolan's duplicity. "Sure, I'm going to write it up," he responds to Dolan's attempt to dissuade him. "I'm a reporter and that's my business." Dolan then offers Magee a bribe, which the journalist rejects with a righteous huff.

Drunk and searching for a way to stop the obstinate Magee from revealing his lie, Dolan punches and accidentally kills the reporter. He immediately passes out alongside the corpse he created and the bottles he spent the evening emptying. The crooked Woods steals Dolan's watch and takes off with the equally conniving Goldie—only to die in a fiery car wreck while attempting to outrun the police. Those inspecting the rubble find Dolan's watch and assume he is the dead driver. Only Phlaxer (Guy Kibbee), a disgraced and aging detective, suspects that Woods's charred corpse is not Dolan when he notices that the boxer is a southpaw and the dead body was not wearing the watch on the appropriate wrist.

Dolan wakes the next morning to the stunning and hungover realization that he killed Magee. The boxer flees west when he sees a newspaper report commenting on his apparent death. Dolan ends up at a farm for disabled children in Pleasant Valley, Utah, run by Mrs. Moore (Aline MacMahon) and her niece Peggy (Loretta Young), who demonstrates a selflessness on par with the fake image Dolan once fashioned to court publicity. The fugitive, who goes by the alias Jack Daugherty, begins to work at the farm and teach the kids how to box. Dolan's narcissistic worldview gradually shifts as he spends more time with Peggy and her innocent wards.

Although his colleagues consider the Dolan case closed, Phlaxer believes the boxer is alive and continues searching for him. Scouring newspapers, the detective comes across a story on "Daugherty" training the kids and travels to Pleasant Valley to investigate. Phlaxer arrives just before Dolan is set to fight in a match against King Cobra (Sammy Stein) to raise money for the cash-strapped farm. Knowing Phlaxer is on his tail, the boxer abandons his southpaw style to conceal his identity from the wily old gumshoe. Phlaxer, however, is not fooled and apprehends the fugitive after the match. But when the detective notices Dolan's moral transformation, he opts to let him go. "Say, maybe I got the wrong guy," Phlaxer says knowingly as he releases Dolan to resume the newly virtuous life he established with Peggy and the kids.

Beyond showing its protagonist's conversion, *The Life of Jimmy Dolan* emphasizes how media combine to create boxing as a public commercial spectacle. Dolan builds his image through manipulating the press and radio. The prospect of Magee exposing Dolan's phony but valuable persona in the press is so threatening that the boxer resorts to manslaughter—albeit unintentional— to prevent the report from reaching newsstands. And Phlaxer relies principally on the newspaper coverage boxing attracts to conduct his detective work.

Boxing films also traced how prizefighting aided radio's transformation into a primarily domestic medium and helped to construct the gendered contours surrounding the changing medium's consumption. Instead of attending Frankie Morgan's final match as *The Big Chance* ends, Morgan's love interest Mary—who convinced the boxer not to throw the bout despite the financial benefits—listens to the radio broadcast at home with her son Arthur. The fight scene cross-cuts between Morgan struggling through the grueling match and Mary listening at home in agony. Similarly, Peggy and the children stay at the farm and listen to the radio broadcast of Dolan's fight against King Cobra. When the announcer reports that Dolan is losing, the kids begin to sob and Peggy, unable to listen further, turns off the set. The scenes demonstrate radio's potential to convey unfolding events across spatial distance—and they employ this breach to intensify the women spectators' emotional longing and helplessness in the face of the boxers' masculine struggle. These film depictions also encode the domestic sphere as feminine and indicate that radio broadcasts allow women and children to experience boxing at a remove from its corrupting brutality and seediness. Morgan and Dolan reunite with their virtuous love interests, but outside the realm of prizefighting. Morgan even proposes to Mary via a postfight radio interview: "Let's get married right away," he says into the microphone to the woman he knows is listening at home. The films' gendered depictions of the radio broadcasts' consumption emphasize the domestic sphere's purity and boxing's comparative ruggedness while connecting these seemingly disparate zones. Such representations extended into the television era and became a common trope in the boxing film to stress the intersecting gender relations marking sport and media.

W. S. Van Dyke's *The Prizefighter and the Lady* (1933) shows how boxing propelled convergence among the multiple media that combined to build its spectacular status. The film stars heavyweight fighter Max Baer as Steve Morgan, a short-fused barroom bouncer. Morgan impresses a washed-up and alcoholic former trainer, the Professor (Walter Huston), after dispatching a belligerent patron. The Professor convinces Morgan he has potential and begins to mold the raw talent into a contender. Morgan encounters the beautiful nightclub singer Belle (Myrna Loy) as his career takes off. The singer, who is in a relationship with the gangster and nightclub owner Willie Ryan (Otto Kruger), initially rebuffs Morgan's swaggering flirtations. But Morgan eventually persuades her to leave Ryan and marry him.

Like *The Big Chance* and *Winner Take All*, *Prizefighter and the Lady* uses a montage of newspaper clippings to trace Morgan's rapid rise through the professional ranks. It also includes musical sequences of a vaudeville show starring Morgan that, like *The Jack Dempsey Revue*, was produced to capitalize on his swelling celebrity. The media-driven fame Morgan so quickly acquires goes to his head just as rapidly. He begins philandering and stops listening to the Professor's instruction. As a result, Morgan's partnership with the sagacious trainer dissolves. Similarly, Belle leaves the untrustworthy fighter and returns to Ryan. Sensing Morgan's mounting hubris, Ryan arranges for the prizefighter to take on the champion Primo Carnera, who plays himself. "Carnera will knock his fat head into the East River," Ryan confidently wagers. The gangster books the match through Jack Dempsey Enterprises, a fictional promotional company run by Dempsey, who also appears as himself and aims to turn the fight into a happening on par with his Tunney bouts. "It can only be big," Dempsey explains to the boxers as they sign the contract, "when you convince Old Man Public you're giving him a real fight." As Ryan gambled, Morgan arrives at the championship match out of shape and without the Professor's expert guiding hand. Carnera dominates the early rounds and seems headed for a decisive victory. But Belle can no longer stand to see Morgan get punished and convinces the Professor to rejoin his corner. The trainer swallows his pride and coaches the fighter to an unlikely draw. Although Ryan initially rebukes Belle for helping Morgan, he eventually gives her his blessing to get back together with the humbled boxer. *The Prizefighter and the Lady* was released while Carnera was heavyweight champ and benefitted from the celebrity's inclusion. The film again spiked in popularity after Baer beat Carnera for the title in 1934—a victory that Baer claimed was aided by his experience sparring with Carnera during the film's production.[63]

Prizefighter and the Lady demonstrates the overlapping media that fused to build Morgan's celebrity and generate interest in his eventual championship tilt. Morgan, for instance, uses talking with sportswriters—a professional necessity given the publicity their coverage offers—as an excuse to get out of the house so he can carouse. "Got a lot of sportswriters here and they're figuring ways to plug me as a contender. You know, same old stuff," he tells the suspicious Belle. The exposure drives radio broadcasts of his fights, the vaudeville show, and the extra editions that newsies hawk outside of the title fight at Madison Square Garden. Prior to the championship, the film presents a montage of photographers snapping pictures, printing presses shooting out papers, radio microphones capturing sound, and newsreel cameras recording the scene. Like earlier boxing film depictions of newspapers and radio, the montage highlights the spectacle surrounding Morgan and Carnera's fight. But this scene blends these

The Boxing Film through the Golden Age • 31

media and suggests they cannot be unwoven within the multifaceted sports media landscape in which the Morgan-Carnera match is taking place. It also reinforces Dempsey's role in helping to catalyze this convergent media environment by including him as the promotional engine behind this multiplatform spectacle.

Aside from depicting the intermingling media that transform prizefights into nationally experienced spectacles, *Prizefighter and the Lady* began adopting their narrative practices—a convention other Hollywood boxing movies employed to approximate how fans consumed fights. The film presents Morgan and Carnera's fight from the perspective of a radio broadcast that sets the scene by remarking on the presence of celebrities and other media at the fight. The broadcaster (Dan Tobey) mentions that Al Jolson, Anne Morgan, and Grantland Rice are at the match (though they do not have cameos), and the film cuts to journalists and photographers covering the bout. The narrative technique reinforces radio's position as the dominant way fans experienced prizefights at the time and uses the medium's conventions to build realism that complements the film's inclusion of venues like Madison Square Garden and boxers such as Baer, Carnera, and Dempsey. Moreover, the visual accompaniment the film provides to its presentation of a live radio broadcast offers a precursor to television coverage a decade before the medium took hold. *Prizefighter and the Lady* demonstrates how the boxing film institutionalizes, makes sense of, and even anticipates the multimedia culture surrounding boxing.

Prizefighter and the Lady also comments on and enacts how commercial media shape boxing's history and cultural politics. Prior to discovering Morgan, the Professor drunkenly waxes nostalgic about boxing's good old days. "There are no more prizefighters," he resignedly slurs. "The present generation of fighters are nothing more or less than an army of Adagio dancers. Where are the Sullivans? The Fitzsimmonses? The Ketchels?" He sees Morgan as a revival of this heroic tradition of old-school brawlers. The Morgan-Carnera title match supports this attitude by trotting out a collection of retired fighters prior to the fight—a common practice at big bouts. The ceremony showcases lightweight Joe Rivers, welterweight Jackie Fields, middleweight Billy Papke, the wrestler Strangler Lewis, and the heavyweights Jess Willard, Frank Moran, and Jim Jeffries—all of whom appear as themselves. The special guests enter the ring to rapturous applause, cameras flashing, and ringside typewriters feverishly chronicling their cameos. The ceremony accents the Morgan-Carnera fight's import as a continuation of the glorious heritage the retired fighters exemplify. It also reinforces the entirely White boxing history about which the Professor reminisces during the film's opening minutes. Jack Johnson was alive—and still occasionally boxing—when *Prizefighter and the Lady* was produced. The film, however, erases the rebellious Black fighter from the sporting tradition it commemorates and continues.

32 • The Boxing Film

Prizefighter and the Lady demonstrates how the proliferation of commercial media ensured boxing's salability by Whitening the sport. It attributes these racial politics in part to Dempsey by casting the namesake of Dempseymania—and the biggest star in boxing's media-driven explosion through the 1920s—as the force behind the championship bout's promotion. Films like *Prizefighter and the Lady* chronicle the cultural attitudes accompanying boxing and media's commercially driven synergy and informing the shape both the sport and representations of it took during the Golden Age of Sports Media. These depictions, however, began to shift along with the rise of future heavyweight champion Joe Louis, who began his professional career one year after *Prizefighter and the Lady*'s release.

2

St. Joe Louis, Surrounded by Films

●●●●●●●●●●●●●●●●●●●●●●●●

Martin Luther King Jr.'s classic civil rights treatise *Why We Can't Wait* (1964) includes a story about a young Black convict in the 1930s American South awaiting execution in the gas chamber, at the time a newfangled technique that was erroneously considered more "humane" than hanging or the electric chair. Prison officials placed an audio recorder in the chamber to offer researchers some ghastly indication of how a person might respond when faced with such singularly terrifying circumstances. When the executioner released the toxic gas, the condemned man did not plead for mercy, issue a confession, or even sneak in a quick Hail Mary. Instead, he bellowed "Save me, Joe Louis! Save me, Joe Louis!" in desperate hope that the heavyweight champion—the second African American title holder after Jack Johnson—might miraculously deliver some form of salvation. "The condemned young Negro, groping for someone who might care for him, and had power enough to rescue him, found only the heavyweight boxing champion of the world," King wrote. "Joe Louis would care because he was a Negro. Joe Louis could do something because he was a fighter. In a few words the dying man had written a social commentary. Not God, not government, not charitably-minded white men, but a Negro who was the world's most expert fighter, in this last extremity, was the last hope."[1] Although probably apocryphal, the folk tale speaks to Joe Louis's mythic significance in Black culture. Louis was heroic enough to make plausible a scenario in which a young man faced with execution might call on the boxer to swoop in and save the day.

34 • The Boxing Film

Despite his exalted status, Louis died nearly penniless after being bilked by his management, haunted by a series of poor investments, and hounded by the IRS for back taxes. The country Louis inspired and the associates he made wealthy virtually abandoned the champion once he exhausted his usefulness. Neo-impressionist artist Jean-Michel Basquiat commented on the fighter's dual role as hero and victim with *St. Joe Louis, Surrounded by Snakes* (1982). The spare and colorful painting, produced one year after the boxer's death, shows Louis seated on a stool in the corner of a ring with a halo floating above his head—a gesture toward his righteousness. Louis is wreathed by a collection of monstrous consultants who at once seem to be watching out for him and conspiring behind his back. Basquiat's Louis—who stoically gazes ahead while fractured by the errant lines and drips characteristic of the artist's style—embodies at once the possibilities of American democracy and the perils of institutionalized injustice.

Boxing, and the heavyweight division specifically, lagged after Jack Dempsey's retirement. Sammons calls the early 1930s a "pugilistic depression" that matched the larger economic hard times. Louis's ascendance rejuvenated the sport. His vitalizing impact extended into boxing films, which had similarly wilted after Dempsey hung up his gloves.[2] Films of Louis's victories were popular—if often illegal—attractions among African American audiences, and the boxer both appeared in and inspired various independent race films made for exhibition in segregated Black theaters. Beyond these niche productions, Louis's popularity precipitated Hollywood's most robust period of boxing films. Although they capitalized on Louis's renown, the mainstream productions did not feature a Black protagonist until *The Joe Louis Story* in 1953—a film released after Louis retired and the heavyweight title was back in White hands. Reflecting the simultaneous exaltation and exploitation that Basquiat's painting addresses, Louis was surrounded by boxing films that profited from the popularity he triggered but avoided depicting worlds that centered on Black fighters or exploring the distinct challenges they faced in and out of the sport. These different productions showcase the conditions under which separate alcoves of film culture would celebrate Louis as well as the lengths to which Hollywood went to suppress the Black agency he represented from the boxing movies he helped to make viable.

Black Moses and Brown Bomber

Louis's trajectory exemplifies the American Dream narrative so central to boxing films—particularly those produced during the Great Depression era when he began his professional career. He was born Joe Louis Barrow in 1914 to a LaFayette, Alabama, family of sharecroppers. In 1926 the Barrows moved to Detroit in search of the factory work that drew many southern African

Americans to the industrializing North and Midwest. As the story goes, Joe's mother Lillie was giving her teenage son money to take violin lessons. Barrow's friends teased him about his delicate extracurricular activity—one he had little aptitude for and only moderate interest in. As a result, Barrow began secretly using the money for his violin classes to rent a locker and learn the appreciably tougher trade of boxing at the Brewster Recreation Center. Lillie soon discovered his truancy and forgave her son on the condition that he give his preferred activity his best effort.

Barrow had a knack for fighting that immediately outshone whatever tunes he managed to wring out of his fiddle. He also saw the sport as a way to make money, something that had always been in short supply. The fledgling pugilist began fighting under the truncated name of Joe Louis with the guidance of an all-Black group of mentors that included comanagers Julian Black and John Roxborough and trainer Jack Blackburn, who shaped him into a pro by the time he turned twenty. As it became apparent that Louis had the potential to compete on a national level—and perhaps someday contend for the heavyweight title—his management developed a plan to help their fighter navigate and mitigate the racist judgment he would inevitably encounter. Although it had been years since Jack Johnson had been champion, Black fighters—especially heavyweights—still lived under the incendiary shadow he cast. Despite many being deserving, no Black heavyweight had even received a title shot since Johnson. "We will not let Louis follow in the footsteps of Jack Johnson," Blackburn matter-of-factly remarked. "He will be an example and a help to the colored race."[3] Louis's handlers realized their fighter could reach the big time only if he affected a persona that would not aggravate the anxieties his Blackness already provoked in a White society deeply uncomfortable with the prospect of a Black heavyweight champ. Louis was directed never to have his picture taken with a White woman or attend a nightclub alone; he was to give maximum effort in all fights, adhere by the rules, and never participate in a fixed match; he could not humiliate opponents, gloat when victorious, or even say anything beyond the most predictable platitudes when talking to reporters; and he had to live clean. Press releases trumpeted the upstanding young fighter as a devoted son who read scripture daily, saved his money, and abstained from drinking and smoking. The publicity fashioned a wholesome and even childlike contender who loved chewing gum and eating ice cream—an obvious contrast to Johnson's libertine lifestyle. As biographer Randy Roberts explains, "Everything Louis did, every image he projected, carried the same message: 'I am not Jack Johnson.'"[4] Louis was a painstakingly curated innocent along the lines of Jimmy Dolan. And, like Dolan, Louis's private life did not always jibe with his abstemious public image.

Undefeated through his first twenty-two bouts, Louis caught the attention of Mike Jacobs, a former ticket scalper for Tex Rickard who established the

36 • The Boxing Film

Twentieth Century Sporting Club promotional company in 1933. Jacobs saw the up-and-comer as a potential star who could boost the nascent Twentieth Century's status. He first organized Louis's March 1935 fight against Natie Brown in Detroit. Following in the footsteps of Rickard and Kearns, the shrewd promoter commissioned a train to shuttle New York City sportswriters to Detroit and thereby ensure the bout would receive national exposure.[5] Along the way, Jacobs continued to push Louis as an exciting and modest contender—a celebrity that newspapers, hungry for the next prizefighting sensation, were happy to puff.

Despite Louis's strict code of conduct and Jacobs's aggressive promotion, the fighter still faced rampant racism. Before Louis was even champion, Jack Dempsey sponsored a "White Hope" tournament to "find a white boy who can wallop Louis" and, in doing so, make him a less viable title contender.[6] Sportswriters routinely used animal metaphors to describe Louis and quoted him as speaking in minstrel dialect. Grantland Rice called him a "jungle cat," and illustrators depicted the fighter as a big-lipped and shuffling oaf. While the Brown Bomber was the nickname that eventually stuck, Louis absorbed an abundance of other racially driven and lazily alliterative monikers that included the Black Menace, Chocolate Cobra, Dark Destroyer, Ebony Elephant, Harlem Hammer, and Tawny Tiger. Louis tolerated most of the indignities. But he drew the line when one photographer asked him to pose while eating a slice of watermelon.[7]

Although Louis was frequently mistreated by mainstream media outlets, his importance in the Black community is difficult to overstate. Like Johnson, Louis shattered racist norms that imposed ceilings on African American achievement. *New York Sun* reporter Edward Van Every called him a "Black Moses" who would usher "broader tolerance on the part of his white brother." By the middle 1930s, Louis was the most famous Black man in the United States—and probably the world. "Americans, especially Black Americans, simply could not see, read, or hear too much about him," Roberts explains. "It was almost impossible to glance through a Black newspaper without encountering Louis's face and dozens of articles touting his exploits."[8] Like Dempsey's, Louis's fights became cultural events. But unlike Dempsey's matches, Louis's bouts were wrapped up in the broader struggle for African American equality, which primed them for dramatization.

Louis's first match in New York City—against the Italian Primo Carnera— began to show his fights' potential to serve as provocative storylines that would attract interest beyond die-hard boxing fans. At the time, Italy was undertaking military action against the comparatively weak African state of Abyssinia (now Ethiopia). Jacobs framed Louis-Carnera as a distillation of this racial and geopolitical rift. Louis's sixth round victory by knockout composed a symbolic defense of Blacks over White imperialist bullies. Louis's next fight, against the popular former champion Max Baer, composed the highest profile match in which a Black heavyweight had competed since Johnson's career. And it was billed as yet another proving ground for racial superiority—a narrative that helped the nationally broadcast bout, which Louis won with a fourth-round knockout, attract the largest gate since Dempsey and Tunney's 1927 rematch.

Louis took on the German former champion Max Schmeling in June 1936—a fight most viewed as a warm-up that Louis would win easily on his way to a title shot against James Braddock. Although the match itself was not expected to offer much excitement, it resonated with and intensified the racial and political stories that built interest in Louis's bouts against the Italian Carnera and the Jewish Baer. The German Nazi Party, still relatively obscure on the global stage at the time, trumpeted Schmeling as an emblem of its white supremacism. Nazi leader Adolf Hitler saw great benefit to having a White German as the heavyweight champion, and he endorsed the fight despite resistance from far-right German newspapers, which called for Schmeling to boycott "on the grounds that no self-respecting Aryan should lower himself by entering the ring with a black man."[9] Arguing from the opposite end of the ideological spectrum, the NAACP registered its disapproval because of the Nazis' racism. The controversy only boosted the match's profile. But Louis—perhaps convinced by the many reports of his inevitable victory—trained haphazardly for the match. Schmeling capitalized on Louis's lackadaisical preparation and delivered the younger fighter his first professional defeat with a twelfth-round knockout. Like the Dempsey and Tunney rematch, reports surfaced of twelve people dying from stress while listening to the radio broadcast.[10] Germans used films of the match as propaganda, deeming them "politically valuable" and possessing "educational value" because they showcased "German victory over the colored race." Moviegoers outside a Vienna theater reportedly gave Nazi salutes and hollered "Heil Schmeling!" and "Heil Hitler!" after watching the fight film.[11]

Stunned and embarrassed by the loss, Louis rededicated himself to training and won his next seven matches. The impressive rebound combined with Louis's general popularity secured him a title shot against Braddock without having to fight Schmeling again. Braddock initially contracted with Madison Square Garden to defend his championship against Schmeling at the arena. Jacobs and the Twentieth Century Sporting Club, however, cooked up a handsome deal—one that included 10 percent of their earnings from Louis's future fights—that convinced Braddock to break his contract and fight Louis in Chicago. Louis knocked out Braddock in the eighth to become the first Black champion in twenty-two years. Such a banner moment for African Americans sparked widespread celebrations in Black communities. But the victory did not prompt the racial discord that accompanied Johnson's win over Jeffries—a testament to Louis's comparative acceptance due to the public relations strategy his team devised.

While Louis was arguably the United States' first "crossover" African American sports star, the circulation and exhibition of Louis versus Braddock films demonstrate the limits of America's racial tolerance. *Variety* observed that the film, "like previous celluloid records of Joe Louis's victories over ofay [White] battlers," would play well in the North but would have difficulty finding an audience in the South. It also pointed out that the film of Schmeling's victory over Louis played widely in the South and was one of the region's "biggest fight [film] grossers in years." The Louis-Braddock film, *Variety* continued, "can't be expected to get more than half the biz the German's victory film enjoyed."[12] The *Chicago Defender*'s Luther Carmichael reported that while two Black theaters in Nashville programmed the Louis-Braddock film, only one of the city's many White-oriented movie houses showed it. "The attitude of the local theatre operators following the recent fight is exactly the reverse of the course they pursued following the Louis-Schmeling fight of a year ago," Carmichael explained, "when practically every downtown theatre showed the films for a two-week period, a record run for any type of movie in this city."[13] These exhibition practices show the racial enmity surrounding Louis. Southern exhibitors were more willing to schedule films of a victorious instrument of Nazism than a triumphant Black American.

Intending to leave no doubt that he deserved the title he gained from Braddock, Louis scheduled a June 1938 rematch against Schmeling. Political tensions between the United States and Germany had escalated since the first fight. The rematch extended the racial animosity Louis and Schmeling signified into a broader battle between democracy and totalitarianism, particularly since Louis publicly identified with patriotic "popular front" efforts to combat fascism. The fight's political contours made it even an even bigger spectacle than Louis-Braddock with seventy thousand attending the bout at Yankee Stadium and a record-breaking hundred million listening to the live radio broadcast worldwide. Louis's first-round knockout, one of the most convincing victories of his career, made the champion's superiority over Schmeling unquestionable. The quick fight—now often cited as the most important boxing match ever because of its political implications in the run-up to World War II—quieted those who viewed Schmeling's 1936 victory as proof of Aryan supremacy and solidified Louis's position as an African American hero. "There was never anything like it," wrote the *Daily Worker* of postfight celebrations in the Black enclave of Harlem, which was just walking distance from Yankee Stadium. "Take a dozen Harlem Christmases, a score of New Years eves, a bushel of July 4ths and maybe—yes, maybe—you get a faint glimpse of the idea. . . . There were parades, meetings, demonstrations, snake dances, speeches, Ethiopian and American flags, home-made confetti, in which every strata of the Negro people took part." Contrasting the Viennese moviegoers' responses to films of Louis and Schmeling's first bout, Harlem revelers reportedly issued mock Nazi salutes and jubilantly cried "Heil Louis!"[14]

Given the fight's brevity—just over two minutes—films of the Louis-Schmeling rematch presented relatively little value to U.S. exhibitors. Hitler decided the film of the rematch lacked the "educational value" Nazi censors ascribed to the 1936 bout and discouraged its exhibition. Those films of the fight that did manage to circulate in Germany were reportedly doctored to make Schmeling appear more competitive by inserting snippets from the 1936 match—allegations German authorities denied. But the documentary evidence the film provided of Louis manhandling Schmeling—much like the films of Johnson beating Jeffries in 1910—were disruptive enough to warrant containment in Germany.[15]

Louis did not rest on his well-deserved laurels after earning the championship and beating Schmeling. He defended his title twenty-five times—a marked contrast to Dempsey, who barely fought while champion in favor of milking the promotional opportunities the title offered without jeopardizing the status it delivered. Louis had to fight since he did not receive the same diversified flood of opportunities outside of the ring that were lavished upon his White predecessor. Moreover, he likely would have been accused of cowardice had he mirrored Dempsey's inactivity. But critics still managed to find fault in Louis's actions and belittled the parade of overmatched challengers he faced as the "Bum-of-the-Month Club." A key element that made these continuous and predictable bouts profitable was the possibility that one of the mostly White challengers would unseat Louis. While Louis enjoyed far greater acceptance than Johnson, the many boxing films produced during his career make it clear that mainstream America would still have preferred a White champion.

Our Joe and Their Joe

Fictional race melodramas used Louis to fashion inspirational tales of Black uplift. Louis starred as Joe Thomas in Harry L. Fraser's *Spirit of Youth* (1938), a film loosely based on the fighter's biography. "We have observed certain experiments with films using all-colored talent. There is no question but there is a demand for pictures of the right type," said *Spirit of Youth* producer Clarence Muse, who also played the role of Thomas's manager Frankie Walburn. Muse explained that Louis composed "a personality we may well be proud to present to any audience in America" and that *Spirit of Youth* would offer a story "that is elevating to the Negro race, entertaining to all movie fans."[16] Muse figured that Louis's agreeable image would allow *Spirit of Youth* to attract a Black audience without provoking controversy beyond its target demographic.

Adapting Louis's life story, *Spirit of Youth* has Joe Thomas leave Alabama—along with his mother (Cleo Desmond) and childhood sweetheart Mary (Edna Mae Harris)—to find employment in Detroit. He works a series of menial jobs and discovers his uncanny fistic talent after flooring an abusive boss

40 • The Boxing Film

who mistreats his companion Crickie (Mantan Moreland). Taking notice of Joe's tremendous punching power, Crickie encourages his buddy to pursue boxing. Beyond the economic benefits, Crickie suggests Joe could use boxing as a tool for social and even racial elevation. "You can make your people proud of you," Crickie says. Joe hires Frankie Walburn to manage him and begins moving up the ranks—a trajectory conveyed with a montage of newspaper headlines. *Spirit of Youth* further borrows from Louis's biography by characterizing Joe Thomas as unusually pious. He orders orange juice with dinner, is humble and soft-spoken when talking to the press, and asks his mother's permission before turning pro. "Whether you win or lose, it's no shame if you do your best," Mrs. Thomas lovingly responds. "But don't ever bring disgrace on your family." Like Crickie, Thomas's mother suggests there is more than just money to be gained from his burgeoning boxing career. However, and in keeping with the film's efforts to remain noncontroversial, neither Crickie nor Mrs. Thomas frame his boxing success as a counter to White racism.

But Joe Thomas's focus drifts and he falls under the spell of the sexy nightclub singer Flora (Mae Turner). Ignoring his mother's advice, the immature fighter is surprisingly knocked out by the White underdog Fritz Baldwin—an evocation of Louis's first Schmeling fight apparent through Baldwin's race and Germanic first name. Again echoing Louis, Thomas regains his discipline and redeems himself by eventually winning the championship. The film ends at a celebratory postfight banquet at which a large group of African Americans are gathered. Walburn toasts the new champion as "Our Joe." *Spirit of Youth* underscores Louis's position as a potent symbol of Black empowerment and suggests that this agency is best achieved through the self-reliance Joe Thomas typifies.

Spirit of Youth gathered mainly negative reviews that focused on Louis's acting. *Variety* panned it as a "hodge-podge of stereotyped clichés and homely philosophy" and cited Louis's "lack of facial and lingual mobility" as its principal offense.[17] Despite the film's hackneyed plot and poor acting, Louis's celebrity was enough to draw a crowd. Moreover, *Spirit of Youth* premiered shortly before Louis's rematch against Schmeling and benefitted from interest surrounding the bout, specifically among the Black community the film courted. "Come see the heavyweight champion in action and see how he will look when he beats Schmeling in the forthcoming fight," wrote a *Los Angeles Sentinel* report on the film. The partisan commentary cited *Spirit of Youth* as a complement to the racial progress Louis's athletic feats delivered. The melodrama remained in circulation at Black theaters through the rest of Louis's career.

Spirit of Youth was popular enough to inspire the very similar race film *Keep Punching* (1939), starring lightweight champion Henry Armstrong as Henry Jackson. Armstrong affected a public image much like that of Louis. *Ring*, in fact, named them its Most Valuable Boxers of 1938—a testament to their complementary mainstream friendliness. Like Louis, Armstrong identified as a patriotic defender of U.S. democracy and encouraged Black Americans to make their way with the opportunities it afforded, however limited. "While the so-called American Way hasn't been kind to my people, it's better than any known system," Armstrong told the *New York Amsterdam News*.[18] *Keep Punching* builds on the bootstraps ethos Armstrong endorses. It immediately engages the theme of Black uplift by opening with a group of African Americans singing "Lift Every Voice and Sing"—also known as the "Black National Anthem"—at a graduation ceremony. The officiant singles out Henry Jackson as "the pride of our community, who has never failed us." *Keep Punching* then cuts to a party that further honors Jackson's academic and athletic feats. His teacher, Professor Washington (uncredited), extols Jackson's monumental potential. "The hope is born within me that there are no heights our Henry cannot climb," Washington says. "My one hope is that little Henry will follow the path that I have planned for him. Little Henry must enter college, pursue his studies, become a lawyer." Mirroring *Spirit of Youth*'s celebration of "our Joe," *Keep Punching* praises "our Henry" as a beacon of hope in the Black community.

Despite Professor Washington's scholarly urgings, Jackson is enticed by the money and glamor pro boxing offers. A gambler (Willie Bryant) and the seductress Jerry (Mae Johnson) conspire to sabotage his big match. But Jackson evades the plot, wins the bout, and quits boxing in favor of the route Washington originally encouraged him to pursue. "Soon there will be no more fighting," he tells Fanny as the melodrama ends. "Soon there will be more schooling, and, if fate is kind, maybe I'll become a lawyer." *Spirit of Youth* and *Keep Punching* suggest Joe Louis and Henry Armstrong's athletic achievements instill optimism and pride in the Black communities these boxers represent and make them, at the very least, marginally acceptable in the White world that surrounds them. The films safeguarded this acceptability by framing the protagonists' struggles more as quests to establish their economic status and manhood than as indictments of racial oppression.

Oscar Micheaux's *The Notorious Elinor Lee* (1940), the pioneering Black independent filmmaker's second boxing movie after *The Brute*, heightens *Spirit of Youth* and *Keep Punching*'s melodramatic themes to offer a bleaker take on race and boxing. Set in Harlem, the production opens with a shot of a newspaper headline celebrating the Benny "Bombshell" Blue (Robert Earl Jones), a young boxer modeled after Louis whose Bombshell nickname evokes his Brown Bomber moniker. The African American gangster's moll Elinor Lee (Gladys Williams) owns Blue's contract and is plotting with White racketeers to build her fighter up and eventually make him take a dive.

Lee's plan for Blue goes awry when he loses to the German Hans Wagner (Harry Kadison). Paralleling Louis's first fight against Schmeling, Blue was expected to breeze through the bout. The self-assured Blue tells his trainers he plans to let the bout last four or five rounds "for the pictures" before he

FIG. 3 Lobby card for Oscar Micheaux's *The Notorious Elinor Lee* (1940). (New York Public Library)

finishes Wagner to ensure the fight films would sell. But like Schmeling, Wagner surprises the undertrained and overconfident Blue with a late-round knockout. The film underscores Blue's standing in the African American community—and the devastation his defeat produced within it—by periodically cutting to a group of dejected Black spectators listening to the radio broadcast of the match. It also alludes to Wagner's alliance with Nazi racial ideologies when the victorious German claims to "have exploded the myth of [Blue's] greatness"—a myth he presumably replaced with a newly racialized narrative of sporting excellence.

Blue, again echoing Louis after the initial Schmeling match, recommits to his training and begins rebuilding his résumé. Wagner refuses to grant Blue a rematch until the German contender secures a fight against the current champion. But, and like Braddock, the champ discovers that he can get a bigger payday by fighting the more popular Benny Blue and grants him the title shot instead of Wagner. Blue wins and finally achieves the exalted status Lee can exploit by fixing his championship defense against Wagner. "Now he's rematched with Wagner and the time's ready for the big killing," she remarks diabolically. Had she a mustache, the melodramatic scoundrel surely would have twisted it.

Once the film establishes Blue as a champion and African American hero, it introduces his girlfriend Fredi (Edna Mae Harris), who complains that the boxer has been ignoring her. "It's just that I've been so busy redeeming myself that I've neglected all things socially," Benny says in his defense. Elinor Lee plans to blackmail Fredi, an escaped convict whom she helped break out of prison, into persuading Blue to throw the Wagner fight. Although beholden to Lee, Fredi is appalled by her devious conspiracy. She tries to dissuade Lee from the plot by arguing that it would not only compromise Blue's reputation but also put the progress of the entire Black race in jeopardy. "In addition to being a great fighter, and the idol of millions, Benny Blue is one of us," she pleads. "As poor as we are, even wretched. And as low as we are, doesn't it mean anything to you, a colored woman, to see this boy on top?" "Not as much as a million dollars," Lee coolly replies. "You see, it's a matter of business with me. I bought his contract and built him up to the championship for this very purpose." Aside from extorting Fredi, Lee recruits Cracker Johnson (Columbus Jackson)—a retired African American former champion—to help achieve her corrupt objective. An obvious reference to Jack Johnson, Cracker Johnson, like Lee, is happy to harm the already fragile Black community to secure his personal gain. Micheaux uses Cracker Johnson's difference from Blue to comment on the vast gulf separating Jack Johnson from Joe Louis and offers a clear suggestion as to which fighter he believes better served African Americans.

Fredi initially proceeds with Lee's plan by luring the previously disciplined Blue into Harlem's vibrant nightlife, where she aims to soften him with its debauched pleasures. The tabloids take notice of Blue's changed lifestyle and suspect he may be drifting into the indolence that helped Wagner beat him. Micheaux integrates a shot of a gossip column that expresses concern about Blue's frequent late nights: "Benny Blue seems to have moved his training quarters from Plattoon Lakes to the night clubs, where in company with the 'vampire' (Fredi Welsh) he is seen every night until? . . . Be careful, Benny. It's obvious that 'night club' training is not so good for a fighter." But despite the risks, Fredi cannot bring herself to carry through with the plot and helps to get Blue back on track. As in the Louis-Schmeling rematch, Blue knocks Wagner out in the first round. Micheaux, in fact, staged the Blue-Wagner fight scene to resemble Louis and Schmeling's 1938 bout, and the camera angles he employed duplicate those used in the fight film. He also combines the Blue-Wagner match with shots of jubilant Black spectators listening to the radio broadcast to suggest the victory amplified the racial pride Fredi ultimately protected by defying Lee. The melodrama ends with a newspaper report that Lee had been murdered— presumably by the White gangsters who expected Blue to take a dive.

The race films Louis inspired were both designed for Black audiences and depicted almost entirely segregated worlds. *The Notorious Elinor Lee*, for example, opens with a title card that highlights its "great all star colored cast."

Moreover, the films showcase educated and affluent Black communities that reflect the aspirational progress Louis personified. While these films did not explicitly critique racism and were exhibited mainly in African American communities, they still incited anxiety from those concerned that the Black empowerment they depicted might unsettle racial hierarchies. A Motion Picture Production Code administrator speculated the *Spirit of Youth* would encounter trouble in the South because it depicted a Black man victorious against White opponents. Similarly, the *Atlanta Daily World* surmised that a scene in *Spirit of Youth* in which Walburn gives a handout to a broken-down White pug—a fighter he presents to Thomas as a cautionary tale—would arouse "southern resentment and resentment in the British and French colonies" that would hamper the film's prospects.[19] Even without directly confronting racial bigotry, these segregated tales of self-reliant Black elevation provoked bitterness.

A spate of Hollywood boxing movies appeared alongside the race films. None of these productions included Black stars; but many tapped into the success of fighters like the Jewish Barney Ross (whose struggles with drug addiction inspired André de Toth's *Monkey on My Back*, 1957) and the Italian American Tony Canzoneri to frame boxing as a pathway toward cultural and economic success for Depression-era White urban ethnics.[20] Films like *Kid Galahad* (Michael Curtiz, 1937), *The Crowd Roars* (Richard Thorpe, 1938), *The Kid Comes Back* (B. Reeves Eason, 1938), *Golden Boy* (Rouben Mamoulian, 1939), *They Made Me a Criminal* (Busby Berkeley, 1939), and *City for Conquest* (Anatole Litvak, 1940) commented on the decade's hardships by depicting boxing as a heroic avenue for betterment that is nevertheless pocked by unfairness and corruption.

While these Hollywood productions focused on White ethnic identity, some included allusions to Louis's familiar story that boxing fans would surely recognize. Michael Curtiz's *Kid Galahad*—which Phil Karlson remade as an Elvis Presley movie in 1962—focuses on Nick Donati (Edward G. Robinson), an Italian American manager who shapes the handsome and clean-living bell hop Ward Guisenberry (Wayne Morris) into a boxing idol. His efforts to build Guisenberry into a contender allude to Louis's early career. "There isn't any room for feelings in this game," Donati reminds his young boxer. "The fighter's a machine not a violin player." Donati urges Guisenberry to make the same macho pivot Louis undertook as a boy when scrapping his violin for boxing gloves. He also encourages Guisenberry to adopt a wholesome persona like Louis by naming him Kid Galahad—a reference to an Arthurian knight known for being pure of heart—and giving him a set of prescriptions to guarantee that his public conduct will fulfill this marketable and romantic identity.

Rouben Mamoulian's *Golden Boy*, an adaptation of Clifford Odets's play, similarly evokes Louis to tell the story of Joe Bonaparte (William Holden), a young Italian American who gives up the violin to pursue boxing. Bonaparte's decision devastates his father (Lee J. Cobb), who dreamed that Joe would become a classical musician. Like Louis, a combination of economics and masculinity moved Bonaparte to quit the violin for pugilism. Bonaparte's friends made fun of his music, and he viewed fighting as a way to make quick money for his poor immigrant family. "Money's the answer," Joe tells his disappointed and idealistic father. "I can get it through fighting."

Kid Galahad and *Golden Boy* comment on boxing's idealized potential to offer White ethnics opportunities for advancement in a society with few economic prospects in general and even fewer for outsiders like Donati and Bonaparte. The films' depictions of ethnic uplift, as Grindon points out, combine with their evocations of Louis to dramatize "the widespread public anxiety about assimilation Joe Louis raised."[21] Though subtle, *Kid Galahad* and *Golden Boy*'s allusions to Louis's well-known biography use that African American story to help explore the opportunities boxing offered disenfranchised Whites during the Depression. And beyond simply evoking Louis, the films attracted audiences by relying in part on his popularity. *Kid Galahad* premiered just before the Louis-Braddock match and was marketed as a primer to the championship bout. Similarly, Odets's drama debuted on Broadway shortly after Louis secured the title. Such productions, therefore, used Louis's story to help fashion marketable tales while keeping his Blackness at a safe distance.[22]

While Hollywood films only indirectly engaged Louis, the boxer's image proved innocuous enough to prompt a repeal of the Sims Act and liberate fight films from the law that officially prohibited them from crossing state lines. The federal ban had never been particularly popular—especially once Johnson lost the title. Jack Dempsey publicly denounced the restriction and estimated that it cost him two million dollars in potential film earnings over the course of his career. Beyond the financial drawbacks, the ban was nearly impossible to enforce, and many theaters—like those that showed films of Louis's early bouts—simply ignored it. The prohibition was also not equipped to withstand the imminent rise of television, which would shuttle moving images of fights across state lines via immaterial radio waves instead of bulky film canisters.[23] New Jersey senator Ralph Barbour, who competed as an amateur boxer prior to his political career, proposed overturning the Sims Act by appealing directly to Louis's difference from Johnson. "The present champion, Joe Louis, is universally admired and the conditions that accompanied the ascension of Jack Johnson to the title did not accompany the ascension of Joe Louis," Barbour reasoned. Dempsey testified in support of the repeal, and the bill was signed into law on July 1, 1940—twenty-eight years after the Sims Act's institution.[24] Previously restricted fight films immediately began showing up in nationally distributed productions. Torch Films' biographical documentary *The Brown Bomber* (1940) relied on footage from fight films of Louis and Archie Mayo's

Hollywood musical *The Great American Broadcast* (1941) integrated sequences from Dempsey and Willard's 1919 fight film. Louis's relatively congenial image—which movies like *Spirit of Youth* helped to construct—freed this valuable footage that previously circulated only in defiance of federal law.

While Louis was safe enough to motivate a repeal of the film ban, Hollywood boxing movies still conspicuously avoided the champion boxer. Republic Pictures hired the heavyweight fighter Billy Conn to star in *The Pittsburgh Kid* (Jack Townley, 1941) shortly after the handsome, charismatic, and White heavyweight nearly beat Louis. The Hollywood film industry offered Conn a more prominent opportunity than Louis had received up to that point because of the excitement generated by the White challenger's brief flirtation with victory. Other Hollywood boxing films during the early years of Louis's championship reflected on the sport's past. *The Great American Broadcast* inaccurately celebrates the genesis of sports radio through the Dempsey-Willard match, *Gentleman Jim* (Raoul Walsh, 1942) commemorates Jim Corbett, and *The Great John L.* (Frank Tuttle, 1945) hails John L. Sullivan. Made during the height of Louis's title run, the historical boxing films express nostalgia for an era before he was champion and, in the case of *Gentleman Jim* and *The Great John L.*, a period before Black fighters were even allowed to compete for the heavyweight belt.

Aware that charges of slackerism almost ruined Jack Dempsey's career, Louis joined the Army shortly after the United States entered World War II—another effort to demonstrate his virtue to a public still reluctant to give him the benefit of the doubt. Louis's management knew the Black champ would not receive the same level of tolerance as Dempsey if he sat out of the war. Immediately after enlisting, Louis donated the purses earned for his 1942 title defenses against Buddy Baer and Abe Simon (who had a bit part in *The Notorious Elinor Lee*) to the Navy Relief Society—gifts that some African American groups criticized because of the Navy's reputation as the military's most discriminatory branch. His service mostly aided U.S. propaganda and morale-boosting efforts through public appearances and exhibitions for soldiers, although he refused to perform for segregated troops. His most noteworthy contribution occurred during a Navy Relief fundraiser at Madison Square Garden when he assured the crowd, "We're going to do our part ... and we'll win because we're on God's side"—a quote the Office of War Information immediately plastered on posters along with an image of "Pvt. Joe Louis" charging forward with a bayonet. As such, Louis became an embodiment of the sacrifices Americans were urged to make during the war and emerged as the key figure through which the government encouraged Blacks to enlist. Louis's role as a propagandist extended into film. In 1943 he appeared in Michael Curtiz's musical *This Is the Army*, an adaptation of Irving Berlin's stage production that donated its proceeds to the Army Emergency Relief Fund. Lionizing Hollywood's participation in the war effort, *This Is the Army* cast actors who served in the military and included their ranks in the credits. The plot centers on a ragtag group of soldiers led by Johnny Jones (Ronald Reagan) who reprise a morale-boosting musical revue produced during World War I. The tale is sprinkled with songs that glorify different facets of Army life.

Louis is the main attraction of the lone musical number *This Is the Army* directs toward African Americans. He first appears backstage just prior to the performance. When a producer (George Murphy) asks if he is nervous, Louis responds with a wooden adaptation of his by then legendary rallying cry. "I quit worrying the day I got in uniform," he says. "All I know is I'm in Uncle Sam's Army and we're on God's side." Curtiz then cuts to the song, "What the Well-Dressed Man in Harlem Wears," which encourages African American military involvement. The performance takes place on a set painted to resemble a cartoonish cityscape with zoot-suit-wearing Black men dancing the jitterbug. The song's lyrics suggest that such stylish and urban African Americans ought to follow Louis's selfless lead and trade in their fancy duds for Army uniforms.

> There's a change in fashion that shows, in the Lenox Avenue clothes,
> Mr. Dude has disappeared with his flashy tie.
> You'll see in Harlem esquire, what the well-dressed man will desire.
> When he's struttin' down the street with his sweetie pie,
> suntan shade of cream or an olive drab color scheme.
> That's what the well-dressed man in Harlem will wear.
> Top hat, white tie, and tails no more,
> they've been put away 'til after the war.

Louis appears on stage and begins hitting the speed bag alongside the song's chorus, offering a percussive accompaniment to the upbeat tune. "If you don't know, take a look at Brown Bomber Joe," the soloist croons as Louis continues working the bag. "That's what the well-dressed man in Harlem will wear." As Louis put his career on hold to serve in the military, the song urges Harlemites—a shorthand for the urban African American community more generally—to make a temporary material sacrifice for the greater good. *This Is the Army* was the highest grossing film of 1943. *Variety* called it a "boxoffice tornado" and cited "Well-Dressed Man" as "the highlight of the entire picture, with sepia entertainers whamming over a terrific score."[25]

One year after *This Is the Army*, Louis played a similarly inspirational role in *The Negro Soldier* (Stuart Heisler, 1944), an extension of Frank Capra's War Department–produced *Why We Fight* documentary series. Partly a response to pressure from African American groups about racial discrimination in the armed forces, *The Negro Soldier* celebrated Black contributions to U.S. military efforts while encouraging World War II enlistment. The documentary opens with establishing shots of churches and cuts to the interior of a chapel in which

48 • The Boxing Film

a congregation of African Americans—many of whom are uniformed GIs—sings a hymn. As the song concludes, the preacher (Carlton Moss) explains that he was suddenly inspired by the military presence and decided to diverge from his planned sermon to discuss the war effort instead. He opens his homily by recalling Louis's 1938 victory over Schmeling. "In that one minute and forty-nine seconds, an American fist won a victory," he says atop film of the fight. "But it wasn't a final victory. No, that victory is going to take a little longer. And a whole lot more American fists." The preacher continues as the image track cuts to newsreel footage of Schmeling training with Nazi paratroopers and Louis conducting exercises with his Army regiment. "Now those two men who were matched in the ring that night are matched again. This time in a far greater arena," he solemnly intones. "This time it's a fight not between man and man, but between nation and nation. A fight for the real championship of the world." After using Louis-Schmeling to explain the war, he emphasizes the conflict's particular relevance to his African American parishioners by quoting a passage from Hitler's *Mein Kampf* that compares Black people to apes and expresses outrage at the equal treatment they ostensibly receive in the United States. "The liberty of the whole Earth depends on the outcome of this contest," the minister gravely says.

The preacher then narrates a rundown of Black contributions to American military history—from the Revolutionary War through World War II. He augments the initially martial focus with a celebration of broader African American achievements by profiling a surgeon, judge, and Joe Louis. *The Negro Soldier* plainly suggests that African Americans are central to the establishment, success, and preservation of American democracy. "The tree of liberty has born these fruits," the minister concludes as the documentary returns to the church where his sermon began. While *The Negro Soldier* lauds a wide variety of Black Americans, it gives Louis's accomplishments special praise. The poster for the documentary features an image of Louis holding a rifle in the foreground beneath a banner that reads, "America's Joe Louis vs. The Axis." Beyond using Louis's notoriety to boost its viewership, *The Negro Soldier* echoes *This Is the Army*'s suggestion that the fighter's wartime sacrifice offers an example that patriotic African Americans would do well to emulate.

Like *This Is the Army*, *The Negro Soldier* mainly drew praise. *Time* called it a "brave, important and helpful event in the history of race relations" and indicated that the documentary would provide useful education for bigots.[26] The poet Langston Hughes, covering *The Negro Soldier* for *The Chicago Defender*, named it "the most remarkable Negro film ever flashed on the American screen."[27] Capra sought to ensure the film would satisfy both African American and mainstream critics by softening some of the more potentially polarizing material that screenwriter Carlton Moss, who played the preacher, included in his first draft. "Moss wore his blackness as conspicuously as a bandaged head," Capra recalled in his memoir. "Time and again he would write a scene, then I'd rewrite it, eliminating the angry fervor. He'd object, and I would explain that when something's red-hot, the blow torch of passion only louses up its glow. We must persuade and convince, not by rage but by reason."[28] As part of this effort to avoid controversy, *The Negro Soldier*'s history of African American contributions to U.S. military efforts made no mention of slavery when covering the period leading to the Civil War and elided segregation when discussing subsequent conflicts. While the documentary was required viewing for all soldiers, and despite Capra's efforts to give it crossover appeal, various southern theaters still refused to show *The Negro Soldier*. But it played well in African American communities. Harlem's Morningside Theatre programmed it as a double feature with *Spirit of Youth*.[29]

This Is the Army and *The Negro Soldier* suggest that Louis enjoyed some exposure in mainstream film during his career—but only in rare occasions when those films, or portions of them, were reaching out to Black audiences. While the wartime productions were distributed more broadly than the race films Louis inspired, they were similarly segregated. Louis's scene in *This Is the Army* was the only section of the popular Hollywood production that included Black soldiers and overtly addressed African Americans. Similarly, the sermon that guides *The Negro Soldier* is directed toward an entirely African American congregation, and the film's exhibition patterns suggest it did not garner much White viewership outside of those soldiers required to see it as part of their official training. These productions, ironically, minimize Louis's importance to the war effort by suggesting his achievement and sacrifice were relevant only to African Americans. They make clear that "Our Joe," when it came to mainstream media culture, was "Their Joe."

During World War II, and partly as a response to the wartime contributions Louis typified and *The Negro Soldier* celebrated, Hollywood promised the NAACP that the industry would give African Americans more consequential roles in front of and behind the camera. Film historian Thomas Cripps explains that segregated race movies like *Spirit of Youth*, *Keep Punching*, and *Notorious Elinor Lee* "seemed to be reactionary vestiges of past oppression" inconsistent with popular front attitudes that constructed, however dubiously, a harmonious American state united against global fascism. Independent race films continued to be produced, and Joe Louis even starred as a noble champ who combats juvenile delinquency in *The Fight Never Ends* (Joseph Lerner, 1948). But Hollywood representatives vowed that the industry would "improve the quality and quantity of black roles" in its comparatively visible and influential films.[30] Hollywood boxing films gradually began integrating roles for African Americans that went beyond the occasional sidekick or outmatched opponent.

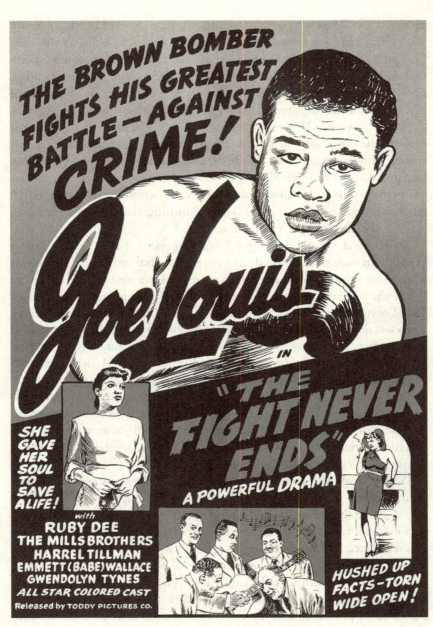

FIG. 4 Poster for Joseph Lerner's race film *The Fight Never Ends* (1948). (Wikimedia Commons)

Joe Palooka, Champ (Reginald Le Borg, 1946), one of many film offshoots of Ham Fisher's popular comic strip (which also had spinoffs in radio and eventually TV), gave both Louis and Henry Armstrong small parts as themselves. Their appearances came amid charges that Fisher's comic strip perpetuated racial inequity because his main character never fought African Americans, and those Black characters that did intermittently appear were typically limited to the roles of servants and comic relief.[31] An earlier Palooka film titled *The Blonde Bomber* (Lloyd French, 1936) even appropriated Louis's handle and redirected it to celebrate the protagonist's Whiteness. Fisher defended his media franchise by suggesting that any Black opponent—like all of Palooka's combatants—would inevitably lose and surmised that their defeat might aggravate racial tensions. Fisher's franchise did not hesitate to engage shifting current events by having Palooka join the war effort and spend much of the 1940s punching out Nazis. But it was reluctant to reflect boxing's changing landscape by including Black fighters beyond cameos that reinforced Palooka's supremacy.

Robert Rossen's *Body and Soul* offered the Hollywood boxing film's first complex Black character with Canada Lee's portrayal of Ben Chaplin. The noir film's narrative functions through a flashback that occurs while the boxer Charley Davis naps prior to a championship fight he has agreed to throw. It traces how Davis used boxing to rise out of a poor, Jewish neighborhood and attain the fame and wealth prizefighting reserves for its biggest stars. Like *Kid Galahad* and *Golden Boy, Body and Soul* represents boxing as an avenue for White ethnics to improve their circumstances. As one proud member of Davis's neighborhood (Shimen Ruskin) exudes, "Over in Europe the Nazis are killing people like us, just because of our religion. But here, Charley Davis is champeen." The pride Davis instills in his Jewish community reflects Louis's standing among African Americans. Friedman, however, points out that this potentially controversial scene was excised from *Body and Soul*'s original theatrical version.[32]

As Davis makes his name in boxing, he connects with the mendacious criminal Roberts (Lloyd Gough), who runs the New York City fight game. Roberts sets Davis up with a fixed championship match against Ben Chaplin, who has a blood clot in his brain that could result in fatal damage if he is hit too forcefully. Roberts tells Ben that Charley will go easy and take the fight to a decision so that the hobbled champion can evade serious harm and salvage some dignity in defeat. The gangster, however, did not inform Charley about the fix or Ben's injury. As a result, Charley gives the fight his all and beats Ben by a knockout. The brutal fight scene was made more realistic through James Wong Howe's pioneering action cinematography, which created heightened authenticity by employing handheld cameras that Howe operated while roller skating around the ring. Ben survives the drubbing but is left with irreparable mental and physical damage. Once he becomes champion Charley gets swept up in the crooked and materialistic world Roberts runs. Like so many boxing movie protagonists before him, Charley loses focus and becomes estranged from his comparatively grounded friends, family, and even his wife Peg (Lilli Palmer). Eventually, Roberts—like Elinor Lee—directs Charley to take a dive. Everyone on Charley's team supports the plot except Ben, whom Charley charitably hired to help him train after their fight forced the onetime champ into retirement. Roberts confronts and berates Ben when he overhears him attempting to dissuade Charley. Their confrontation erupts into a shouting match in which Ben works himself into an enraged frenzy, falls to the ground, and dies from a stroke presumably triggered by the injuries he suffered in his fight against Charley.

The film cuts to Charley waking from his prefight nap screaming Ben's name in distress. Wracked with guilt, he confronts Roberts about Ben's demise and their role in it. "Everybody dies," the gangster replies with frosty indifference as he leaves Charley to follow out his orders. But Charley's remorse about Ben and his escalating contempt for Roberts prompt a moral awakening. He surges to a late-round knockout regardless of the danger that double-crossing the gangster poses. An enraged Roberts confronts the victorious Davis after the match. "What makes you think you can get away with this?" he seethes. "Everybody dies," Charley retorts, repackaging Roberts's amoral response to Ben's passing against the mobster. The reformed fighter reunites with Peg and leaves the arena, as well as the corrupt world of boxing, behind. "Are you alright?," Peg asks. "I never felt better," Charley replies as the film ends. The integrity he salvaged by refusing to throw the fight, the boxer implies, is worth whatever risk Roberts and his goons may pose.

While *Body and Soul* centers on Charley Davis, Ben Chaplin composes the film's most honorable character and propels the protagonist's transformation. He provides what Baker describes as the film's "moral and dramatic center" and, as Cripps adds, "the ethical bridge between the complaisant Charley and the resolute Charley."[33] In addition to stressing Ben's unusual decency in the fight game, *Body and Soul* emphasizes his position as an African American hero. "I always felt so good after a win," Ben reminisces when trying to talk Charley out of throwing the match. "Walk down Lenox Ave. Kids going crazy for you. And proud." Like Louis, Ben is an inspiration in the Black community—a status his reference to Harlem's Lenox Avenue signals. He appeals to the responsibility he feels toward African Americans to discourage Charley from disappointing the Jewish community he represents. With Ben, *Body and Soul* shows the boxing film beginning to explore multifaceted Black characters without segregating them or ignoring their racially inflected mistreatment.

Robert Wise's *The Set-Up* (1949) initially planned to revolutionize the typically regressive boxing film by casting a Black lead. The noir production adapts

Joseph Moncure March's 1928 narrative poem about Pansy Jones, a worn out African American fighter who endures boxing's intersecting corruption and racism. As March's opening lines explain, "Pansy had the stuff, but his skin was brown / And he never got a chance at the middleweight crown."

The racist mobster Tony Diamond arranges for Pansy to take a fall. The thugs Diamond tasks with securing Pansy's cooperation, however, figure he is a sure loser and decide not to tell the fighter about the fix. They can make more money, they surmise, by cutting Pansy out of the scheme. When Pansy surprisingly wins, Diamond assumes the boxer defied their arrangement and has him killed.

Wise's adaptation originally intended to star the Black actor James Edwards and explore racial bigotry through boxing. But the filmmaker decided that he could not find a "black star with sufficient name value to carry the film"—a choice for which he later expressed regret.[34] Wise eventually cast Robert Ryan, a White actor who had boxed in college. He removed the racism angle and transformed the production into a straightforward noir about an aging fighter who is betrayed by his manager. Although Ryan was better known than Edwards, he was not a marquee leading man with the sort of "name value" that Wise claimed dissuaded him from hiring a Black lead. Prior to *The Set-Up*, Ryan appeared mostly in B movies, including a supporting role in the little-known boxing film *Golden Gloves* (Edward Dmytryk, 1940). Wise's eventual decision to cast Ryan in *The Set-Up*—which became one of the boxing film's most lauded productions—was more likely a consequence of his concern that a Black star would repel mainstream audiences.

The Joe Louis Story

Joe Louis retired with the championship in 1949—the same year *The Set-Up* was released. He immediately began Joe Louis Enterprises, which would manage the four leading contenders' contracts.[35] The nascent company stalled, however, when Louis's initial partner abandoned the deal. Louis then joined James Norris and Arthur Wirtz to create the International Boxing Club (IBC). But instead of owning 51 percent of the concern—his planned stake in Joe Louis Enterprises—Louis held only a 20 percent minority share of the IBC. Saddled with debt, the boxer had little leverage to bargain with Norris and Wirtz for a better deal. Moreover, his lack of interest and expertise in running a business reduced his role mostly to a figurehead. With Mike Jacobs fading into retirement, Norris and Wirtz quickly turned the IBC into professional boxing's most powerful force by securing deals with Madison Square Garden, Yankee Stadium, and St. Nicholas Arena. Locking up these prominent venues gave the IBC "control of nearly half of all championship boxing in the United States."

54 • The Boxing Film

"For the first five years of its existence," explains historian Troy Rondinone, "the [IBC] controlled thirty-six of the forty-four championship fights in the United States." It also forced competitors to give the IBC exclusive rights to their matches. If boxers refused the IBC's terms, they would be banished from subsequent big-money bouts the IBC ran. The aggressively monopolistic IBC came to be known as the Octopus because of how its far-reaching tentacles pervaded the fight game through the 1950s.

The IBC's success did not alleviate Louis's crippling debt—most of which he accumulated while serving in the military and making the soldier's wage of twenty-one dollars a month. He owed much of this money to Jacobs, who issued the boxer loans so he could maintain his extravagant lifestyle throughout the war. But neither Jacobs nor the U.S. government was willing to forgive the debt Louis incurred despite the wealth he generated for his manager and the contribution he made to the war effort. The bankrupt fighter returned to the ring one year after his initial retirement and was immediately defeated by the new champ Ezzard Charles. Despite his obviously diminished skills, Louis continued fighting, with some of his purses going directly to the IRS to chip away at his debt. But he retired for good after suffering a humiliating eighth-round knockout by Rocky Marciano in October 1951. The up-and-coming Italian American bruiser dominated Louis throughout the match and at one point nearly knocked the aging former champion out of the ring. Louis's defeat took on additional symbolic importance because it simultaneously marked the rise of Marciano, who won the title the following year, as the next great White heavyweight.

As Louis faded from prominence, Hollywood boxing films further expanded their historically narrow representational scope. *Right Cross* (John Sturges, 1950) and *The Ring* (Kurt Neumann, 1952) center on Mexican American fighters dealing with discrimination and anxieties about immigration. Other sports movies, such as the biographical dramas *The Jackie Robinson Story* (Alfred E. Green, 1950) and *The Harlem Globetrotters* (Phil Brown and Will Jason, 1951), began to star African Americans and were produced while their subjects were actively competing. But it was not until Louis retired and Marciano captured the title that *The Joe Louis Story* (Robert Gordon, 1953) became the first Hollywood boxing film to star an African American by casting the heavyweight contender Coley Wallace in the title role.

Adopting a less syrupy tone than *Spirit of Youth*, the still sentimental *Joe Louis Story* opens with footage of Louis's final match against Marciano. After displaying the embarrassing loss by integrating film of the actual match, the production cuts to a young sportswriter (Herbert Ratner) entering a newspaper office to write up his story. He immediately encounters the veteran reporter Tad McGeehan (Paul Stewart), who is working late. "Hey Tad, you missed the

FIG. 5 Coley Wallace stars as Joe Louis in Robert Gordon's *The Joe Louis Story* (1953). (Wikimedia Commons)

greatest fight of the year. This Marciano is another Dempsey," announces the younger scribe, who is invigorated after the thrilling bout. "Louis is through for real now. He should have quit while he was ahead," the writer continues as McGeehan wearily listens. "Rocky almost knocked him out of the ring. The kid's got a punch like a ten-ton truck. He'll be the new champ for sure." McGeehan interrupts his colleague before he sits to write his fight report. "I'll write the story," McGeehan insists. When the younger writer confusedly protests that McGeehan did not see the match, the senior reporter guarantees that he'll write "the *real* story." McGeehan, who covered Louis throughout his career, is concerned that the former champion's pathetic end will tempt less experienced writers to misunderstand the boxer's legacy. The film continues with McGeehan, who functions as the narrator and a supporting character, loading paper into his typewriter to give Louis the careful treatment he deserves.

The biopic offers a mostly predictable take on Louis that stresses his humble beginnings, victory over Schmeling, and service during World War II. The combination of scripted material, McGeehan's narration, and fight film footage gives *The Joe Louis Story* a documentary quality that complements its historical subject matter. A poster for the production emphasizes the presence of Primo Carnera, Max Baer, Max Schmeling, and Rocky Marciano through the fight films it weaves into the plot. But the ostensibly realistic and biographical *Joe Louis Story* calls only brief attention to the racism that informed nearly every aspect of Louis's career. It instead highlights Louis's remarkable ability to overcome poverty, self-doubt, and the Nazis—obstacles with which White audiences could identify. Along these lines, the biopic presents the fighter's decision to return to the ring after his initial retirement—a choice that McGeehan discourages Louis from making—as a product of the former champion's pride rather than a result of the racially informed exploitation that left him broke.

After tracing Louis's biography, *The Joe Louis Story* returns to the newsroom before the fateful Marciano fight. Although he had covered Louis's entire career to that point, McGeehan elected not to attend the Marciano match and assigned his underling to report on it. He shrugs off the curious decision by claiming that Louis is "past his prime" and suggesting there is no sense in watching his all but certain loss. But McGeehan's crestfallen tone indicates that the reporter cannot bear to witness the legendary fighter's certain humiliation. The veteran sports journalist is unable to resist, however, and watches Louis-Marciano on television at a bar—a recent option for spectators—before returning to the newsroom to have the postfight conversation that sets the film in motion. McGeehan ends the film with a hopeful voiceover that defends the legacy that Louis's loss to Marciano imperiled. "And so tonight I saw the last fight in the career of one of the greatest fighters of all time," he explains. "Out of it all, [Louis] found himself. And for me, who knows him better than most, I can see a beginning, not an end." The *real* story McGeehan offers reminds viewers of Louis's personal and professional excellence despite the humiliations he suffered toward the end of his career.

Beyond celebrating its subject, *The Joe Louis Story* signaled the rise of Marciano—who was champ by the time it premiered. As the junior sportswriter's description of Marciano shows, the powerful White boxer was viewed as a nostalgic throwback to the tradition Jack Dempsey embodied. McGeehan's guiding narration—as well as the paternalistic attitude he effects toward Louis—illustrates the degree to which the White-centered media establishment exerted control over Louis's story and channeled it through narratives that minimized the institutionalized racism that marked his biography and the forces that sustained this inequality, forces that include sports journalism and the film industry. Along these lines, the biopic points toward television's emergent participation in these racial politics as the new and visual medium began to supplant radio and intensify calls for White fighters.

As the first Hollywood boxing film to star an African American, *The Joe Louis Story* is significant within and beyond the genre. But the groundbreaking production was not made until a White fighter once again held the heavyweight title. Louis's distance from the championship informed the film's viability. He was now a safe subject far beyond his prime who could be admired and cheered, rather than feared. The biopic displays how the many boxing movies made during Louis's career participated in the cultural ambivalence surrounding the first Black champion since Jack Johnson. They benefited from the renewed interest in prizefighting that Louis ignited while constructing a sport that often excluded the racial difference he signaled and, when it did represent Black fighters, downplayed their abuse.

3
TV Fighting and Fighting TV in the 1950s

• •

As with cinema and radio, boxing was at the foundation of television and aided its development. Some of Philo T. Farnsworth's earliest experiments with what would become TV adapted fight films into proto-telecasts. In 1928, J. Andrew White—who had gone from delivering the blow-by-blow for RCA's Dempsey-Carpentier broadcast to becoming CBS's president—named boxing matches "the first and most logical application of the television apparatus." And in 1935 film theorist Rudolf Arnheim predicted that fights—not political speeches or election results—would realize TV's potential to allow viewers to "witness immediately what is going on in the world around us."[1] By 1939, NBC televised an exhibition between heavyweights Lou Nova and Patsy Perroni on a limited and largely experimental basis. The nascent medium's technical capacity made the competitors only faintly visible to the lucky handful of New Yorkers who saw the exhibition. But the seed was planted. Boxing, it seemed, might prove an even more entertaining and profitable complement to TV than it had to film and radio because of how the emergent medium combined the imagery of film with the immediacy of radio.

Following a developmental hiatus during World War II, televised boxing began to show signs of fulfilling the promise White and Arnheim identified. Just weeks after D-Day, Mike Jacobs inked a deal with the Gillette Company to stage a fight every Friday evening as part of *Gillette Cavalcade of Sports*, a collection of sports programming that launched on radio in 1942 and expanded

59

to TV in 1944. Boxing composed an ideal vehicle to attract the adult male viewership Gillette sought to make aware of its patented safety razors. *Friday Night Fights* premiered on September 29, 1944, with a Willie Pep and Chalky White bout that reached roughly seven thousand TV sets along the East Coast—a "national" audience at the time. Echoing the boxing film, which TV gradually put out of business, the program quickly became one of the most popular prime-time shows of any genre and spawned imitators across the major networks. Beyond the sport's long-standing popularity, and again reflecting early cinema, boxing was uniquely suited to television's many limitations. "Nothing is so made to order for television as a world's championship prize fight," observed the *Saturday Evening Post*. "The bout takes place in a small, well-lighted arena and can be handled perfectly." "It's the ideal arrangement," added the *New York Times*, "because every seat in front of a video screen is a ringside seat." Moreover, boxing matches' multiple rounds provide natural pauses for commercial breaks. By 1946, the sport accounted for nearly 40 percent of all television programming and was a driving force in TV sets' booming sales.[2]

Louis was at the center of television boxing's emergence—as a competitor, celebrity, and entrepreneur. His June 1946 rematch against Billy Conn was the first televised heavyweight championship and drew a hundred fifty thousand viewers.[3] The IBC used Louis, once he returned from his brief retirement, to expand from staging fights into selling the rights to televise them—via both home TV programs like *Friday Night Fights* and closed-circuit exhibitions held in theaters, arenas, and other public spaces. The IBC demanded one hundred thousand dollars for broadcast rights to Joe Louis and Lee Savold's 1951 match in Madison Square Garden. When no network would foot the bill, the Octopus sold live exhibition rights to eight theaters in six cities. "The IBC regards this as an experiment and doesn't expect to reap much revenue from it," reported the *Washington Post*. "Some say in the future it's going to be the big money-maker." The inaugural closed-circuit exhibition was an unexpected "sensation at the box office" that attracted 39,000 viewers—in contrast to the 18,179 in attendance at the match itself. Participating theater operators were forced to turn away 10,000 more they could not accommodate. Crowds in Chicago smashed through theater doors after being denied admission. "Nothing since the introduction of sound has stirred more general excitement among exhibitors than the drawing power of the Joe Louis–Lee Savold pictures," observed the trade magazine *BoxOffice*.[4]

Meanwhile, TV manufacturers were worried that closed-circuit exhibitions would hinder sales. Seven companies—Admiral, Crosley, General Electric, Motorola, Philco, RCA, and Sylvania—united to outbid closed-circuit distributors and provide a coast-to-coast telecast of Louis and Marciano's October 26, 1951, match on *Friday Night Fights*, the same broadcast McGeehan viewed in *The Joe Louis Story*. The IBC, of course, was happy to sell broadcast rights to whichever entity bid highest regardless of how it delivered the match. The Louis-Marciano fight was successful but unsustainable. Marquee fights wound up being broadcast in theaters via closed-circuit—a distribution practice with higher economic ceilings compared to the onetime fees paid for home TV—and other bouts appeared on programs like *Friday Night Fights*.

As Louis helped TV boxing's rise during the 1950s, the medium's proliferation coincided with his decline and Marciano's ascendance. Undersized, gritty, and White, Marciano was an even more mainstream-friendly champ than the Brown Bomber. As such, he was often cast as a reassertion of traditional racial hierarchies that complemented the decade's stereotypical conservatism. Television boosted Marciano's stardom and the racial politics that constituted it. It also ushered commercialized shifts that many traditionalists argued were further corrupting the sport. Boxing films of the 1950s confronted these conditions and television's role in them.

TV Fights and TV Fighters

By 1955, live televised fights regularly reached eight million weekly viewers. The telecasts spanned all four networks—ABC, CBS, NBC, and the short-lived DuMont—and could be seen virtually every evening in prime time. The most prominent of these broadcasts were *Friday Night Fights* and CBS's Pabst Blue Ribbon–sponsored *Wednesday Night Fights*. The IBC controlled both programs and generated roughly ninety thousand dollars per week from them.[5] Capitalizing on this trend, advertising executive and boxing film collector William Cayton formed Sports Films Inc. and produced *Greatest Fights of the Century*, a series of fifteen-minute syndicated films of classic bouts from his vast archive that surrounded the live telecasts. *Greatest Fights*, which adopted slightly different titles depending on the sponsor, put TV fight programs into dialogue with boxing's filmed history. Just as important, it suggested the regular televised bouts were part of the vaunted heritage *Greatest Fights* commemorates. Sports Films Inc. struck a deal with the IBC from 1952 through 1957 to acquire film rights to its bouts for use in *Greatest Fights*. The deal ensured that the IBC's fights would eventually be included in the tradition Cayton's program curated. Syndicators also strategically programmed *Greatest Fights* segments to complement whatever matches they were supporting. For instance, *Greatest Fights* films of Louis's 1938 victory over Schmeling aired immediately after the fading pugilist's loss to Marciano. *Broadcasting* praised the arrangement as "sage programming" because of how it offered a sympathetic reminder of Louis's onetime greatness to accompany his sad decline.[6] Syndicators combined Marciano's first title defense—a 1953 rematch against Joe Walcott— with a *Greatest Fights* segment on Dempsey's 1923 victory over Luis Firpo. The scheduling put Marciano into dialogue with Dempsey and the racialized nostalgia that informs the Manassa Mauler's place in boxing history.

But critics cited the television broadcasts as considerable threats to boxing. The *New Yorker*'s A. J. Liebling charged TV boxing with sapping prizefighting of its humanity and sociality. "Watching a fight on television has always seemed to me a poor substitute for being there," he wrote. "Before television, a prize-fight was to a New Yorker the nearest equivalent to the New England town meeting." The venues that provided this apparent sense of community became less important as television matured into boxing's chief revenue stream. Select closed-circuit theatrical exhibitions strove to reproduce the atmosphere Liebling mourned by staging broadcasts in the types of arenas where boxing matches would take place, combining them with live undercards, and even suspending large screens above boxing rings. Despite these occasional efforts, Liebling located TV—at home or in the theater—as irreparably spoiling his beloved "sweet science." "Television gives you so plausible an adumbration of a fight, for nothing, that you feel it would be extravagant to pay your way in. It is like the potato, which is only a succedaneum for something decent to eat but which, once introduced to Ireland, proved so cheap that the peasants gave up their grain-and-meat diet in favor of it."[7] For Liebling and other purists, telecasts turned boxing's sizzling steak dinner into a tepid and lumpy plate of mashed potatoes.

More specifically, the naysayers pointed out that TV had harmed the economy of boxing—in particular the clubs housing those fights that are too obscure to demand airtime. "Television has decimated boxing as a business," wrote Charles Einstein of *Harper's*. With the small clubs shuttering, aspiring boxers had fewer opportunities to prepare for their graduation to TV. "There aren't that many good prizefighters anymore," the *New York Times*' Arthur Daley opined. "They are brought up before they are ready for that quick buck." *Ring* editor Nat Fleischer estimated that the pool of pro fighters diminished by half through the 1950s because of TV. "We've got to convert the fireside seat back to the ringside seat," the Pennsylvania Boxing Commission's Frank Wiener warned, "or we'll dry up our talent, kill the small promoter and ruin boxing."[8] Liebling even conjectured that TV had made boxing more dangerous by forcing greenhorn pugs into tough matches before they were ready. Heavyweight Ed Sanders, for instance, died after being knocked out in the eleventh round of a televised 1954 fight against Willie James. It was only Sanders's ninth pro bout. Before television, Liebling pointed out, a rookie fighter like Sanders would not have been competing in matches of that grueling and hazardous length so quickly. The TV-driven shifts hastened Sanders's premature rise and contributed to his untimely death.[9]

Television also changed how featured boxers competed and were evaluated, a trend that provoked Fleischer to worry that the medium was turning prizefighting into "another puppet show." Despite Fleisher's concerns, *Ring* briefly published annual special issues devoted to TV and gave a "TV Fighter of the Year" prize to the most entertainingly telegenic—not simply the most proficient—competitor. These "TV fighters" often favored a brawling approach that would satisfy dilettantes watching at home or in bars over the more technical fighting that purists venerated. "The fine old art of fisticuffs is rapidly being replaced by a pugilistic soap opera—more blood, more violence, less skill," lamented John Lardner, who mockingly called *Friday Night Fights* "the regular coaxial bloodbath" because of the clumsy and unscientific fighting it fostered. As the *Chicago Tribune* added, "Too many promoters pick up a fighter and say, 'He can't fight, but he's a good-looking boy, and what does the television audience know anyway?' So they match the stiff out of his class."[10]

Welterweight Chuck Davey was ideally suited to television, and his popularity offers some perspective on the history of gender and sexuality in sports TV. The handsome White fighter had served in the Air Force, graduated from Michigan State after competing on the boxing team, and even earned a master's degree in education. His looks, pedigree, and flashy southpaw style made him a television darling. While he drew fans, Davey was only a mediocre pro boxer. The fighter, as the *Chicago Tribune*'s David Condon snidely observed, "could not have boxed cigars in a Tampa tobacco house." But promoters orchestrated the dashing crowd-pleaser's ascendance by matching him with competitors who suited his style. He was, as the *Atlanta Journal and Atlanta Constitution*'s Furman Bisher put it, "advanced by the cathode ray tube." "Legions of boxing fans, never closer to the prize ring than TV viewing range in their living rooms, are convinced that the fancy-boxing Davey is truly cloaked with invincibility," wrote the *Washington Post*. Before long, Davey had a title shot against Kid Gavilán. Experts considered Davey a ten-to-one underdog. Fans, however, were convinced he could win. Gavilán knocked Davey out in the tenth round with a performance so dominant that some accused him of carrying the popular White challenger to ensure the fight's TV sponsors received sufficient commercial breaks. "The cameras recorded Davey's downfall as clearly as they had shown his ascent," and the fans moved on to the next promising fighter who came along to charm the airwaves.[11] Davey retired shortly after the Gavilán loss.

Davey and other good-looking TV fighters also expanded boxing's traditionally male audience. Many of Davey's biggest fans were women—a circumstance that made the sport even more attractive to advertisers. The women viewers extended the long-standing connection between female spectatorship and boxing's public repute. As John Lardner wrote, the influx of female viewers marked "the final, complete merger of boxing and respectability" and created a form of "universal suffrage" that came "only with television."[12] The 1955 edition of *Ring*'s "TV Fights" special issue features a husband, wife, and child

64 • The Boxing Film

enjoying a boxing broadcast together at home. The grinning wife sits closest to the TV and is engrossed in the spectacle with her fist clenched while watching the shirtless men struggle.

Women traditionally receive but a tiny fraction of the sports TV coverage men garner, and the attention women get often emphasizes those competitors who complement conventional heterosexual standards of beauty instead of the best athletes. In other words, this coverage privileges women's physical appearance over their athletic skill—a sexualized double standard to which men are not commonly held.[13] But Davey offers an early and rare example of a middling male athlete receiving a disproportionate amount of attention because of his appearance. In fact, Davey parlayed his looks into a job hosting the TV program *Chuck Davey's Corner*, which aired after *Wednesday Night Fights* in 1954. The telegenic fighter moved permanently to TV—a career to which he was ultimately far better suited than boxing. Other popular TV fighters followed Davey's lead. Former middleweight champ Rocky Graziano—who lost to Davey as his career came to an end—took various television roles in retirement that built on the familiarity he established as a TV fighter. Graziano's autobiography was eventually adapted into Robert Wise's *Somebody Up There Likes Me* (1956)—a production his TV fame aided.

Television boxing during the 1950s unsurprisingly gave special privilege to White fighters like Davey, Graziano, and especially Marciano. The visual medium increased demands for Whites and motivated broadcasters to feature them disproportionately—a practice that Marciano's success emboldened. "White boxers of all [weight] classes received better television exposure and were routinely pushed along faster than their black counterparts," writes boxing historian Russell Sullivan, "even if they happened to possess less talent, ability, or flair." The IBC's Truman Gibson, an African American and onetime member of FDR's "Black Cabinet," admitted that the organization's television sponsors urged it to set interracial bouts because of their exceptional drawing power among majority White audiences. "All-black boxing matches like all-black [TV] shows, were not desirable," Sammons explains.[14] As with other TV genres, boxing broadcasts—on home and closed-circuit television—reinforced which bodies mattered most in 1950s America. The new medium at once radically altered the sport and stabilized the cultural attitudes surrounding it.

Boxing Films on TV

Beyond TV boxing's impact on the sport, *Variety* reported that the pervasive broadcasts were harming ticket sales to see Hollywood boxing films.[15] The phenomenon of the TV fighter functioned in part by re-creating the dramatic archetypes fictional boxing movies established. These productions have a long history of commenting on the sport's corruption and using it as a narrative device to build the often-seedy environments they showcase—from *Body and Soul* to *The Set-Up*. The changes the IBC and television brought about gave 1950s boxing films new targets at which to hurl their occasional critiques—even as they increasingly mimicked TV aesthetics to approximate how fans most commonly experienced the sport. The broader economic impact television was having on boxing movies only incentivized the productions to level these dramatic barbs.

Mark Robson's *The Harder They Fall* (1956), a noir adaptation of Budd Schulberg's 1947 novel of the same title, composes 1950s Hollywood's most direct takedown of prizefighting. The film stars Humphrey Bogart (in his final role) as Eddie Willis, a cynical and recently unemployed sports columnist whom the shady promoter Nick Benko (Rod Steiger) hires to hype his new fighter Toro Molina (Mike Lane). Molina is a giant but untalented and naïve Argentinean loosely based on Primo Carnera. Benko sees extraordinary potential in Molina's ability to draw fans despite his pugilistic inadequacies. "I can get a million bums who can box," he tells Eddie. "But Toro's got it in him to fill a stadium." As Benko continues, "The fight game today is like show business. They're all actors, the best showman becomes the champ."

Eddie is tasked with creating a persona that will turn Molina into such an attraction. Discouraged by his wife and voice of conscience Beth (Jan Sterling), Eddie expresses some initial reluctance to abandon his journalistic scruples in favor Benko's con. However, he longs for a comfortable living that his journalistic career never could furnish and eventually convinces himself that crafting Molina's image will be no different from any other sales gig. "You sell a fighter, you sell soap. What's the difference?" he explains to a skeptical Beth. Eddie devises a campaign that brands Molina as the exotic "Wild Man of the Andes." They barnstorm the country in a Molina-themed bus—complete with the boxer's likeness painted on the sides—to create buzz as Eddie spins yarns about the fighter to reporters scouring for juicy copy and Benko schemes behind the scenes to fix his matches. Their combined efforts eventually turn Molina into a contender. They do such a good job that even the dim-witted Molina thinks he has succeeded through his own merits.

The Harder They Fall puts the fight game's wickedness on grisly display when Molina kills Gus Dundee (played by the retired pro fighter Pat Comiskey), a punch-drunk boxer who broke his neck in a recent loss to the champion Buddy Brannen (Max Baer). In an effort to set himself up for retirement, the desperate and haggard Dundee agrees to take a dive. Molina lands a lucky and relatively weak punch early in the match that sends Dundee to the canvas awkwardly. The bloodthirsty crowd boos at the suspicious knockout as Dundee is carted out of the ring and taken to the hospital, where he dies. As it turns out, Molina's feeble blow simply capped the brutal punishment Brannen gave Dundee in the previous match. Dundee's strange demise was based on a 1933 incident when Carnera killed Ernie Schaaf. Like Molina, the lumbering Carnera had aggravated an injury Schaaf suffered in an earlier fight with Max Baer. While Molina and Eddie are deeply unsettled by Dundee's death, Benko views it as a fortunate promotional opportunity. He directs Eddie to tell the tale in a way that colors Molina as a ruthless executioner. The storyline, he rightly wagers, will inflate the gate for his upcoming title fight against Brannen and lengthen the odds for the unfixed match, which will make Benko even more money when he finally bets against Molina. Although Eddie is repulsed by Benko's blind greed, he opts to stay involved through the championship bout. He also owns a piece of Molina's contract and stands to earn a handsome payout from his inevitable loss.

Eddie's shame finally compels him to tell Molina that he is a fraud who will suffer potentially life-threatening harm from Brannen. Molina, however, is so taken in by the hype and fixed fights that he initially does not believe Eddie. "I don't know my own strength," the ignorant fighter says, parroting Eddie's publicity copy. Eddie is forced to prove his point by having the aging trainer George (played by former heavyweight champ "Jersey" Joe Walcott) give Molina an easy beating. While this revelation tempts the despondent and confused Molina to quit altogether, Eddie convinces him to stay on through the title match so he can retire wealthy and return to his homeland. Eddie and George develop a strategy to help Molina last long enough to give a good show while minimizing the damage he absorbs from Brannen. But Molina lacks the skill or cunning to follow the plan and is beaten to a gruesome mash. "Some guys can sell out and other guys just can't," George frankly states after the bout as a doctor wires shut Molina's broken jaw.

Benko makes a bundle off the loss and immediately sells Molina's contract to an even less scrupulous promoter who seeks to turn the fighter into a traveling punching bag. When Eddie protests, the new promoter bluntly reminds him that "fighters ain't human" and chuckles at the publicist's sensitivity. The hospitalized Molina had sent Eddie—the only one he thinks he can trust—to collect his share of the take from Benko. But Molina's payment amounts to a miniscule $49.07 after Benko deducts the varied expenses. "You let him get beaten to a bloody pulp and then you leave him with a hole in his pocket," Eddie fumes. The unrepentant Benko calmly explains that their arrangement was completely legal and spelled out in the contract, an agreement Molina clearly did not understand. While Molina is left with nothing but his injuries, Eddie made $26,000 off the sham. The guilt-ridden publicist recovers some dignity by giving his profits to the battered fighter and sneaking him onto the next flight back to Argentina. He then returns to his journalistic roots by starting an exposé that will reveal the wicked greed in fighting that lines promoters' pockets and leaves fighters devastated.

Columbia Pictures marketed *The Harder They Fall* as the "film they tried to suppress." One poster promised the production would offer up "THE FIGHT RACKET EXPOSED!" Another provoked, "WHY? . . . did 'they' try to stop the filming of this picture in New York, Chicago, Kansas City and Los Angeles? . . . WHY did 'they' want to prevent us from bringing Budd Schulberg's sensational novel to the screen? . . . BECAUSE . . . *The Harder They Fall* tells the whole unvarnished story of 'big-time' boxing!" The conspicuously anonymous "they" in question, of course, is the boxing establishment. The IBC refused to let Robson gather crowd shots during a 1955 match between Marciano and Archie Moore for use in *The Harder They Fall* because of the film's critical take on prizefighting. While touring to promote the film, Joe Walcott claimed that he accepted the part of George because he believed *The Harder They Fall* might force boxing to reform—comments that prompted a subpoena calling for him to elaborate on his vague allegations.[16] Moreover, the film's decisions to cast real fighters such as Walcott, Comiskey, and Baer and to reference ripped-from-the-headlines controversies like Schaaf's death align it with the actual sports world.

The Harder They Fall's crusading ethos complemented 1950s "social problem" films such as Richard Brooks's *Blackboard Jungle* (1955) and, more specifically, Elia Kazan's *On the Waterfront* (1954), which Schulberg scripted. Although *On the Waterfront* principally confronts corruption on the New York City docks, it uses boxing to construct its hardscrabble backdrop. Terry Malloy (Marlon Brando) is a has-been fighter who works as muscle for the crooked union boss Johnny Friendly (Lee J. Cobb)—a different but equally nefarious version of Benko. Malloy's boxing career came to an untimely end after he took a dive for Friendly's benefit—a compromise his brother Charley (Rod Steiger), who works as the gangster's top lieutenant, encouraged. But Malloy begins to question Friendly's reign after he unwittingly aids in the murder of the local whistleblower Joey Doyle.

With the encouragement of the local priest Father Barry (Karl Malden) and Joey's sister Edie (Eva Marie Saint), with whom Terry falls in love, Malloy eventually opts to testify against Friendly. The film's signature scene—one of the most famous in all of cinema—has Charley attempting to dissuade Terry from snitching. Charley offers Terry a better job at the docks and even half-heartedly threatens him with a gun, all the while insisting that he is simply looking out for Terry's best interests. Terry, however, reminds his big brother that he convinced him to take the dive that ruined his boxing prospects—giving him, as he memorably puts it, "a one-way ticket to Palookaville." "You was my brother, Charley! You shoulda looked out for me a little bit," Terry moans. "I coulda had class! I coulda been a contender! I coulda been somebody, instead of a bum, which is what I am!" Charley lets Terry go and is killed as a result. Although

Terry is tempted to seek revenge through violence, Father Barry convinces him to avenge his brother by testifying against Friendly and toppling his criminal empire. Like Eddie Willis, then, Terry Malloy eventually does the right thing and helps to clean up the dirty world that had temporarily seduced him with easy money. Both films present boxing as part of a criminal milieu and indicate that their protagonists' manhood is ultimately best proven by their ability to stand up to the crooked world it exemplifies. In fact, Columbia promoted *The Harder They Fall* by comparing it to *On the Waterfront*. "If you thought *On the Waterfront* hits hard," an advertisement for the boxing film claimed, "wait till you see this one!"

The key difference that separates Robson's *The Harder They Fall* from Schulberg's book is the film's focus on television—still maturing when Schulberg published his work—as an agent of boxing's corruption. Like Chuck Davey, Molina is a TV fighter whose image is tailored to the shallow medium and reliant on its reach. In one instance, Benko anonymously donates twenty-five thousand dollars to secure Molina's inclusion in a nationally televised bout that a charity is organizing. Benko watches the fixed fight at home across the country, satisfied at the exposure his fighter is getting. The film cuts from a shot of the telecast to Eddie sitting comfortably at ringside next to the philanthropist they paid to get the match. "There's not a kid in New York who wouldn't recognize him," Benko says of Molina as the fighter's reputation swells. "That's the power of television today." Television, the film suggests, is the key force Benko and Eddie must harness to achieve their plot.

The ending reiterates TV's role in boxing's degeneracy. Benko and his goons burst into Eddie's apartment searching for Molina, who had left for Argentina. No longer willing to be bought, Eddie tells Benko that he plans to write a piece that reveals the promoter's villainy. "You go ahead and write, it's been tried before," Benko hollers in response. "People still read, don't they?" Eddie replies. "The people," Benko snorts. "The people . . . they sit and get fat and fall asleep in front of the television set with a belly full of beer. That's the people for you." Eddie optimistically insists that his project might "wake them up" and reminds the menacing Benko that he "can still write from a hospital bed." Benko storms off and Eddie sits down to his typewriter as Beth brings her reformed husband a cup of coffee to stoke his creative burst. The inspired writer begins typing a piece titled "The Harder They Fall" that opens with the scathing lead: "Boxing should be outlawed in the United States if it takes an act of Congress to do it."[17] Aside from signaling Eddie's transformation from cynical accomplice to principled crusader, the finale suggests that boxing needs careful journalists who will counteract TV's manipulative superficiality and serve as watchdogs to the dishonesty and exploitation the medium aids.

Other boxing films of the 1950s similarly tied TV to boxing's corruption. Released the same year as *The Harder They Fall*, the less prominent *World in*

My Corner (Jesse Hibbs, 1956) follows the rise of Tommy Shea (Audie Murphy), a scrappy club fighter who was "born in a dump and educated in an alley." Trainer Dave Bernstein (John McIntire)—who works for the millionaire Robert Mallinson (Jeff Morrow)—sees promise in Shea and invites him to train at Mallinson's posh Long Island estate. Bernstein takes his time coaching Shea and carefully selects the raw fighter's opponents—a methodical contrast to the trend of rushing to bring up fighters so they can supply TV's insatiable demand.

While in training Shea falls for Mallinson's daughter Dorothy (Barbara Rush), an aspiring writer who yearns to escape her overbearing father. But only a high-profile and televised match will provide the sort of money Shea needs to support Dorothy. These opportunities are controlled by the devious gangster Harry Cram (Howard St. John), another iteration of the Benko and Roberts archetype. For instance, after Shea's old friend and manager Ray (Tommy Rall) visits one of his club fights in New Jersey, he asks the boxer why he is wasting time in such backwater venues when he could be competing in the limelight for Cram. "I ain't been catching none of your fights in a coast to coast hookup," Ray says after Shea's victory. "You can't get nowhere scrounging around for nickels and dimes in the sticks like this." Ray reminds Shea that "without Cram, the New York crowd, and TV you might as well be fighting in a closet." Ray's observations illustrate TV's impact on the small and lower-paying clubs. To leave the clubs and benefit from the larger crowds that TV accesses, however, Shea will have to play by Cram's rules and take a dive on his way up the ladder.

Like Bernstein, Cram sees potential in Shea—first and foremost as a TV attraction. "TV crowd's crying for new faces," Ray tells a convinced Cram. "Tommy's got color." Like Davey, Shea is handsome, charismatic, and White. Desperate and lovesick, the fighter eventually agrees to throw a bout for Cram. Upon Dorothy's urging, however, Shea has an abrupt change of heart. Cram's crew beats Shea up the night before his big fight against Al Carelli (played by the popular TV fighter Chico Vejar) so he will lose. But the already battered Shea surprisingly wins the match as Dorothy watches longingly on TV back at the Mallinson estate. Although victorious, Shea is so tattered that a doctor commands him never to fight again. Like Eddie Willis and Terry Malloy, Shea opts to stick by his values rather than sell out to the corrupt and TV-driven boxing establishment.

Amid the critical noir takes *The Harder They Fall, On the Waterfront,* and *World in My Corner* provide, other boxing films of the 1950s persisted in glorifying the sport as a vehicle for economic and spiritual uplift. *Somebody Up There Likes Me* shows how prizefighting provided the poor and unruly Rocky Graziano (Paul Newman) with discipline and hope that transformed him from a listless juvenile delinquent into an upstanding champion. Alvin Ganzer's similarly romantic *The Leather Saint* (1956) centers on Father Gil (John Derek), an Episcopalian minister who boxes recreationally and is blessed with a devastating right hook. Without divulging his primary occupation or identity, Gil books some prizefights to purchase an iron lung and swimming pool for needy children in his parish. His generosity jarringly contrasts the greed *The Harder They Fall* and *World in My Corner* present as boxing's guiding ethos. Gil's only transgression is the white lie he tells his colleagues about the money that starts pouring in from his clandestine fights, which he attributes to an anonymous donor in the "leather business," an allusion to his leather boxing gloves. Gil strikes opponents only the fewest number of times necessary to win, always makes sure his adversaries are unharmed after the match, and quits boxing as soon as he earns enough to fulfill his altruistic goal. Understated and highly technical in this approach, Gil eschews the flash that TV fighters like Davey rode to fame. While *The Leather Saint* paints boxing as an avenue to economic betterment, it suggests that Father Gil's humble and self-effacing contrast to these more typical and media-friendly boxers contributed to his saintliness.

IBC-controlled network programs like *Friday Night Fights* and *Wednesday Night Fights* naturally avoided Hollywood's indictments of boxing and TV. However, live network teleplays offered an alternative view of prizefighting from the promotionally driven telecasts. In October 1955, NBC's anthology drama *Playwrights '56* adapted Ernest Hemingway's short story "The Battler" (1925), a selection from his *Nick Adams Stories*. Directed by eventual "New Hollywood" auteur Arthur Penn, the production has the restless Nick Adams (Dewey Martin) leaving his restrictive home to strike out on his own. The naïve Adams immediately finds a harsh and uninviting world. He is robbed by the truck driver who gives him a ride and thrown off the train he hops by a sadistic brakeman. The destitute and bruised traveler winds up in a hobo camp where he meets Ad Francis (Paul Newman), a punch-drunk former champion. Francis is mentally unstable from years of taking punches in the ring and drinks to deal with the dementia and soothe his physical discomfort. "Listen, I'm not quite right," the erratic Francis tells Adams. "I'm crazy." Soon thereafter, the scattered former fighter inexplicibly becomes enraged and attacks Adams. Francis's African American companion, Bugs (Frederick O'Neal), is forced to knock him out. "I don't like to thump him," Bugs glumly tells Adams. "But it's the only way to do it when he gets that way. Sort of have to keep him away from people." Bugs recounts Francis's tragic story while the fighter is unconscious.

The Battler's second act explains Francis's heartrending decline through a flashback to his wife (Phyllis Kirk) attempting to convince him to abandon prizefighting. Their argument takes place in a boxing ring outside of a party being thrown to celebrate Francis's championship victory. The staging suggests this marital clash is as significant as the fight he just won. "I'm tired of this whole business," Francis's concerned wife tells the stubborn fighter. "You want me to give up fighting? What for? It's my big feeling out of life!," Francis defiantly snaps. His wife, however, warns that his career is coming to an end and that he needs to quit before he suffers serious injury. "Pretty soon you won't know your left hand from your right hand," she cries. But Francis refuses to retire, and his wife leaves as her grim prophecy materializes.

The final scene returns to the hobo camp as Francis is about to awaken from his forced nap. Bugs advises Nick to move along lest Francis gets ornery again. Apparently scared straight, Nick decides to return home rather than take his chances in the cruel world Francis represents. *The Battler*, then, presents Francis as a cautionary tale. Unlike Tommy Shea in *World in My Corner*, Francis refused to leave the sport when he should have. While it places most of the responsibility on Francis's shoulders, *The Battler* presents boxing as unsympathetic and happy to drain whatever physical and mental abilities he is willing to give.

The following year, CBS's *Playhouse 90* produced Rod Serling's *Requiem for a Heavyweight*—directed by Ralph Nelson and a hallmark of television's "Golden Age." Once the fifth-ranked boxer is his division, Harlan "Mountain" McLintock (Jack Palance) is now a burned-out pug forced into retirement after 111 fights. Serling described McLintock as "a simple, trusting guy who prided himself on his boxing career. Now, after fourteen years, all he has left is his self-respect." Serling was inspired by reports that Joe Louis began to wrestle in retirement to make ends meet—a tale that "struck a special chord with him" because of the fighter's decline from a national hero into an impoverished sideshow.[18] But, and like Robert Wise with *The Set-Up*, Serling made his Louis-based protagonist White to amplify the teleplay's salability.

Requiem opens with McLintock losing what would be his final match. But he did not lose fast enough for his slippery manager Maish (Keenan Wynn), who bet McLintock would not last beyond the third round and, as a result of the fighter's unexpected endurance, is in debt to some leg-breaking gangsters. "What'd I do wrong?," McLintock asks Maish in the locker room after the loss. "You aged, kid," the crooked manager sighs. The doctor (Edgar Stehli) who gives McLintock his postfight exam declares that he is in danger of going blind and must retire. "When I first came in they used to lay them out in front of me," the physician tells Maish with a gloomy shrug at the inhumanity of their profession. "They were human beings; young men. You know what it's like now, Maish? It's like grading meat at the packing plant."

Although McLintock was once a contender, he is not much better off than Terry Malloy after his forced retirement and seems destined to end up like Ad Francis. In one scene, McLintock is passing time at a bar where a community of retired fighters gather to tell old war stories. McLintock begins a tale and suddenly loses his train of thought. The scattered fighter urgently orders a drink to cope with the frustrating memory loss his career yielded. While the boxing business has mercilessly left McLintock behind, the loyal trainer Army (Ed Wynn) helps him begin searching for work outside the ring. With only a ninth-grade education and nothing but fights on his résumé, McLintock's experience does not easily map onto a career path. "I don't fill in all these holes here," he says to the kindly employment counselor Grace Carney (Kim Hunter) while completing a questionnaire. The greatest professional qualification he can think of is never taking a dive, a testament to his uncommon integrity in a licentious world. "I'm real proud of that," he tells Carney.

Carney admires McLintock's earnestness and thinks he might make a good youth coach (who would, ironically, teach kids to pursue the unforgiving trade that left him broken). But the conniving Maish, scrambling to settle his debts, tries to convince McLintock to start wrestling instead, which would allow him to use his athletic skills and avoid some of boxing's physical risks. Although the ever-loyal McLintock wants to help his manager, he views wrestling as a morally bankrupt profession that would undermine the honesty so central to his identity and eradicate what little self-respect he has retained. "Maish, don't make me," McLintock begs while looking into a dressing room mirror to see himself dressed as an oafish frontiersman. "He was somebody," Army protests to Maish. "Don't turn him into a geek." In the process of pushing McLintock to go through with the wrestling match Maish lets it slip that he had bet against the fighter's final bout. "You're not a winner anymore," Maish says to the betrayed McLintock. "Only thing left; make money on the losing." The treacherous revelation finally prompts McLintock—physically and emotionally scrambled but with his pride still hanging by a thread—to abandon Maish and return to his native Tennessee. The production ends with a faint twinkle of optimism when McLintock meets a young boy on a train heading out of town and gives him some boxing pointers—a hint that he might pursue the new life in coaching that Carney recommended.

Though it ends on a marginally hopeful note, the world of boxing that *Requiem* depicts is as inhumane and corrupt as the environment Robson builds in *The Harder They Fall*. *Requiem* was similarly praised for its unflinching perspective. The *New York Times'* Jack Gould called it "a searing, inspired indictment of the worst side of the prizefight game."[19] *Requiem* gathered a pile of accolades, including the first Peabody Award given for TV writing, to make it the most acclaimed boxing production of the 1950s.

While *The Harder They Fall* and *World in My Corner* offer filmic commentaries on television's role in boxing's corruption, *The Battler* and *Requiem* show television itself confronting the sport's grimy underbelly. These critical accounts surrounded live prime-time telecasts of the sport and reflect their relationship to those broadcasts. Though *The Battler* paints boxing as a dangerous business, it individualizes Francis's decline and attributes it mostly to his pride. NBC was carrying *Friday Night Fights* at the time. Explicitly probing boxing's institutionalized crookedness would have irked Gillette and compromised one of NBC's most popular properties. CBS, on the other hand, had stopped carrying *Wednesday Night Fights* the year prior to *Requiem*'s premier. The network's separation from boxing freed it to be more critical of the sport and the forces that ran it. Moreover, the teleplays, as live productions, share aesthetic space with the network boxing broadcasts. Their critiques of boxing's seediness reflect the widespread allegations that television had reduced boxers into actors and transformed promoters into writers who prioritize gripping entertainment over legitimate or safe competition. Their depictions suggest that perhaps all boxing broadcasts were, to greater and lesser degrees, teleplays.

Requiem for the Boxing Film

In 1962, Columbia Pictures released a theatrical remake of *Requiem for a Heavyweight*, also directed by Ralph Nelson. The film opens by panning across an interracial group of bar patrons watching a telecast of protagonist Mountain Rivera (Anthony Quinn) being pummeled by the charismatic up-and-comer Cassius Clay, who plays himself. Bleary shots from Rivera's wobbling point of view complement the realism the film achieved by casting Clay. The *Requiem* reboot appeared during a lull in the Hollywood boxing film when the genre, according to Grindon, went "nearly dormant for twenty years."[20] Grindon attributes this dip to television and, secondarily, the virtual disappearance of viable White heavyweight contenders after Marciano's 1956 retirement as undefeated heavyweight champion—a transition Clay's ascendance heralded. *Requiem*'s opening moments showcase the industrial and racial conditions that precipitated this generic latency.

Boxing also came under heightened suspicion between *Requiem*'s 1956 premier on TV and its 1962 film adaptation. Ongoing investigations, spearheaded by Tennessee senator Estes Kefauver, centered on the IBC's grip on the fight business. A federal court deemed the Octopus anticompetitive in 1957—a ruling the Supreme Court upheld in 1959. The investigations, as Kefauver put it, demonstrated a "massive conspiracy between racketeers and other undesirables to suppress competition and maintain monopoly control over major boxing contests throughout the country." The inquiries broke up the IBC and revealed the endemic corruption that films like *The Harder They Fall* and *World in My Corner* helped to expose. For instance, former middleweight champion Jake LaMotta admitted to throwing a 1947 fight against Billy Fox. Martin Scorsese re-created the match in *Raging Bull* by showing the prideful LaMotta lowering his gloves to absorb a flurry of Fox's punches but refusing to go down. A *Sports Illustrated* article published shortly after the Supreme Court decision and LaMotta's confession observed "that public skepticism about the wholesomeness of the sport has never been deeper than it is today." Kefauver called for federal

74 • The Boxing Film

oversight of boxing to reinstall some faith in the sport and ensure that young fighters like LaMotta were not "obligated to engage in the shame of collusive matches."[21]

The investigations cited television as a catalyst in boxing's escalating corruption. "Most of the ills of recent years have stemmed from the control over television through the auspices of Jim Norris, the IBC, and their associates," said James Farley of the New York State Athletic Commission. "They reduced boxing to the shell we have today." The IBC's Truman Gibson maintained that television had an even more debasing impact on the sport than organized crime.[22] Marquee championship bouts continued to draw via closed-circuit exhibitions, but the regular telecasts dwindled. "Interest in boxing," the *Chicago Daily Tribune*'s David Condon wrote, "has descended lower than a well digger's elbow."[23] The TV networks—beleaguered by broader industrial ignominies like the infamous quiz show scandals—became increasingly wary of associating with the suspicious sport. NBC even canceled the stalwart *Friday Night Fights* in 1959. Gillette moved the program, along with the rest of its sports advertising budget, to ABC, which scheduled it on the less popular Saturday evening. While ABC gave Gillette's weekly boxing show relatively low priority, it used the economic windfall to invest in sports programming and eventually form ABC Sports, the network department that established modern sports television's main formal practices and industrial status.[24] Once again, boxing sat at the foundation of a sports media sea change.

Aside from changing the main character's name and ethnicity, Nelson's *Requiem* remake was a mostly faithful adaptation that expanded the teleplay's length to that of a theatrical feature and took advantage of aesthetic affordances (more locations, stylized editing, and so forth) film offers that elude live TV dramas. The remake's few shifts in storyline reflect the amplified distrust that had enshrouded boxing since the production of Serling's original. Most notably, it abandons the teleplay's hopeful conclusion by having Rivera wrestle as a cartoonish Native American wearing braids, a head dress, a blanket, and a tomahawk. "I'll do anything for you," Rivera bellows to Maish (Jackie Gleason), "but don't ask me to be a clown." Participating in the humiliating match, however, is the only way to save Maish from the vicious gangsters. The dispirited Rivera pathetically limps into the ring and begins whooping for the ravenous and imbecilic crowd. Army (Mickey Rooney) weeps as Rivera surrenders himself to the indignity. The *Requiem* remake ties boxing's heightened depravity to television—the entry point through which its opening scene introduces the inhumane world that eventually reduces Rivera to a worn-out laughingstock. TV at once provided a target at which boxing films of the era could direct their critiques of the sport's many problems and sent the robust genre into remission.

4

Muhammad Ali, *The Super Fight*, and Closed-Circuit Exhibition

•••••••••••••••••••••••

Although the Hollywood boxing film dissipated during the late 1950s, prize-fighting remained a staple of theatrical spaces and exhibition. Live closed-circuit broadcasts in theaters, arenas, and other public venues were the sport's biggest moneymaker and the principal way marquee fights were consumed from the mid-1950s through the mid-1970s. They combined television's immediacy with cinema and sporting events' communal qualities. As Anna McCarthy outlines in the only study of the media practice's relationship to sport, closed-circuit exhibitions provided "the basis for public participation in cultural politics" in ways that domestic telecasts did not.[1] The politicized participation this under-examined form of TV entailed also reflected the circumstances surrounding particular exhibition sites.

Cassius Clay, who changed his name to Muhammad Ali and converted to Islam after winning the heavyweight championship in 1964, propelled closed-circuit's rise and was boxing's biggest star during its brief heyday. But his religious conversion transformed the so-called Louisville Lip from an endearingly audacious loudmouth who dubbed himself "The Greatest" and predicted his fights' outcomes via witty rhyming couplets into an enigmatic threat. Ali became even more controversial after voicing his opposition to Vietnam two years later. These changes remade closed-circuit exhibitions of Ali's fights into spaces where debates about the boxer took place leading to and surrounding his 1967 suspension from boxing and criminal conviction for draft evasion.

75

76 • The Boxing Film

Ali's banishment prompted a scramble to capitalize on and make sense of the excommunicated boxer's contested place in U.S. culture. A key strain of these productions appeared in the theatrical spaces from which Ali's matches were suddenly absent. The most peculiar and instructive was Woroner Productions' 1970 *Super Fight*—a film based on a computer-simulated match that pitted Ali against Marciano to determine which undefeated former champion was the greatest ever. The manufactured bout, which Marciano won, evaded Ali's suspension and the controversies surrounding closed-circuit exhibitions of him while reasserting the sociopolitical norms the boxer so brazenly disrupted. The popular and profitable *Super Fight* eased Ali's eventual reinstatement into professional boxing, which kindled a resurgence of closed-circuit boxing and reinvigorated the Hollywood boxing film. It illustrates how the politics and business of closed-circuit exhibition fanned Ali's celebrity, informed his expulsion, and brokered his reintegration. Moreover, it shows how attitudes surrounding Ali shaped close-circuit's history, transformation, and intersection with cinema culture.

Closed-Circuit Exhibition and Ali

Domestic boxing telecasts dwindled as closed-circuit claimed most big-ticket fights. By 1959 ABC was the only network airing a regular boxing program, *Fight of the Week*, which it canceled in 1964 because "major championship attractions, with few exceptions, were lost to closed-circuit theater television."[2] ABC still attempted to license championship fights but had little success, as promoters preferred closed-circuit's potentially boundless economic ceilings compared to the onetime fees networks paid for broadcast rights. Sonny Liston and Cassius Clay's February 1964 championship bout in Miami, which Clay won by technical knockout in the seventh round, took closed-circuit boxing to new heights of visibility, stature, and profitability. Marketed through Clay's boisterous charisma and Liston's icy antiheroism, the fight was closed-circuited in a record 355 U.S. locations.[3] It also became the first bout transmitted to Europe live via satellite when Nate Halpern, president of Theater Network Television (TNT), made a deal with NASA to use its new relay satellite. At the time, NASA reserved the satellite for "affairs of international significance" and prohibited commercial use. Consequently, Halpern provided the bout for free to 165 million Europeans to take advantage of the prestige the cutting-edge transmission would offer and to market the fight as a global event that transcended sports. TNT also developed novel ways to show the match by using handheld cameras and constructing a catwalk above the ring from which camera operators could take overhead shots.[4]

The Liston-Clay event grossed a record $3.4 million and solidified a relationship between boxing and closed-circuit exhibition that *Independent Film*

Journal described as a "perfect match."[5] The broadcast also negotiated the local politics surrounding exhibition sites. Liston had an antisegregation clause in his contracts and pulled the fight from two New Orleans theaters that refused to show it to an integrated audience.[6] The *Los Angeles Sentinel* praised the fight and TNT for giving "Negro producers a chance for the first time to present the closed-circuit fight pics in their cities." As Dootsie Williams, the African American owner of Compton, California's, Dooto Music Center, remarked, "It seems that many people like to attend events of this kind in the company of their friends." To foster this sociality, Dooto staged a fashion show before the match and gave out door prizes.[7] Such instances positioned the Liston-Clay exhibitions as politicized markers of community that took official measures to guarantee Black participation.

Clay announced his conversion and name change the day after beating Liston to become champion. A rematch was originally booked at the Boston Garden but was canceled because law enforcement suspected a fix and heard rumors of threats against Ali in retaliation for Malcolm X's February 1965 assassination by Nation of Islam members. The fight wound up taking place 130 miles north in Lewiston, Maine's, comparatively puny St. Dominic's Arena. But the closed-circuit broadcast's projected $5 million take made the venue an afterthought. "Liston and Clay would fight in a bathtub before an audience of silverfish as long as the closed-circuit cameras were plugged in," wrote *Los Angeles Times* columnist Jim Murray. "The 'live' rights they shop around like a guy with a hot diamond who can't be too choosy." "The live gate in Lewiston may not reach $200,000," added the *Washington Post*'s Shirley Povich. "Who cares?" The closed-circuit operator SportsVision, which handled the fight's ancillary rights, purchased a seventy-two-hour $1 million insurance policy against Ali's life in case he was attacked. The morbidly practical media company had far more to lose than those staging the actual fight.[8] Ali knocked Liston out in the first round with a suspicious "phantom punch." Many incensed theatergoers demanded refunds, and one San Pedro, California, patron even filed suit against the theater he visited to recover the $5.40 ticket price. "At least in baseball they give you nine innings," snapped a disgruntled Pittsburgh spectator.

Regardless of the attending controversies, the exhibition broke the records Ali and Liston's first match set and, according to SportsVision president Fred Brooks, was "seen on live TV by more people than ever saw a bout" as far away as Kuwait, New Zealand, and Singapore.[9] The Liston matches established Ali as the biggest celebrity in a sport driven by closed-circuit exhibition. The new champion, for instance, received $10,000 to make an appearance on the closed-circuit broadcast of Floyd Patterson and George Chuvalo's February 1965 match, which otherwise lacked the star power he delivered. He also regularly showed up on ABC's prerecorded Saturday afternoon anthology program *Wide World of Sports* to spar verbally with the sportscaster Howard Cosell. Although

78 • The Boxing Film

ABC could not afford to license Ali's fights, it showed replays of them and conducted interviews with the champion. The relatively inexpensive segments gave *Wide World*—which specialized in obscurities like bobsledding and demolition derbies—a ratings jolt while offering Ali a nationwide forum.

Despite his prodigious athletic success and palpable charm, Ali's religion, name change, and political outspokenness alienated him from both White and Black audiences and made him the most controversial fighter since Jack Johnson. This hostility intensified in February 1966 when his draft status was reclassified from ineligible to eligible. The reclassification prompted Ali to express his disapproval of Vietnam on religious and racial grounds. "I ain't got no quarrel with them Viet Cong," he memorably remarked when asserting his position as a conscientious objector. "Nothing alienated him from his detractors more than this," observes biographer Michael Arkush. "For the athletic and political establishment," Randy Roberts adds, "Muhammad Ali was the enemy."[10]

One month before his draft status reclassification, Ali separated from the Louisville Sponsoring Group—a consortium of wealthy White Kentuckians that supported his professional career—and formed Main Bout Inc. to handle the ancillary rights to his matches. Deliberately contrasting the Louisville group, the majority of Main Bout's five principal stockholders were Black. Two of these shareholders, Main Bout president Herbert Muhammad and treasurer John Ali, were prominent Nation of Islam members. Closed-circuit operator Michael Malitz, attorney Bob Arum, and professional football player Jim Brown joined Herbert Muhammad and John Ali to serve respectively as Main Bout's vice president, secretary, and vice president of publicity. Main Bout, sport historian Michael Ezra explains, complemented Brown's work with the National Negro Industrial and Economic Union and gave "blacks control of boxing's most valuable prize, the world heavyweight championship."[11]

Main Bout faced immediate backlash when attempting to organize and sell closed-circuit rights to Ali's March 1966 match against Ernie Terrell in Chicago. Critics like the *Chicago American*'s Doug Gilbert worried that Main Bout gave the Nation of Islam a dangerous amount of power. "If the Muslims own Clay, and also own the television rights to all of his fights," Gilbert reasoned, "then they have what amounts to a hammerlock on all that's lucrative in boxing."[12] The Illinois State Athletic Commission banned the fight shortly thereafter by citing Ali's politics. Main Bout's subsequent efforts to relocate the competition were continually blocked in cities where promoters showed interest. "I got calls from promoters all over the country wanting to hold the fight," Arum explained. "[But] the day after a promoter would call me, the governor of his state or the mayor would announce there'd be no Clay fight in this town or state."[13] Jim Brown argued that the blackballing was as much a consequence of anxieties about the Black economic power Main Bout signaled as Ali's political views. "For the first time Negroes own stock in closed circuit TV and will be in some of the big money," Brown said. "The only difference between this and previous closed-circuit television is that we have Negro participation." The *Los Angeles Sentinel*'s Brad Pye agreed: "No matter what Clay said or did when White folks were in the driver's seat and were handling the closed-circuit TV end of things, the major theatre outlets around the world didn't boycott his bouts. But when Clay started letting the world know that Main Bout Inc., which includes mostly Negroes, stood to make a WHOLE lot of those pretty little green ones from this and all of his future matches, then the flag wavers from every bigoted hot spot came out of their holes."[14] Closed-circuit exhibition rights were at the center of this racial and economic controversy.

Toronto's Maple Leaf Gardens finally booked the match, from which Terrell immediately withdrew because of dissatisfaction about his cut of the purse. Promoters replaced him with the White Canadian George Chuvalo, whose race and nationality they figured would help the gate and provide a clear foil for the newly villainous Ali. Ontario labor minister Leslie Rowntree emphasized that Toronto's decision to host the fight "in no way condones or supports the previous actions, affiliations, or public statements made by either of the major participants in this fight."[15] Nevertheless, the match provoked widespread outrage that focused on quashing media coverage. Sponsor boycotts forced the fight off national radio. Threats to protest closed-circuit exhibitions and subsequently boycott the establishments hosting them cropped up across the United States. Exhibitors in Denver and San Francisco received menacing dispatches "threatening not only destruction to their buildings but violence to their patrons if the fight were shown."[16] Main Bout had originally contracted 280 North American theaters to carry Ali-Chuvalo, but only 32 ended up showing it. The exhibition was banned in Boston, Miami Beach, Sacramento, and San Antonio and did not play (but was not officially barred) in Cincinnati, Milwaukee, Minneapolis—Saint Paul, and Kansas City. Ali's hometown of Louisville was the only southern city willing to carry the match. "We'd be crazy to show the fight," said a Detroit theater owner. "The American Legion would be on our necks in a minute, and I couldn't blame them if they picketed our place." "It'll be interesting to see how the Black Muslims look in red," gloated *Detroit Free Press* columnist Joe Falls about the financial losses Main Bout was likely to incur because of the protests and boycotts.[17]

The California Athletic Commission asked affiliated venues not to carry the Ali-Chuvalo broadcast "because of the extremely unpatriotic and selfish remarks made by Clay." Only two Los Angeles–area theaters showed the bout—one of which was Williams's Dooto Music Center. "Cassius may be unpopular in most circles, but he rates as the best, most colorful as well as the most controversial fighter in modern times," Williams said regarding his decision to show the fight. Although Williams framed his remarks apolitically, the *Los*

Angeles Sentinel credited his theater with affording African American Angelenos an opportunity to view the match without traveling to Toronto.[18] There were, of course, clear economic advantages to Williams's near monopoly on the exhibition in Los Angeles. But given the racialized threats made to exhibitors, Williams also took significant risk to give his mostly Black patrons a rare chance to watch and support the heavyweight champ.

Unsurprisingly, the Ali-Chuvalo match—which Ali won by decision—was a financial disaster. Initially predicted to gross $4 million, it yielded only $150,000. The commercial failure provoked Arum to declare Ali "a dead piece of merchandise" in the United States. "He's through as far as big-money closed-circuit is concerned. If we can, we'll try to put the fight on home TV here. If not, we'll forget about it. The money we made on this one certainly wasn't worth the effort."[19] Main Bout scheduled Ali's next three fights in Europe, where the champion was less controversial. Ali-Chuvalo also deflated the market for broadcast rights to the degree that ABC could finally afford them. The network packaged Ali's European fights as special live presentations of *Wide World*. It also humanized the embattled fighter by highlighting his markedly different image abroad. Prior to his first European bout—against Henry Cooper in London—*Wide World* presented a short introductory piece on Ali's time in England that depicted the champion jovially wandering around London. "People in London don't view him the way so many Americans do," said Cosell said in a voiceover to the upbeat prematch profile. Ali handily beat Cooper and won the next two European matches—against Brian London in London and Karl Mildenberger in Hamburg—just as easily. Moreover, the fights occurred without incident and gathered some of *Wide World*'s highest ever ratings. This success enabled Main Bout to book Ali's next match in Houston against Cleveland Williams and return to the business of closed-circuit exhibition.

Held at Houston's massive new Astrodome, Ali and Williams's November 1966 bout broke indoor attendance records. It also played in 120 U.S. closed-circuit locations—many of which refused to carry Ali-Chuvalo—and received more international exposure than any of Ali's previous matches, a development his European sojourn helped.[20] Despite the seeming recovery since Ali-Chuvalo, the Ali-Williams exhibitions attracted nowhere near the domestic interest Ali's pre–Main Bout matches gathered and still provoked discord. Miami Beach banned it from the city-owned Miami Beach Convention Center, and the Allegheny County VFW picketed showings in Pittsburgh. But the Ali-Williams broadcasts also attracted exceptionally large African American audiences.[21] Ali guaranteed as much by flexing his authority with Main Bout. When he learned the match would be shown at only one Baton Rouge venue, he made arrangements for it to be exhibited at the city's historically Black Southern University. He also paid the exhibition costs at several other southern Black colleges and let those schools keep the proceeds. After the fight, which

Ali won by TKO in the third round, the champ said he was most proud of the economic opportunities the closed-circuit exhibitions provided African Americans. "You know Negroes all over the country were able to share in the profits of the closed fight television," he told the *Pittsburgh Courier*. "We put the fight on in Negro colleges all over the country. They made money. Little Negroes in other cities shared in the promotion of the TV rights. Nothing has ever been done like this before."[22] Ali and Main Bout asserted economic control and fostered cultural solidarity by ensuring Black audiences could watch the fight in welcoming environments while sharing its profits.

Ali won two more fights—against Ernie Terrell and Zora Folley—before being summoned to report for military induction on April 28, 1967. As expected, he refused to take the step to signify his intention to enter the armed services. The New York State Athletic Commission immediately stripped his title and boxing license—a decision the United States' other commissions all followed. The next month, a federal court found the deposed champion guilty of draft evasion, sentenced him to five years in prison, and fined him ten thousand dollars. Ali managed to stay out of jail through funding appeals, but he could not compete in the United States and his passport was revoked, which eliminated the possibility of international bouts. The combined suspension and conviction forced the undefeated heavyweight champion out of the ring and pushed Main Bout out of business.

"A New Era in Theatrical Sports Entertainment!"

Just one week after Ali's suspension, Big Fights Inc.—a production company William Cayton formed with fellow film collector Jim Jacobs in 1959 to produce boxing-themed programming—rereleased *Greatest Fights of the Century* for syndicators to purchase. Although *Greatest Fights* had not aired regularly since the mid-1950s, Ali's expulsion as undefeated champion reignited debates about the best ever fighters that the show took as its topic. As a trade journal advertisement for *Greatest Fights* asked, "Was Joe Louis the greatest of all time? Or could Clay (PARDON ME—'Muhammad Ali') have beaten him in his prime?"[23] Big Fights marketed the suddenly timely vintage program through the disputes Ali's actions and banishment incited.

The following year Big Fights Inc. made the theatrically released documentary *Legendary Champions* (Harry Chapin), which offered a cultural history of boxing through 1929. The film focuses mostly on Jack Johnson and was advertised through the "never-before-seen films" of him that it included from Cayton and Jacobs's library. Although *Legendary Champions* does not explicitly connect Ali and Johnson, the documentary uses Johnson's story to contextualize Ali's predicament. Ali finally shows up during the film's closing moments when narrator Norman Rose briefly runs down the "acknowledged greats" since 1929. *Legendary Champions* concludes with footage of Ali knocking out an opponent as Rose mentions "the highly controversial champions that stand the years to this very day." The footage halts to a still of Ali triumphantly lifting his arms as Rose prophetically says, "Someday, in the distant future, perhaps they too will become legendary champions" and the film ends. The Academy Award–nominated documentary aligns Ali with the tradition Johnson represents while stressing that the unseated champion's legacy is not yet determined. *Legendary Champions* debuted the same month that Howard Sackler's *The Great White Hope* premiered on Broadway. Sackler's play, which Martin Ritt adapted for film in 1970, told the story of a fictionalized Jack Johnson named Jack Jefferson. The drama had been scripted for several years but was produced only after Ali's suspension stoked renewed interest in Johnson. "It's about me," said Ali about the hit play. "Moves were made to strip him of the title, like what happened to me. He had a jail term comin' up, as I have. And at ringside fellows would yell, as they did at my fights: 'Knock that nigger out!'"[24] *Legendary Champions* and *The Great White Hope* put Ali back into the theaters from which his fights had vanished while situating his banishment within the long history of racism in sports.

Miami-based radio producer Murray Woroner's 1967 *All-Time Heavyweight Tournament* took a different approach to participating in the debates Ali's suspension stirred. The manufactured radio event set out to decide the greatest ever heavyweight boxer by programming the National Cash Register Company's NCR-315 computer with 129 variables for sixteen fighters during the peaks of their careers. Woroner polled 250 experts on qualities that ran from easily measurable factors like "speed" to less tangible and highly subjective metrics including "courage" and "killer instinct." "We know a computer can't program heart or courage," Woroner admitted. "But experts can judge guys they saw fight on those grounds. What we did was use the computer as an impartial arbiter on the probabilities of the way certain boxers would fight in their prime."[25] Woroner scripted the fights, hired announcer Guy LeBow to read the commentary, and mixed in crowd noise to transform the computer's calculations into dramatic stories, while ensuring those sporting yarns lasted long enough to give sponsors the twelve commercial breaks he guaranteed.

The *All-Time Heavyweight Tournament* aired weekly from September through December 1967 and culminated with Rocky Marciano beating Jack Dempsey. It played on 380 U.S. stations and 40 more abroad, including Voice of America. "All we've really done is start more arguments," Woroner remarked of the program that *Sports Illustrated* called "one of the most astonishing marketing successes in radio history."[26] Perhaps the radio tournament's greatest provocation was having Ali lose to Jim Jeffries in the quarterfinals. Considering the culturally resonant parallels between Ali and Jack Johnson, the decision to have Jeffries beat Ali had obvious racial undertones.[27] Moreover,

Woroner's script reinforced critiques of Ali as a cowardly braggart by attributing his loss to overconfident laziness. Ali, in this sense, lost the computerized radio match because of intangible characteristics rated by the boxing experts Woroner polled—authorities who represented the establishment that banned Ali before his criminal conviction. The result betrays the racial politics underlying the ratings and the computer program they fed. Ali took exception to the *All-Time Heavyweight Championship*'s results and filed a one-million-dollar defamation lawsuit. Woroner viewed the suit as an opportunity to make more money—something that Ali, mired in legal fees and surviving by working the college lecture circuit, desperately needed. They settled out of court for one dollar and agreed that Woroner would do a separate filmed computer *Super Fight* that pitted Ali against Marciano.

As with the radio tournament, Woroner's *Super Fight* fed the NCR-315 multiple variables on Ali and Marciano. The data were run through the computer five times with different results and Woroner picked the one he thought would make the best show.[28] Beyond Ali and Marciano's status as the only undefeated heavyweight champions, the *Super Fight* exploited their divergent images. "Ali was the screamer, convert to a religion that made whites uncomfortable, finally a draft resister," explains the *Boston Globe*'s Bud Collins. "Rocky was a champion people could understand; they saw him as uncomplicated, a family man who trained hard, punched people thoroughly well and was good to his parents."[29] Marciano had regularly expressed disapproval for Ali's brash demeanor and political dissidence. "It's a bad situation now because there's a lack of respect for the present champion, and that creates a lack of respect for all past champions," he lamented before Ali's suspension. "People just don't treat you the same since he came along."[30] Like Jeffries, Marciano received widespread pleas to leave retirement and fight Ali, which he wisely never indulged. A Texas oil tycoon reportedly offered him four million dollars if he could beat Ali and put the title back in White hands.[31] The *Super Fight* milked these tensions.

Woroner secretly filmed seventy minute-long rounds in a Miami sound stage that was empty apart from the fighters, their corner men, a referee, and the crew. The forty-five-year-old Marciano shed fifty pounds and bought a new toupee to look his best against Ali, who at twenty-seven was still in his prime. The fighters pulled head shots during filming and performed scenarios typical of their respective styles—with the smaller Marciano burrowing in close and the quicker Ali dancing from a distance. Woroner filmed all seven possible endings: two knockouts, two TKOs, two decisions, and a draw. He then edited the footage to complement the script he penned—again with LeBow's commentary, crowd noises, prematch interviews, and his own between round analyses.

A poster hyped the *Super Fight* as "A New Era in Theatrical Sports Entertainment." As Woroner confidently projected, "Because of the nature of the

84 • The Boxing Film

match-up, and because this is a onetime deal, we feel this show has the potential to make the largest single night gross in theatrical history, as well as the greatest gate in sport's history."[32] Although shot on film, the *Super Fight* would be exhibited in the style of a closed-circuit broadcast, with North American venues showing it simultaneously at ten o'clock Eastern on January 20, 1970. Woroner shrouded the event in secrecy to drum up ticket sales. He claimed that only he, his editor, and his sound operator knew the fight's outcome, which *World Boxing* magazine labeled "one of the most closely guarded secrets since the Normandy invasion." "I didn't even tell my wife," Woroner declared.[33] Woroner also had the film lab processors leave in two endings so he could personally cut the finale and hide the result. Once the *Super Fight* was completed, Woroner Productions placed the finished films into sealed containers—to be opened only by projectionists—and hired armed guards to deliver them to exhibition sites no more than thirty minutes before the *Super Fight*'s showing. The guards were instructed to destroy all prints after the exhibition—except one that Woroner planned to deposit at the Library of Congress for posterity and another he would keep for his personal collection.[34] "There will be no second run," the *Super Fight*'s trailer pledged. "The fight will never be seen on television or in newsreels."

Although the *Super Fight* did not meet Woroner's grandiose projections, it was exhibited in fifteen hundred sites—a thousand of which were in the United States. The exhibitions grossed $2.5 million, the most of any of Ali's real or imagined fights since before Main Bout. "P. T. Barnum would have loved it," joked the *St. Louis Post-Dispatch*.[35] Some venues, like the Boston Garden, paired the *Super Fight* with a live undercard as they would with closed-circuit broadcasts of championship matches. Most locations charged five dollars for admission—significantly more than a regular movie ticket but less than a live closed-circuit exhibition—because of its unique and one-time-only status. Beyond the secrecy, scarcity, and novelty Woroner used to promote the *Super Fight*, Marciano's tragic death in a plane crash between the match's filming and exhibition added intrigue and amplified his role as the sentimental favorite.

The *Super Fight* opens on a still shot of an empty ring along with electronic sound effects to emphasize the technologized novelty driving the staged event. In this sense, it resembles early twentieth-century fake fight films. But while these early boxing film reproductions strove to appear realistic through adopting conventions like putting spectators in the stands, the *Super Fight*'s vacant ring and unfamiliar sound effects stress the production's status as a synthetic computer invention. "The film you will see is the result of more than three years of research by leading sportswriters around the world and by members of the World Boxing Historians Association," says Woroner in an introductory voiceover that underscores his role as the visionary behind the experiment. While Woroner emphasizes the *Super Fight*'s status as an imaginary simulation, he guarantees its authenticity and scientific reliability. "The computer applied formulae, four million of them, to each round to tell us each man's condition," he continued. "It told us about cuts, knockdowns, gave us round-by-round scores, and, of course, who the ultimate winner would be, and in what round it would end and how. But make no mistake, you are actually going to see Rocky Marciano and Muhammad Ali at their best, because that's the way the computer saw them."

Like a regular boxing telecast, the *Super Fight* opens by introducing the fighters and offering expert predictions about their impending encounter. It also reinforces the NCR-315's apolitical objectivity. "I'm happy that this fight is taking place on the computer because there will be no home town decisions and there will be no prejudice in this fight," Marciano divulged in a prematch interview. "It will be done by a machine with all the human elements taken out of it, and I'm very pleased about that." Each round concluded with teletype readouts that offer an assessment, statistics, and score up to that point. The readouts use a mechanical font, are accompanied by the crunching sound of a printer, and move vertically up the frame as if they are being emitted from a machine. The trope distances the *Super Fight* from human intervention and indicates that the polarizing differences separating Ali and Marciano are irrelevant to the NCR-315's calculations.

But Woroner's script seasoned the computer's apparently objective findings with drama that played into the fighters' respective images. Since the NCR-315's projections made differing determinations regarding precisely how the match would take shape, Woroner took creative liberties to build a gripping narrative. For instance, LeBow remarks that Ali opened the ninth round with "a bit of a cautious start" after knocking Marciano down in the previous round. He adds that "Muhammad Ali knows that Rocky comes on after some adversity." Sure enough, Marciano surges to tie the score by the end of the twelfth. "THE FIGHT IS ALL EVEN," reads the teletype summary. "Ali is now in as much danger of being knocked out as Rocky is of losing by TKO," Woroner comments between rounds. Marciano knocked Ali out in the thirteenth round—the same round during which he beat Joe Walcott to earn the title in 1952. The comeback both was histrionic and fulfilled Marciano's role as the *Super Fight*'s popular favorite. The film ends with a shot of a chastened and solitary Ali regaining his senses—a contrast to the triumphant image on which *Legendary Champions* ends—as the computerized soundscape that opened the film returns to emphasize again its position as a novel but manufactured spectacle.

Despite the *Super Fight*'s appeals to mechanized impartiality, the cultural deck was stacked against Ali. The *Los Angeles Sentinel* dismissed Woroner's production as "nothing more than a cheap money hustle" and claimed "there was no way Clay would have won at this time" given his suspension and Marciano's recent passing.[36] A Marciano victory certainly made better financial sense considering the heightened public affection for the recently deceased former champion and the fact that Ali could still potentially perform for future productions. But the *Super Fight* also fulfilled the White Hope narrative simmering just beneath the experiment's surface and informing the calls for Marciano to leave retirement and fight Ali—an observation Ali made after watching the film. "But that computer doesn't know what color you are," protested a reporter. "It acts like it," replied Ali, who later bitterly speculated "that computer must have been made in Alabama."[37] As the *Washington Post*'s Kenneth Turah pointed out, "Computer decisions are as human as the people who decide what information to feed the machine and what to withhold." Accordingly, the *Super Fight*—a production that boxing historian Jeffrey T. Sammons called "a soothing tonic to many Americans who longed to see Ali dethroned in the ring"— reflected and reinforced the racial discourses surrounding it.[38] Contrasting Marciano's prematch comments, there undoubtedly was "prejudice in this fight."

Although its outcome irked Ali, the *Super Fight*'s exhibitions transpired without hostility. *World Boxing* reported a "few picketers were in sight" outside of the Miami Beach Auditorium, the same venue where local government banned Ali-Chuvalo, but noted that the exhibition proceeded as planned.[39] Other locations attracted disproportionately White crowds but cited no violence, protests, or boycotts. The *Boston Globe*'s Harold Kaese reported that fewer than 100 of the 7,330 spectators at the Boston Garden exhibition—just twenty-five miles from Marciano's hometown of Brockton, Massachusetts— were Black and guessed that an Ali victory would have incited a riot.[40] The *Super Fight*'s result ensured more peaceful exhibitions. These calm showings made the possibility for additional computerized bouts, which Woroner intended to produce, more likely. The computer had cultural and economic incentives to deem Marciano victorious and comparatively few enticements to give Ali the win.

Beyond its harmonious and lucrative exhibition, the *Super Fight* garnered critical praise for its technical verisimilitude. The production "had all the techniques of the best movie fights and more realism," enthused the *St. Louis Post-Dispatch*'s Bob Posen. NCR scientist David Glick, however, pointed out that while the computer could program according to the fighters' skill sets, records, and tendencies, it could not "emulate the human condition" with complete precision. "You can't get emotion, anger, ring taunting, one race fighting another," Glick explained. "By using probability," Turah agreed, "[*Super Fight*] eliminated the 'anything can happen' aspects that make live sport so enticing, and it removed the 'human factor' occurrences that enlivened Hollywood efforts like *Champion* and *Body and Soul*."[41] On the contrary, the *Super Fight*'s decision to have the White sentimental favorite come from behind and emerge victorious over his mysterious antagonist owes a debt to the fictional boxing film.

Woroner, in this sense, created a different type of boxing movie that—much like *Champion* and *Body and Soul*—exalts and dramatizes the White boxer's triumph and fulfills narrative convention. In doing so, it reproduces and revives the racial politics of the genre that Marciano's retirement and Ali's rise helped put into remission.

Although Woroner claimed the *Super Fight* would be shown only once, he almost instantly rereleased it—a decision he justified by claiming to be honoring the Marciano family's wishes.[42] The *Super Fight* enjoyed a brief theatrical run and served as a cost-efficient accompaniment to male-oriented films like *How the West Was Won* (John Ford, Henry Hathaway, and George Marshall, 1962) and even X-rated productions like *The Minx* (Raymond Jacobs, 1969). Theaters also programmed the *Super Fight* as the lead-in to closed-circuit exhibitions of Joe Frazier and Jimmy Ellis's February 16, 1970, championship match to boost the competition that was otherwise attracting only modest interest. *Super Fight*'s initial showing out-rated the title bout.[43] Nearly three years after his suspension commenced, Ali's fictional fight was a bigger draw than the real matches of the champion who succeeded him—a fact he used to goad Frazier and stoke interest in an eventual match.

Ali became less polarizing as Vietnam gradually sank in popularity. In fact, as time went on he was lauded for his principled stance against the costly and divisive war. The *Super Fight*'s commercial success and smooth exhibition testified to the former champion's sustained profitability and cooled image. Woroner's production participated in this softening by having Ali humbled by a symbol of White masculinity. Interest in an Ali-Frazier fight gradually overshadowed Ali's excoriation, and by September 1970 his license was reinstated. The *Super Fight* aided Ali's reentry into professional boxing by showing his commercial potential, demonstrating the diminished controversy surrounding the fighter and publicly exhibited representations of him in action, and buttressing the traditional sociopolitical order Ali so obstreperously upended.

The Fight of the Century

Unable to set a match with Frazier immediately after his reinstatement and eager to get back in the ring, Ali scheduled his initial return bout against Jerry Quarry in Atlanta. While Quarry lacked Frazier's professional pedigree, his Whiteness amplified interest in the fight. "Here is a chap who was licked by Jimmy Ellis, knocked out by Joe Frazier and stopped, too, by George Chuvalo, and still will collect a $150,000 guarantee to fight Clay," wrote Povich of Quarry. "There has been such a plethora of talented black fighters and so few white ones that for promoters intent on stimulating gate receipts, white is beautiful."[44] Ali-Quarry was promoted through the racial drama that marked the *Super Fight*. The *Los Angeles Times*' Don Page described it as "a reincarnation of Jack Johnson vs. Jim Jeffries, with Quarry representing those who wish to see Ali blasted from public view."[45] "Who could be more respectable in Georgia than a White Hope ranked as top contender in the World Heavyweight Division?," Ali asked. Quarry, in fact, embraced his role as White Hope, and Ali channeled Johnson by continually projecting Big Fights Inc.'s recently released biographical documentary *Jack Johnson* (1970) on a bed sheet while training. "I planned to dedicate Quarry to Jack Johnson," Ali later wrote in his memoir. "To dress up like Johnson, come in the ring in a pearl-gray derby, striped black coat over my boxing shorts, announce to the Georgia audience that I was dedicating my first fight after exile to him, and say, 'Jack, wherever you are, rest easy in your grave. This White Hope won't get away.'"[46] *Wide World of Sports* contracted with Woroner to air the *Super Fight* two days before Ali-Quarry to capitalize on the production's renewed relevance and racial undertones. ABC's *Super Fight* replay achieved the biggest rating in *Wide World*'s history—outperforming even its live telecasts of Ali's European fights.[47]

Ali easily and unsurprisingly beat Quarry by TKO in the third round. But the racial dynamics and excitement surrounding Ali's return helped the otherwise lackluster fight become the second highest grossing bout since Liston and Clay. The closed-circuit broadcast played in 206 U.S. venues and drew no notable conflicts. As Robert Lipsyte explained, the fight "re-established Ali's credibility with the closed-circuit television network that has become the most important element in a successful prizefight. He was alive, he showed up, no Federal Marshalls blocked him at the ring steps, he was fit to fight and he filled the screen."[48] Testing the *Super Fight*'s results with an actual match, Ali-Quarry indicated that closed-circuit broadcasts featuring Ali were profitable and, equally important, noncontroversial.

Big Fights' documentary profile *A.K.A. Cassius Clay* premiered two weeks after Ali-Quarry to punctuate Ali's return to the ring and theaters. Building on *Legendary Champions* and the *Super Fight*, *A.K.A.* includes Ali and famous trainer Cus D'Amato speculating on how he would have fared against former champions—including Marciano—and features dramatic on-screen narration by the actor Richard Kiley, who waxes poetic about Ali's persecution and resilience. Although a mostly disjointed documentary that was hastily released to cash in on Ali's return, *A.K.A.* became one of the season's top box office hits and even broke records at Chicago's Clark Theatre to reestablish Ali's viability as a theatrical attraction.[49]

This success emboldened Ali to assert greater control over subsequent closed-circuit broadcasts. He threatened to pull out of his next postsuspension fight, against the Argentinean Oscar Bonavena at Madison Square Garden, if New York City–area theater blackouts were not lifted and ticket prices lowered. "We're getting letters and phone calls . . . from all over, from kids and old ladies, from the people who can't afford $10," Ali said. "They're asking us to help them

Muhammad Ali and Closed-Circuit Exhibition • 89

see the fight in theaters where they live—in Harlem and Spanish Harlem and the Bronx."[50] The fight was subsequently made available at five local theaters. Less than three months into his reinstatement, Ali realigned the consumption of closed-circuit broadcasts with his politics and ensured that the Black community would be able to see his match, which he won with a fifteenth-round TKO. Ali not simply was back in theaters but also leveraged his economic clout to politicize these spaces.

Ali finally booked a title fight against Frazier shortly after the Bonavena match. In addition to the bout's championship implications, Ali and Frazier had developed a promotionally rich rivalry. Although Black, Frazier was more accepting of the status quo than Ali. And like many conservatives, Frazier insisted on calling Ali "Clay" despite his name change. The combination of Frazier's conformist persona and slugging style, in fact, prompted many to call him the "black Marciano."[51] Ali and Frazier's March 8, 1971, match in Madison Square Garden both resonated with the *Super Fight* and drew the biggest distribution of any bout since the computerized match.

Hollywood-based entertainment promoter Jerry Perenchio marketed Ali-Frazier as the "Fight of the Century." "This is not just a boxing match," Perenchio promised, "this is one of the greatest entertainment events in history." With financial backing from Los Angeles Lakers owner Jack Kent Cooke, Perenchio guaranteed Ali and Frazier $2.5 million each—the biggest boxing purse ever and a key plotline in the event's promotion that *Time* magazine made its March 8, 1971, cover story. Budd Schulberg called the fight "an event as significant to the *Wall Street Journal* as it was to *Ring* magazine." "In size of the money outlay and spectator interest," the *Boston Globe* added, "the attraction dwarfs such spectacles as the Super Bowl football game and baseball World Series in the United States, the World Cup and even the colorful Olympic Games." Perenchio issued six hundred press credentials for the affair—one of which went to Frank Sinatra, whom *Life* hired as its ringside photographer.[52]

The Fight of the Century, which Frazier won by unanimous decision, generated a record gate of $1,352,961. "But the live gate is not the primary factor," Perenchio reminded "The closed-circuit TV network is."[53] The fight appeared in four hundred theaters and was the first to show in all fifty states. It played in forty additional countries via closed-circuit or home TV to reach an estimated total audience of three hundred million. Closed-circuit venues charged up to twenty-five dollars per ticket, resulting in a roughly twenty-million-dollar take—another financial record. Recognizing television's crucial importance to the event and its success, Perenchio enhanced the fight's suitability to the medium by darkening the ring's canvas and adjusting the color of the towels each corner used. He also prohibited radio broadcasts except for Armed Forces Radio, which he originally blocked but decided to permit after receiving backlash from the same patriotic contingent that had castigated Ali for his draft

90 • The Boxing Film

resistance. Mutual Broadcasting System had to sue for the rights to air round-by-round radio updates. A judge ruled in Mutual Broadcasting's favor but limited the bulletins to fifty words and prohibited the use of sound effects that might insinuate it was reporting live from the event.[54] Like Woroner, Perenchio said no films of the event would be shown for at least six months. Also like Woroner, Perenchio circulated films across the world almost immediately after the match.

While Ali's fights against Quarry and Bonavena transpired smoothly, the Fight of the Century's distended profile sparked renewed anxieties among closed-circuit distributors and exhibitors. Citing Ali's politics, Manchester, New Hampshire's *Manchester Union-Leader* did not accept ads for the fight and refused to cover it. Oklahoma City prohibited the fight from playing in its publicly owned Civic Center Music Hall, and veterans protested exhibitions in Hershey, Pennsylvania. Guided by very different motives, the Southern Christian Leadership Conference picketed three Philadelphia venues in response to their ticket prices and because none of them were Black owned.[55] Despite these skirmishes, the exhibitions occurred without much hostility and with no reports of racially motivated conflict. As *Variety* reported, "Theatre men attuned to closed-circuit sports events were relieved, fundamentally, that it [*sic*] was not any interracial fisticuffs." The only reports of trouble surrounded the destruction of property by people turned away from full houses or by patrons frustrated because of technical complications. Fans at Chicago's Coliseum and International Amphitheater threw chairs off the balcony because of a faulty projector, for instance, and the Chicago police turned fire hoses on others who stormed the gates after being denied entry to the sold-out venue.[56] The differences separating the clashes at Ali-Frazier exhibitions from those at closed-circuit broadcasts of Ali's earlier fights are telling. The confrontations at Fight of the Century showings were not attempting to prevent the broadcast but expressing disappointment over not being able to see it. Despite these divergences, the closed-circuit industry's fortunes remained intimately tied to Ali and attitudes surrounding him, and the *Super Fight* was instrumental in creating this economic and cultural change.

5

The 1970s, *Rocky*, and
the Shadow of Ali

• •

The hibernating Hollywood boxing film began to stir as closed-circuit faded. This resurgence was set in motion mainly by *Rocky*, a surprise 1976 hit written by and starring Sylvester Stallone. The low-budget production took inspiration from both the *Super Fight* and closed-circuit. Its working-class and undersized Italian American protagonist, Rocky Balboa, evokes Marciano and even has a shrine to the former champion on the mantle of his disheveled Philadelphia apartment. "I was looking around for a suitable vehicle, one that would be appropriate for me," Stallone reflected. "Someone had shown me a tape of Rocky Marciano fighting Ali; it was a computer analysis of what would happen. I saw the juxtaposition of style and contrast and I was interested." Balboa gets his big break through a novelty match not dissimilar from the *Super Fight* in which the charismatic Black champion Apollo Creed (Carl Weathers) offers the no-name fighter an undeserved title shot knowing the White challenger will guarantee big TV ratings. Stallone also cites as an influence a 1975 closed-circuit exhibition he watched of Ali fighting the White long shot Chuck Wepner, who surprisingly knocked Ali down and lasted fifteen rounds before finally succumbing to the superior fighter. Wepner's unlikely success and unusual determination gave Stallone a template for Balboa. Ali, in turn, inspired his invention of Creed. "Apollo Creed was a thinly disguised impersonation of Ali," Stallone divulged. "If Ali didn't exist, I don't think people would have bought the premise of *Rocky*."[1] *Rocky* combined the *Super Fight* and Ali-Wepner to tell the story of a tenacious White underdog based partly on Marciano who takes on and humbles a boisterous Black celebrity athlete modeled on Ali.

Rocky became "the most popular boxing film in screen history" and collected three Academy Awards—including Best Picture—out of ten nominations.[2] The film's racial politics, critics suggest, drove its unprecedented resonance by aligning with 1970s "New Right" conservative responses to the social cleavages Ali represented and depicting a return to traditional values through Balboa's achievement. *Rocky* kindled what Grindon calls "the most important cycle of boxing films since the close of the studio era."[3] These productions continued to reinstate the customs Ali and his publicly projected image disrupted. Some reinforced *Rocky*'s conservatism with tales of White triumph. Others offered Black-centered stories of achievement that took Ali as their inspiration and even subject. These shifts illustrate how the revival of boxing films during the 1970s was guided by dual efforts to capitalize on Ali's polarizing image and negotiate the cultural hierarchies it upset.

A Black President and White Struggle

The late 1960s and early 1970s saw Hollywood's biggest recession since the Great Depression. The classical studio era's blockbuster-driven model lost viability and the film market fragmented. This splintering resulted in multiple and divergent shifts—from the emergence of iconoclastic "New Hollywood" auteurs like Arthur Penn and Martin Scorsese to low-budget blaxploitation productions that catered to urban African American audiences with Black-cast films. While blaxploitation grew out of the race film tradition, the genre contrasted its predecessor's conventional acquiescence with overtly provocative representations. Blaxploitation engaged the Civil Rights Movement and responded to Hollywood's traditional caricaturing, and often exclusion, of African Americans with liberated and powerful Black characters who challenged oppressive, corrupt, and frequently White-run institutions. It routinely paired these images of Black power with heavy doses of sex and violence—a mixture that foundational blaxploitation flicks like Melvin Van Peebles's *Sweet Sweetback's Baadasssss Song* (1971) and Gordon Parks's *Shaft* (1971) pioneered.

Ali inspired blaxploitation's politics and epitomized the genre's tendency to rail against the White establishment. Boxing offered a convenient backdrop from which to engage blaxploitation's thematic hallmarks. Bruce Clark's *Hammer* (1972) stars Fred Williamson—a handsome and bold former professional football player who called himself the Muhammad Ali of football—as B. J. Hammer, a dockworker who moonlights as a prizefighter. The gangster Big Sid (Charles Lampkin), who runs the docks and uses them to smuggle heroin, notices Hammer's fighting prowess after he pummels a racist coworker and recruits the boxer to fight under his management. Once Hammer compiles a respectable record—a collection of matches that, unbeknownst to him, Big Sid had fixed—the gangster commands him to throw a bout against the White fighter "Irish" Joe Brady (George Wilbur). Like in *Body and Soul* and *World in My Corner*, Hammer flirts with corruption but ultimately refuses to take the dive.

While Muhammad Ali does not appear in *Hammer*, the film uses him as an emblem of Black pride and integrity. In one scene, a detective (Bernie Hamilton) tries to persuade Hammer, who had been enjoying the material spoils his partnership with Big Sid bestows, against throwing the fight. Hammer leans against a jukebox with an image of Ali displayed above it as he considers the gumshoe's perspective and eventually decides against Big Sid's criminal path. Ali symbolically looks on as Hammer chooses honesty over greed and, in doing so, transforms himself from a mob-owned goon into a virtuous competitor. Hammer again evokes Ali after beating Brady and reuniting with his girlfriend Lois (Vonetta McGee). "If you're with me," he says to Lois as they jauntily leave the arena, "I can whip the whoooole world!" Delivered in the style of Ali's showboating smack talk, the final lines tie Hammer's triumph to the fighter.

Richard Fleischer's nineteenth-century plantation melodrama *Mandingo* (1975), an adaptation of Kyle Onstott's 1957 best-selling novel, takes *Hammer* in salacious new directions. The film stars professional boxer Ken Norton, who was known as Black Hercules and gained widespread fame after beating Ali in 1973. Norton plays Mede, a muscular and handsome slave descended from the Mandingos, an African tribe famous for fighting. The Maxwell family, helmed by the wicked patriarch Warren (James Mason), purchases Mede and brings him back to their Falconhurst plantation to fight other slaves—sometimes to the death—for their owners' entertainment. The melodrama unfurls when Warren Maxwell's comparatively sensitive son Hammond (Perry King) falls in love with and impregnates the slave girl Ellen (Brenda Sykes). Hammond's jealous wife Blanche (Susan George) throws Ellen down the stairs, which causes her to miscarry, and then blackmails Mede into sleeping with her. Blanche becomes pregnant after the vengeful tryst and delivers a multiracial child, whom Warren Maxwell orders the doctor to kill in order to conceal the indignity. The shocking birth prompts a violent denouement in which Hammond poisons Blanche, shoots Mede, and then drowns the Mandingo fighter in a cauldron of boiling water. One of Mede's fellow slaves kills Warren Maxwell during the melee to leave Hammond weeping over his father's corpse and with Falconhurst in shambles.

Film historian Donald Bogle describes *Mandingo* as "*Gone with the Wind* inside out."[4] Although critically panned, the film earned enough money to generate the sequel, *Drum* (1976), which takes place at Falconhurst fifteen years later and again stars Norton as the titular slave fighter. *Drum* was even more provocative than its predecessor. As one poster for the film promised,

"Mandingo lit the fuse, *Drum* is the explosion!" Like Mede, Drum is a Mandingo whom Hammond Maxwell (Warren Oates) purchases to use as a fighter. Soon after Drum arrives at Falconhurst, Hammond's daughter Sophie (Rainbeaux Smith) unsuccessfully attempts to seduce him as well as the slave Blaise (Yaphet Kotto). Embarrassed by the rebuffs, Sophie accuses Blaise of rape, which prompts her father to chain him up. Maxell's fellow slave owner Bernard DeMarigny (John Colicos)—who had also attempted to sleep with Drum and bitterly vowed revenge after being denied—urges Maxwell to castrate Blaise as punishment. But before they can exact the gruesome penalty, Drum unchains his compatriot and leads a violent uprising. DeMarigny shoots and kills Blaise during the revolt. Drum avenges his friend by castrating DeMarigny with his bare hands—a grisly reversal of the slave master's sexualized sadism. Drum, however, spares Maxwell as his fellow slaves torch Falconhurst. The film ends with Drum sprinting through the night toward freedom as the White establishment he overtook burns.

Ali regained the heavyweight title amid blaxploitation's proliferation. His 1974 "Rumble in the Jungle" victory over George Foreman in Zaire—a global spectacle organized by the African American promoter Don King—emboldened the film genre's often-Afrocentric message of Black empowerment. And Ali's second championship brought the fighter greater mainstream acceptance. *Sports Illustrated* named him its 1974 Sportsman of the Year, and President Gerald Ford invited him to visit the White House. "Ali was now an American hero," observes biographer Jonathan Eig, "a symbol of national identity."[5] The onetime pariah gained widespread approval without changing his political positions.

William Greaves and William Klein's respective Ali documentaries accompanied and celebrated the boxer's return to prominence. Greaves's *Ali, the Fighter* (1974) was the first Ali documentary made by an African American and extended the filmmaker's socially conscious work for National Educational Television's *Black Journal* (1968–1977) to emphasize the boxer's position as a pillar of the Black community. Klein's *Muhammad Ali: The Greatest* (1974) documents Ali's dramatic transformation—as an athlete and public figure—during the ten-year period separating his 1964 championship win over Liston and the Rumble in the Jungle. Klein, for instance, includes revealing interview footage with members of the Louisville Sponsoring Group shortly after Ali—then Cassius Clay—initially won the heavyweight title. It pans through the group of wealthy White men as they introduce themselves, announce their prestigious occupations, and offer some thoughts on the boxer they bankroll. The bourbon scion W. L. Lyons Brown insists that he does not seek to profit on his investment in Ali, but admits he is "inclined to feel" the newly minted champ "is a little ungrateful" for the support the Louisville group gave him. Brown continues to divulge that his relatives likely owned some of Ali's ancestors but asserts that they were benevolent enough to free their slaves. He implies, then, that Ali owes him gratitude and deference—for far more than supporting his athletic career. The scene demonstrates the paternalism that eventually drove Ali to separate from the Louisville Group and form Main Bout Inc. with mostly Black partners.

By showing Ali's eventual break from the Louisville group and transformation from a plucky youngster into a powerful global icon, Klein suggests the boxer's refusal to be intimidated by establishmentarians like Lyons—whose tone-deaf protestations of generosity reek of entitled racism—and the traditions they represent is precisely what makes him so praiseworthy. *Muhammad Ali: The Greatest* ends with a Pop Art rendering of Ali and Gerald Ford's 1974 meeting along with speech bubbles that imagine their exchange. "You're the greatest," Ford tells the fighter. "Yea.... And I'm the next president, too," Ali retorts as a buoyant Afrobeat song celebrating the fighter plays in the background. "President of the USA.... President of the Universe.... Greatest President of all times!!!"[6]

The blaxploitation films and Ali documentaries celebrated cultural shifts that threatened the racial order productions like *The Super Fight* worked to repair and solidify. The few early 1970s boxing films that featured White fighters contrasted these depictions of Black power with images of White hardship. John Huston's *Fat City* (1972), a neo-noir adaptation of Leonard Gardner's 1969 novel, centers on Billy Tully (Stacey Keach), a washed-up and alcoholic former fighter in Stockton, California, who can't hold down a job and wallows in a hopeless haze since his wife left him. Tully—who was once known as "The Pride of Stockton"—meets the young boxer Ernie Munger (Jeff Bridges) while attempting to sweat out a hangover at the local YMCA. Tully thinks the fresh-faced and rangy Munger has potential and encourages him to meet with his former manager Rueben (Nicholas Colasanto). Rueben believes Munger might be able to sell tickets to local fans thirsting for a White Hope. "There's a white kid who come in," he tells his uninterested wife as she drifts to sleep one night. "I got nothing against coloreds, there's just way too many of them in the game. Anglos don't wanna pay to see two colored guys fight. They want to see a white guy fight." Rueben cannily bills Munger as "Irish" Ernie Munger—even though he is not Irish—so those reading the newspaper will know he is White and possibly come see him. Munger, however, has little talent, which makes his Whiteness only moderately useful.

Along these lines, Tully has been fired and laid off from so many jobs—box factory laborer, fry cook, etc.—that he resorts to manual labor in the nearby fields. "He felt being white no longer made a difference," Gardner wrote of Tully's circumstances in his novel.[7] Huston's film, for which Gardner penned the screenplay, depicts the racial dimensions of this lack of opportunity by making Tully one of the only White men working the land. The onetime Pride of

96 • The Boxing Film

Stockton effectively lost his only advantage and finds himself on the lowest rung of society. Tully, however, clings to his puerile fantasies of someday making a comeback. He even begins training and wins an ugly match against the injured Mexican fighter Lucero (Sixto Rodriguez), who is pissing blood before the bout and is so hobbled that he can barely step into the ring. "Lots of people have asked about the title of my book," Gardner told *Life* magazine. "The title is ironic: Fat City is a crazy goal no one is ever going to reach."[8]

The film closes with a drunk Tully stumbling into Munger one night. Munger, who had continued boxing and shown some modest improvement, is returning home to his family and has little interest in catching up with Tully, who has become more of an embarrassing nuisance than an old pal. But Tully insists they go to a nearby diner. Munger indulges his onetime mentor and impatiently sips coffee as Tully yammers about life and boxing in an unsteady tone that drifts from resentment to nostalgia. Contrasting the boxing film's typical stories of achievement and transformation, neither Tully nor Munger is better off than when the film began. Amid his scattered reveries, Tully smugly points out an Asian man working in the diner and asks Munger: "How'd you like to wake up in the morning and be him? Jesus—a waste! Before you get rolling your life makes a bee-line for the drain." Irritated and perplexed, Munger counters that maybe the man is happy—a possibility Tully dismisses as preposterous before asking, "Would you believe he was young once?" "No," Munger replies in monotone. "Maybe he wasn't," Tully concludes as the diners continue nursing their coffees until Munger finally rises to leave. "No, stick around a while," Tully pleads. Munger indulges Tully and the twosome returns to sitting in silence as the film ends—a muteness Gardner's screenplay describes as "so prolonged it becomes bizarre, so absolute that it is like a truth, a profound spiritual expression by two men facing the void." The awkward and melancholy finale encapsulates *Fat City*'s ironic title. By any obvious indication, the man working at the diner is doing far better than Tully; and he certainly seems more content than the sloshed, embittered, and burned out blowhard. But Tully has fooled himself into believing he is superior and destined for greater things if he can catch a few lucky breaks—an illusion of upward mobility that betrays the shred of privilege Tully's Whiteness offers while only exacerbating his increasingly pathetic existence and punctuating film's overall existential malaise.

Walter Hill's *Hard Times* (1975) presents a slightly more hopeful depiction of a White fighter facing privation. The production stars Charles Bronson—building on his popular role as a soft-spoken but merciless vigilante in *Death Wish* (1974)—as Chaney, a solitary Depression-era wanderer who rides the rails and makes money as an underground bareknuckle brawler. Chaney washes up in Baton Rouge, where he connects with the fast-talking hustler Speed (James

Coburn) and Poe (Strother Martin), an opium-addled cut man. The motley trio heads to New Orleans to capitalize on Chaney's barbaric skill.

Economic circumstances lead the stoically masculine Chaney to take up fighting, a talent he possesses but does not relish. When Lucy (Jill Ireland), a hard luck woman with whom he begins an affair, expresses surprise at his unusual and dangerous job, Chaney responds, "It's better than working at the bus station changing tires for two bucks a day." Searching for some competitive or spiritual rationale to explain his primal trade, Lucy asks him what it feels like to knock someone out. "It makes me feel a hell of a lot better than it does him," he curtly responds. "There's no reasons about it," Chaney asserts in deadpan. "Just money." Chaney makes it clear that he would pursue another profession if it paid as well. In fact, he plans to stop brawling once he earns enough to make his next move. Speed, however, owes money to some dangerous gamblers, and Chaney must fight one last time to get him off the hook. Although victorious in this final bout, Chaney is far from triumphant. He silently hops a train and leaves the same way he entered the film—both Chaney and the world he occupies remain the same as when the story began. He will presumably continue fighting as long as it proves to be his most pragmatic means of survival.

Fat City and *Hard Times* bleakly contrast the blaxploitation films' and Ali documentaries' depictions of Black conquest. While B. J. Hammer can "whip the whoooole world," Drum burns Falconhurst to the ground, and Ali is "the greatest president of all times," Tully bitterly drinks his life away and Chaney aimlessly hops trains until he is hungry enough to fight. These racialized differences reflect the increased challenges working-class White men faced amid the economic downturn that hit America after Vietnam. Civil Rights–driven increases in African Americans competing for jobs accompanied this recession. These shifts were met with conservative responses that blamed minorities for the economic downturn's emasculating effects. The 1970s boxing film engaged these contentious changes by both celebrating the Black triumphs and lamenting the White struggles.

Filling in Gaps

The 1976 U.S. bicentennial celebration inspired nostalgia and a renewed sense of patriotism amid the widespread economic difficulties. *Rocky* became the bicentennial's most popular and celebrated film of any genre. The production centers on Rocky "The Italian Stallion" Balboa, an underachieving Philadelphia mob debt collector and club fighter who—by a strange happenstance that borders on divine intervention—is given a chance to fight for the heavyweight title when Apollo Creed's original opponent drops out. Prepping under the guidance of the surly trainer Mickey (Burgess Meredith), Balboa's goal is simply to "go the distance" with Creed—something none of the Ali-inspired champ's challengers had yet achieved. In the process, Balboa rekindles his self-esteem, falls in love with the timid pet shop clerk Adrian (Talia Shire), and transforms himself into something greater than another "bum from the neighborhood." Film critic Frank Rich described *Rocky* as a "fairy tale" that "tapped the spirit of the present. The old-fashioned bicentennial vision of America."[9] Stallone embraced the film's blatant romanticism: "I believe the country as a whole is beginning to break out of this . . . anti-everything syndrome . . . this nihilistic, Hemingwayistic attitude that everything in the end must wither and die. . . . I want to be remembered as a man of raging optimism, who believes in the American Dream," he continued. "Right now, it's as if a big cavernous black hole has been burned into the entertainment section of the brain. It's filled with demons and paranoia and fear. Where are all the heroes?" *Rocky* countered this pessimism with its relatable underdog's reaffirmation of the American mythos of upward mobility.[10]

Stallone billed himself as a real-life Balboa by crafting a heavily embellished origin story that the production exploited to great promotional effect. Prior to *Rocky*, Stallone was a struggling actor with a child on the way. He had a few small roles—including an uncredited part in *Mandingo*—but his career was languishing. "On my 29th birthday, I had $106 in the bank," he told *Playboy* shortly after striking it big. "My best birthday present was a sudden revelation that I had to write the kind of screenplay that I enjoyed seeing. . . . I relished stories of heroism, great love, dignity and courage, dramas of people rising above their stations, taking life by the throat and not letting go until they succeeded." He found a template after spending the last of his entertainment money to see Wepner nearly go the distance against Ali via a closed-circuit broadcast. "They said Wepner wouldn't last three rounds," Stallone reflected. "But as the fight progressed, this miracle unfolded. He hung in there. We had witnessed an incredible triumph of the human spirit and we loved it. . . . That night, Rocky Balboa was born—a man of the streets, an All-American tragedy, a man without much mentality and few social graces. But a man with deep emotion and spirituality and patriotism. And a good nature, though nature was not particularly good to him. He had to have his shot, too."[11] The actor and screenwriter claims to have composed the script by hand at his kitchen table in a three-day fever of inspiration. Like Balboa, Stallone would take his big chance regardless of the odds. "His own phenomenal, long shot success story was the ultimate proof of the sweet positivism of his film," the *Boston Globe* wrote of Stallone.[12] The young artist adopted Balboa as an alter ego and largely made the story of the film's production about his own life—a personal connection he strengthened by giving his brother, father, and dog roles in *Rocky* and having his wife shoot photographs on set.[13]

United Artists liked Stallone's script and issued a bid, which gradually inflated as the writer refused to sell unless he could play Balboa.[14] United Artists finally consented, but paid Stallone just twenty thousand dollars along with a percentage of the profits for his acting. Because of *Rocky*'s mostly unknown lead, United Artists budgeted the film for a little over a million dollars and signed journeyman filmmaker John Avildsen—another obscure entity—to direct. The production company had middling hopes for the small film and even considered selling it directly to TV before its eventual theatrical premier in November 1976.

When the film begins, Balboa seems destined to end up like Billy Tully or Mountain McLintock. The down-and-out Philadelphian makes meager pay in the ring when not working as a reluctant "legbreaker" for the local gangster Tony Gazzo (Joe Spinell). But while Tully is characterized by doomed stasis, Balboa transforms along the lines of *On the Waterfront*'s Terry Malloy and *Somebody Up There Likes Me*'s Rocky Graziano by gaining confidence in the ring and by coupling with Adrian—the painfully shy sister of Rocky's churlish friend Paulie (Burt Young). In keeping with Stallone's avowed nostalgia, the film heavy-handedly signals its aesthetic lineage. It opens with a mural of Jesus before panning out to display the smoky Resurrection Athletic Club—a converted church that establishes a foundation for Balboa's story of rebirth— where Rocky is fighting Spider Rico (Pedro Lovell), another graceless local heavyweight. Balboa wears light purple trunks and eventually wins the sloppy fight by knocking Rico through the ropes—references to George Bellows's iconic *Dempsey and Firpo* (1924) painting. Balboa collects for Gazzo at the docks but lacks the ruthlessness his job requires—both of which reflect Terry Malloy prior to his moral awakening. The homages connect *Rocky* to boxing's visual heritage and reinforce its engagement with the romantic stories Stallone believed had been abandoned in favor of grim tales like *Fat City*.

Although Balboa clumsily wins his first match against Rico—the only bout *Rocky* shows aside from the final fight—the spectators treat him with disgust. They throw debris into the ring and a woman calls him a "bum" as he heads to the locker room after the bout. Upon returning to his filthy apartment, Balboa looks glumly in the mirror at his busted-up face and then at a picture of himself as a child. The impoverished fighter is clearly displeased with how his life has turned out. He is literally and metaphorically fractured as the film begins; and so are the people around him. Adrian is insecure, Paulie is unhappy and volatile, and Mickey is bitter at having never reached his potential as a fighter. But the gang of White misfits unite around and transform through Rocky's big shot.

As Rocky trains by beating on sides of beef in the slaughterhouse where Paulie works—an unorthodox and primitive regimen that typifies his underdog status—his ill-tempered pal, between covert swigs from a pint of cheap scotch, asks the boxer why he's attracted to the introverted Adrian. "I don't see it. What's the attraction?" Paulie asks Rocky. "I don't know," the inarticulate but sincere Rocky responds. "Fills in gaps, I guess. . . . She's got gaps, I got gaps, together we fill gaps." After Balboa reaches his goal and goes the distance against Creed, the battered fighter shows no interest in the reporters who swarm him for interviews. All he wants is to be united with Adrian—a yearning he signals with his signature bellow from the ring: "Adriaaaaaaaan!" His cries for Adrian, in fact, drown out the ring announcer's faintly audible declaration that Creed won the decision. Triumphant though not victorious, Balboa is indifferent to the bout's outcome. His quest creates a new family among Adrian, Paulie, and Mickey. Like the fighter, these underdogs have found purpose and are no longer "bums from the neighborhood." Again echoing *On the Waterfront*, they become "somebody" through Rocky's achievement. By extension, the hopeful bicentennial film suggests the United States furnishes opportunities for unlikely heroes like Balboa to fill the trying gaps many similarly splintered Americans withstood through the 1970s.

But *Rocky* also works to fill the cultural gaps that ruptured White masculinity during the 1970s. Film critic Andrew Sarris called Balboa "the most romanticized Great White Hope in screen history."[15] The wealthy and Ali-inspired Creed functions as the main barrier to the achievement Rocky represents. The film depicts the champ as a superficial racial opportunist who is more interested in the economic rewards of business than the honor of competition. Apart from the final match, the champion only appears on camera while wearing a suit and making deals to promote the fight. Creed, in fact, conceived the idea to fight Balboa. "Without a ranked contender what this fight is gonna need is a novelty," he says to his managers and promoters after his initial opponent drops out. "This is the land of opportunity, right? So Apollo Creed on January first gives a local underdog fighter an opportunity. A snow-white underdog." "Apollo, I like it," responds the promoter George Jergens (Thayer David). "It's very American." "No Jergens," Apollo retorts. "It's very smart." Creed selected Balboa because, like Rueben in *Fat City*, he realizes the fighter's racially coded nickname will build the gate. "Apollo Creed meets the Italian Stallion. Sounds like a damn monster movie," Creed says with a contented smirk.

Unlike the clumsy and unpolished Balboa, Creed is a creature of media who effortlessly navigates and harnesses its promotional power. The film introduces Creed via an Ali-esque TV appearance that Balboa watches at the Lucky 7 Tavern down the street from his shabby apartment. Creed later humiliates Balboa when they appear together on television to promote their fight. Balboa, of course, has no idea how to behave at a press conference and looks foolish compared to the sharply dressed and quick-witted champion. Creed's savoir faire and privilege reinforce Balboa's disadvantage. The film presents the other Black characters Balboa encounters as similarly chastening impediments to his success. Early in the film, Mickey boots Balboa out of his gym locker and gives it to a Black fighter named Dipper (Stan Shaw). Mickey justifies the decision by maintaining that Dipper is "a contender" with a bright future—not a dead-end "tomato can" like Balboa. "I dig your locker, man," Dipper taunts after Balboa protests his eviction. Rocky faces similar humiliation by a Black female TV reporter whom Paulie, attempting to make some money off the attention his friend is suddenly receiving, invited to the meat locker to do a story on Balboa's strange training program. Prior to the interview, Balboa requests that the journalist "don't take no cheap shots"—a response to the lessons he learned after Creed embarrassed him on the air. Though she does not level any obvious jabs, the journalist issues a subtly condescending report that treats the fighter more as a laughable clod than as a legitimate challenger.

These instances—all of which magnify Rocky's lowly station—racialize the circumstances that make Balboa a long shot bum. As film scholars Michael Ryan and Douglas Kellner point out, *Rocky*'s "edifying story of accomplishment just barely hides the spirit of resentful white working-class racism that motivates it." Stallone dismissed charges of *Rocky*'s subtle racism—in particular that Creed was an offensive Ali caricature. "The movie's about a white underdog," he objected, again conflating himself with Balboa. "I'm being more racist toward myself than anybody else, because I lose the fight." Stallone elaborated on the implications of Balboa's transformation in a separate interview with the *Chicago Tribune*: "I wanted the champion to come out of his corner and throw 15 punches in a row without Rocky connecting, I wanted Rocky to be hit 15 times in a row, because by then the audience would be feeling such exasperation that Rocky can't hit the champ, that when Rocky does hit him for the first time, all of the frustrations of Rocky's life, all the anxieties, all of the failures, will come forward in that one blow and *deck* the monster, *deck* this symbol, *deck* this institution."[16] Creed, as Stallone argues, represents the establishment that subordinated Balboa. And Rocky's eventual triumph marks a reversal of the hierarchy Creed signifies.

Balboa, then, functions similarly to Marciano in Woroner's *Super Fight*. And the film continually emphasizes Balboa's similarities to Marciano—from his name and ethnicity to his fighting style. "You know, you kinda remind me of the Rock [Marciano]," Mickey tells Balboa early in the film. "You move like him and you have heart like he did." While readying for the fight, Mickey notices a problem with Balboa's footwork and has him adopt a method Marciano once employed. Mickey also gives the fighter one of Marciano's boxing glove cufflinks—the trainer's most prized possession—as a good luck charm. The keepsake, which Balboa puts on a necklace, becomes a recurrent talisman in the franchise that the fighter eventually passes on to his own son in *Rocky V* (1990). Like the 1950s heavyweight on which he is partly based, the Italian Stallion represents a bygone tradition that figures like Ali and Creed replaced.

102 • The Boxing Film

And like *The Super Fight*, *Rocky*'s depiction of White triumph found an enthusiastic audience.

Reflecting its main character and screenwriter, *Rocky* defied the odds to become the highest grossing film of 1976 and one of the decade's biggest hits. It not only won the Academy Awards for Best Picture and Best Director but beat out eventually canonical films like Sidney Lumet's *Network* (1976) and Martin Scorsese's *Taxi Driver* (1976). Critics and audiences identified *Rocky* as a refreshing throwback to Frank Capra's sentimental "Capra-corn" titles like *Meet John Doe* (1941) and *It's a Wonderful Life* (1946). Capra, in fact, praised the film. "I think it's the best picture of the last 10 years," he enthused. "When I saw it, I said, 'Boy, that's a picture I wish I had made.'" Like Capra, *Rocky* sought mass appeal through celebrating the American Dream and reinforcing dominant attitudes regarding which Americans ought to have privileged access to it. "I pitched it straight to a mass audience," Stallone said. "You could say that's very calculated, and you'd be right, but it's calculated to be entertaining."[17] *Rocky* propelled both a resurgence of the boxing film as well as a broader renaissance of the mainstream blockbuster—a politically conservative contrast to the New Hollywood productions and blaxploitation movies that arose during the first half of the 1970s. Andrew Britton identified *Rocky*, along with George Lucas's *Star Wars* (1977), as heralding a "general movement of reaction and conservative reassurance in contemporary Hollywood." It marked the front wave of the moralistic and reactionary blockbusters that characterized the Regan era—*Top Gun* (Tony Scott, 1986), *RoboCop* (Paul Verhoeven, 1987), etc.—and worked to repair further the cultural gaps *Rocky* aspired to fill.[18]

Rocky Exploitation

Rocky touched off a "revival of the screen boxer" across genres.[19] *Bare Knuckles* (Don Edmonds, 1977) continued blaxploitation's consistent engagement with boxing. *Every Which Way but Loose* (James Fargo, 1978), which starred Clint Eastwood as a trucker who moonlights as a street fighter and runs with an orangutan sidekick, and *Matilda* (Daniel Mann, 1978), about a boxing kangaroo that a creative promoter (Elliott Gould) starts matching against humans, combined the boxing film with zany animal humor. Howard Zieff's *The Main Event* (1979) used boxing as the backdrop for a screwball comedy starring Barbara Streisand and Ryan O'Neal. Stanley Donen's *Movie Movie* (1978) and Michael Preece's *The Prize Fighter* (1979) spoofed 1930s boxing films, and Franco Zeffirelli's *The Champ* (1979) offered a tear-jerking remake of King Vidor's 1931 melodrama of the same title. *The Champ* stars Jon Voight—who previously played a fighter in *The All-American Boy* (Charles K. Eastman, 1973)—as the drunken former champion Billy Flynn who tries to get his life on track while raising his precocious son TJ (Ricky Shroeder). The reboot exploited *Rocky*'s nostalgic sentimentalism through Billy and TJ's unconventional but loving relationship. Similar to *The Champ*, the NBC TV movie *Goldie and the Boxer* (David Miller, 1979) featured O.J. Simpson as a down-on-his-luck pug who looks after his deceased sparring partner's White orphaned daughter, who ultimately becomes his manager. The majority of these films, and all of the mainstream Hollywood productions, reproduced *Rocky*'s racial politics. Despite the fact that Black fighters continued to dominate the sport on which these boxing movies were based, they were as likely to have a kangaroo in a leading role at this time as an African American. Little had changed in Hollywood since the 1940s.

But *Rocky*'s impact stretched well beyond boxing films. It became a template through which underdogs—especially White long shots—were sold across media, sports, and popular culture. ABC Sports' live telecast of Roberto Duran and Edwin Viruet's September 1977 match from Philadelphia opened with Bill Conti's "Gonna Fly Now (Theme from *Rocky*)" to dramatize the fight. That same year, Don King conceived a tournament to create a U.S. boxing champion. King capitalized on *Rocky* by billing the tournament as a chance for obscure fighters to live out the film's inspiring story. Howard Cosell praised the tournament, which ABC Sports contracted to televise, as "a dream come true for the many faceless hardworking fighters who toiled in backwater arenas for a couple hundred bucks and the use of a locker." But sportswriter Jack Newfield charged that the ostensibly meritocratic event cynically built on *Rocky* and continued the TV fighter tradition by ensuring that a lopsided amount of White boxers participated, regardless of their qualifications. The tournament was ultimately canceled because of the suspicious rankings used to justify the inclusion of its disproportionately White roster of competitors.[20]

Rocky's immense success earned Stallone enough clout to convince United Artists to let him direct *Rocky II* (1979). The sequel doubled down on its predecessor's romance and politics. It opens with Balboa recovering from his brutal fight against Creed. The bout took such a toll on Rocky that his doctor, much like in *Requiem for a Heavyweight*, warns that continued competition could blind him. Having proven his valor against Creed, Balboa opts to leave the ring, find a less taxing job, and start a family with Adrian. But the uneducated and unskilled former fighter cannot secure gainful employment. Again echoing *Requiem for a Heavyweight*, Balboa visits job counselors and can list only boxing on his résumé. The vocational services have nothing for him outside of manual labor. Paulie eventually gets the dejected Balboa a gig at the slaughterhouse—a position he loses almost immediately because of seniority rules. "It was nobody's fault," he tells Adrian. "They was just cutting back. It was economics." Moreover, Balboa is terminated by a Black man—a suggestion that these unfair economic circumstances are particularly tough on working-class Whites. The pregnant Adrian offers to help out by picking up some shifts

104 • The Boxing Film

at the pet store, a position she quit after marrying Rocky. "But I'm the one who's supposed to support," the woebegone Balboa protests. Rocky then asks Mickey for a job helping out around the gym. Mickey initially refuses in the interest of preserving Balboa's crumbling ego. "You're like royalty here," the crusty trainer growls. "You want those guys to see you carrying towels and buckets around? Where's your dignity?" Balboa, the film indicates, has lost whatever dignity he once possessed. Like Tully in *Fat City*, the freshly retired fighter is reduced to menial labor and the racial identity that drove his title shot provides no apparent advantage.

Embarrassed after almost losing to Balboa, Creed begins a campaign to goad him into a rematch that preys on Rocky's unraveling masculinity. The local newspaper runs a cartoon that depicts Rocky as the "Italian Chicken," and locals again begin to dismiss him as a gutless loser. "I'm supposed to be a fighter," Balboa muses, "I think I'm becoming nobody again." Creed's relentless taunting finally brings Balboa to his breaking point, and he resolves to return to the ring despite Adrian's wishes and his doctor's advice. When Adrian objects, Balboa silences her by appealing to his gendered duties. "I never asked you to stop being a woman," he says. "Don't ask me to stop being a man." Adrian, however, gives birth prematurely after overexerting herself at work—a result of her return to the pet store to compensate for Balboa's inability to provide—and falls into a coma. Ravaged with worry and guilt, Rocky suspends his training to watch over his ailing wife. When Adrian wakes, she gives Balboa her blessing to fight, and he begins training with a restored sense of energy and focus. His routine consists of running through the streets of Philadelphia and up the city's museum steps to build endurance, chasing a chicken around a coop to boost quickness, and whacking tires with a sledgehammer to increase strength. The old-school training program—which is most memorably captured when a group of Philadelphians spontaneously join Balboa on his run through the city as Bill Conti's theme blares—composes a gritty and populist counter to Creed, who works out in his pristine mansion as the artist LeRoy Neiman sketches the celebrity athlete.

Their grueling rematch ends with the equally exhausted Creed and Balboa both falling to the canvas as time expires. Balboa, however, musters the tenacity to rise just in time to prevail. Again, the boxer is less concerned with the victory and more interested in sharing the triumph with Adrian—still recuperating after her health scare—who proudly watches on TV at home as Rocky bawls, "Yo, Adrian! I did it!" Intensifying its predecessor's cultural politics, *Rocky II* has Balboa entering the ring to protect his interrelated financial well-being and masculinity by defeating his rich, confident, and Black adversary. *Rocky II* rode these themes to similar success, which, as Ryan and Kellner suggest, reflected the conditions prompting many members of the White working class to vote Republican and stoked resentment toward African Americans as the Reagan era dawned.[21]

Rocky and *Rocky II* producers Robert Chartoff and Irwin Winkler used the popular franchise to secure funding for Martin Scorsese's *Raging Bull*—an adaptation of Jake LaMotta's 1970 autobiography that now stands as the boxing film genre's most critically revered title. Like *Rocky*, *Raging Bull* centers on an Italian American fighter and owes aesthetic debt to Classical Hollywood films like *On the Waterfront*. But Scorsese carefully distinguished his film from *Rocky* and the predictable boxing stories it spawned. As the filmmaker sarcastically explained, "There were so many boxing pictures being made in the seventies that I dreaded the moment when I wouldn't be able to sleep and the only thing on TV would be the poorest of them and nothing else."[22] He separated *Raging Bull* from the glut by shooting in black and white—an homage to boxing's cinematic heritage that paid particular tribute to James Wong Howe's groundbreaking cinematography in *Body and Soul*.[23]

Just as noticeable as its stark visual palette, *Raging Bull* moved against the saccharine wistfulness driving *Rocky* and its similarly mawkish ilk. Jake LaMotta is an abusive, self-absorbed, self-loathing, and self-destructive contrast to the earnest, generous, and trusting Balboa. Robert De Niro won an Academy Award for his brutal and shapeshifting depiction of LaMotta that traced the temperamental fighter's transformation from a chiseled young brawler into a tubby middle-aged has-been. As Grindon puts it, LaMotta "shares Balboa's animal nature, but turns its associations upside down."[24] *Raging Bull* offers up a discomfiting version of masculine sporting heroism that undercuts *Rocky*'s sentimentality. While Balboa fawns over Adrian, LaMotta beats his wife Vicky (Cathy Moriarty) and repeatedly accuses her of infidelity. While Balboa is an emblem of meritocracy, LaMotta participates in the fight game's endemic corruption. But despite its formal and thematic divergences, *Raging Bull* partly maintains *Rocky*'s cultural politics by continuing the cinematic tradition of elevating White boxing protagonists—whether inspiring or contemptible.

The racial assumptions driving the boxing film's renaissance were not lost on Ali. "I have been so great in boxing they had to create an image like Rocky, a white image on the screen, to counteract my image in the ring," he told *Chicago Sun-Times* film critic Roger Ebert. "America has to have its white images, no matter where it gets them. Jesus, Wonder Woman, Tarzan, Rocky."[25] Ali's biopic, *The Greatest* (1977), was wrapping up production as *Rocky* debuted. An adaptation of Ali's 1975 memoir (coauthored with Richard Durham) that starred the boxer, *The Greatest* builds on *The Joe Louis Story* with a tale of its main character's rise, struggles, and triumphs. It also contrasts *The Joe Louis Story* by celebrating Ali's refusal to compromise his values to satisfy social norms. Ali used *Rocky*'s colossal success to promote his film, which premiered in May 1977, by employing the same kind of trash talk he used when hyping his fights. He charged that Stallone stole his story, challenged the actor to an exhibition match, and even sent him a backhandedly congratulatory poem before the 1977 Academy Awards:

> You fought and you worked,
> you're a determined guy.
> *Rocky* is great,
> and we love you, Sly.
> And if you get an Oscar,
> remember, please do.
> *The Greatest* will also get one,
> 'cause I'm prettier than you.

The Academy Awards ceremony staged an Ali appearance in which the boxer rushed the podium as Stallone presented the award for Best Supporting Actress. "You stole my script!," Ali hollered as he joined Stallone, and they playfully tussled on stage. The exchange mirrored Ali's confrontations with so many prizefighting adversaries and indicated that *The Greatest* would be battling *Rocky* at the box office.[26]

While Ali's digs were lighthearted, *The Greatest* offered a blaxploitation response to *Rocky*. Ali called himself the "black Clark Gable" and insisted that he had been fashioning a drama over the course of his career that was even more successful than the one Stallone conjured up at his kitchen table. "I've been acting in real life, not just before the cameras," the boxer insisted. "I didn't go to acting school; I wrote my own scripts; I directed my own scenes; and they all fell for it. The world was my stage. And now I have your ear, listening to my latest act." Ali took further ownership over the biopic by rewriting parts that he did not believe accurately reflected Black culture. "He's a good writer," Ali said of *The Greatest*'s screenwriter Ring Lardner Jr., "but a good white writer. What I did was make it more soulful. I erased some lines and told him, 'Hey, man, we don't talk like that.'" While *The Greatest* deliberately catered to Black audiences, Ali distinguished it from blaxploitation's often-provocative themes. "No sex in my picture, no profanity," he maintained. "No *Mandingos* for me, no *Super Flys*."[27]

The Greatest's focus on Black culture, as the *Boston Globe*'s Bruce McCabe observed, turned *Rocky* "on its head."[28] As *Rocky* presents complacent and arrogant African Americans like Creed and Dipper as Balboa's main obstacles, *The Greatest* reminds viewers of the profound racism Ali faced throughout his entire career, and his ability to succeed despite these structural challenges. Moreover, in *The Greatest* Ali takes ownership of the brashness *Rocky* uses to bill Creed as a superficial opportunist. In one scene, for instance, Ali comments on Jerry Quarry's marketable Whiteness prior to their 1970 match. "He's white," Ali says to the promoters and managers. "We all stand to get rich now." The scene mirrors Creed's scheme to find a "snow white underdog." While the scene evidences Ali's similar business acumen, it also showcases the racism that shaped it—a point *Rocky* overlooks. "Yes, I'm arrogant and I coined that phrase 'The Greatest' because that was the bait which drew people all over the world to come and see me fight," Ali said while promoting the film. "They wanted to see this arrogant nigger get whupped so they paid. That arrogance was a pose for a purpose." Ali reminds that his famous egotism—the basis for Creed's character—was an economically driven effort, but one that was borne out of racism. "I made more money as a fighter than any other world champion," he continued. "This nigger ain't going to die poor or broke washing cars." He was not, in other words, about to end up like Joe Louis. Ali suggests his persona is a response to the institutionalized racism *Rocky* suppresses when fashioning its narrative of White struggle and triumph. *The Greatest* brings this discrimination into focus and contends that Ali faced an even tougher road than Balboa—one that was perhaps made all the more difficult because he lacked the racially sympathetic attitudes Stallone used to dramatize his protagonist's achievement.

Cannon Films expanded on *The Greatest* with George Bowers's *Body and Soul* (1981), a blaxploitation remake of Robert Rossen's 1947 film. The production starred Leon Isaac Kennedy—who began his acting career with a small role in *Hammer*—and his wife Jayne Kennedy, a model and cohost of CBS's *NFL Today* pregame football program. Based on his performance in Jamaa Fanaka's prison boxing film *Penitentiary* (1979), Cannon signed Leon Kennedy to a three-picture deal to act, write, and produce. Cannon and Kennedy figured a *Body and Soul* reboot would at once benefit from the success of *Penitentiary*, which was popular enough to spawn the sequels *Penitentiary II* (1982) and *Penitentiary III* (1987), and broaden the blaxploitation film's audience by engaging the Classical Hollywood tradition that Rossen's production represents.[29] Mirroring Stallone in *Rocky*, Kennedy both penned the screenplay and starred in the film.

Bowers reimagined *Body and Soul*'s tale of a fighter forced to choose between greed and righteousness through blaxploitation's tropes of Black empowerment, violence, and sex. Kennedy plays Leon Johnson, an aspiring physician who boxes for extra money. Johnson puts his professional goals on hold when his sister (Nikki Swasey Seaton) is diagnosed with sickle cell anemia—a malady that disproportionately impacts people of African descent. Much to the disappointment of his mother (Kim Hamilton), who wants Leon to "be somebody," Johnson begins fighting full-time to pay his sister's medical bills. He seeks out and convinces Muhammad Ali, who plays himself, to help him train. With Ali's help, Johnson reinvents himself as Leon "The Lover" and amasses a popular following—especially among the many women who are bewitched by his

108 • The Boxing Film

looks and magnetism. He also develops a relationship with the beautiful and intelligent reporter Julie Winters (Jayne Kennedy), who is put off by his macho bluster until she realizes the selfless goals that ultimately drive his prizefighting.

But Johnson is gradually seduced by the many temptations his fame yields. He becomes involved with the profiteering White gangster Big Man (Peter Lawford) and sinks into the hedonistic world over which he presides—a development that estranges Johnson from Ali and Julie. After steadily grooming Johnson with money, drugs, and women, Big Man—like Roberts in the original *Body and Soul*—pressures the boxer to throw a fight. Predictably, and much like in *Hammer*, Johnson does some soul searching, remembers the virtues that drove him to the sport, and reconciles with Julie. She convinces him not to take a dive and bets all her money that he will win—a vote of confidence that inspires Johnson to reconnect with Ali and begin training for the match. He wins the fight and celebrates with Julie, Ali, his mother, and his sister—the characters that represent virtue. Though Julie won a bundle from her bet, Johnson is happier at having salvaged his integrity than winning the bout, and the film presents this moral awakening as his ultimate achievement. When Big Man threatens Johnson for not obeying his crooked commands, the boxer dismisses him with the same final lines Charlie Davis delivered to Roberts: "Everybody dies." Johnson, like Davis, would rather lose his life than give up the honor he nearly let drift away.

Like *Hammer* and *The Greatest*, *Body and Soul* elevates Ali as a symbol of Black power and virtue. The fighter both helps to mold Johnson into a successful boxer and inspires him to stand by his principles. "I've never thrown a fight and you shouldn't either," Ali advises Johnson early in the film. Aside from shepherding Johnson away from corruption, Ali eventually helps him stick it to the White gangsters who sought to control and exploit him. The *Body and Soul* remake links its protagonist's eventually commendable gallantry to the integrity Ali epitomizes and imparts.

While he thought Kennedy's script fell short of Abraham Polonsky's Academy Award–winning screenplay for the original *Body and Soul*, the *Chicago Tribune*'s Gene Siskel praised the remake as "the black version of *Rocky*."[30] Like Stallone, Kennedy faced considerable adversity on his road to success in Hollywood. Unlike Stallone, these disadvantages continued after he achieved stardom. As part of his efforts to promote *Body and Soul*, Leon appeared with Jayne Kennedy in *Playboy*'s July 1981 issue. The celebrity couple posed for a nine-page pictorial that included stills from the film's steamiest moments. The Kennedys drew immediate flak for the photoshoot. Leon, however, disputed these moralistic critiques by maintaining that the high-profile appearance was necessary to publicize the film, which was providing rare opportunities for African Americans in Hollywood and might lead to more depending on how well it performed. "The positive aspect of all this seems to have been overlooked," Kennedy defensively asserted. "In Hollywood, there are almost no Blacks working at all, but Jayne is working continuously and I am able to put a movie together. I have been able to write, produce, and star in a movie. I managed to put together more than $2 million for the making of *Body and Soul*. I bought the rights to the old John Garfield movie and I rewrote the script. It is a good movie and we were able to hire more than 20 other black people including our director."[31] Kennedy implies that he would not have had to go to lengths like appearing in *Playboy* if there were consistent and sustaining opportunities for African Americans in Hollywood. The provocative photoshoot and Kennedy's explanation of it reveal the film industry's racial inequities—within and beyond the boxing film. Stallone did interviews with *Playboy*; Kennedy had to pose in the magazine.

"The Public's Perception of a Fighter"

Blaxploitation films like *The Greatest* and *Body and Soul* did little to dull the impact *Rocky* had on mainstream representations of boxing. For instance, the June 14, 1982, issue of *Time* magazine featured Neil Leifer's cover photo of the White heavyweight contender Gerry Cooney posing next to Stallone as Balboa. Cooney was set to challenge Larry Holmes for the heavyweight title, and Stallone was about to star in *Rocky III*, in which Balboa takes on the sadistic Black ex-convict Clubber Lang (Mr. T). Balboa provided a familiar myth through which Cooney was depicted as a similarly inspirational White Hope.

Leifer, however, suggested that Balboa's fictional image did not simply make sense of Cooney, but composed an alluring simulacrum that overshadowed the actual fighter. "My biggest problem was trying to make Gerry Cooney look as much like a heavyweight champion as Sly," Leifer admitted. "Rocky Balboa's body is the public's perception of a fighter, while Cooney's is not."[32] The *Rocky* franchise provided a White Hope as the Black-dominated sport on which it was based wandered further from the nostalgic racial fantasies it offered, a situation that Mike Tyson's antiheroic ascendance during the 1980s made abundantly clear. The boxing films that followed through the 1980s—including the jingoistic Cold War melodrama *Rocky IV* (Sylvester Stallone, 1985) and *Rocky V* (John Avildsen, 1990)—regurgitated the marketable framework of White masculine conquest on which *Rocky* so successfully traded. Films like *Tough Enough* (Richard Fleischer, 1983), *Dempsey* (Gus Trikonis, 1983), *Last Man Standing* (Damian Lee, 1987), *Split Decisions* (David Drury, 1988), *Homeboy* (Michael Seresin, 1988), *The Opponent* (Sergio Martino, 1988), *Thunderground* (David Mitchell,1989), and *The Big Man* (David Leland, 1990) continued to fill in the vulnerable cultural gaps *Rocky* confronted by featuring White guys kicking ass in a world where such scenarios seemed increasingly far-fetched.

6

HBO Sports
• •
Docu-Branding Boxing

Emerging in the 1970s alongside *Rocky* and blaxploitation, cable television reflected network TV's development, as fledgling cable outlets gravitated toward prizefighting to gather viewers. Home Box Office (HBO) most aggressively pursued TV rights to the sport. The premium cable outlet is now best known for prestigious original series like *The Sopranos* (1999–2007), *Six Feet Under* (2001–2005), and *Game of Thrones* (2011–2019). Consequently, scholarship on the outlet has unsurprisingly focused on these productions and their role in building HBO's brand as a landmark of "quality TV."[1] But sports programming—and boxing in particular—similarly contributed to HBO's repute by building the subscribership that bankrolls its expensive and renowned original series. "We'll always have our mainstay of boxing that continues to drive massive ratings for the network," remarked HBO Sports president Ross Greenburg.[2] Documentary accompanies boxing as a key contributor to HBO's image. HBO uses documentary's stereotypical refinement among TV genres to position itself as a journalistically rigorous, artful, and even socially conscious outlet that seeks both to educate and to profit. It also deploys the genre's edifying reputation to balance the salacious and tawdry focus of programs like *Cathouse* (2005–2014).[3]

Moreover, HBO's documentaries promote its boxing coverage and, just as importantly, stress the media outlet's importance to the sport—a status the channel's sports division HBO Sports emphasizes by branding itself as "The

Heart and Soul of Boxing." Beyond its documentaries, HBO participates in a range of related activities that similarly mediate boxing's reality and emphasize the media outlet's significance to it. These docu-branding efforts—which include docudramas, brand placements in films, video games, and reality TV programs—build renditions of boxing's past and present that put HBO Sports at its cultural, economic, and historical center. They demonstrate HBO's expansive and documentary-driven efforts to publicize its boxing coverage and situate itself as the historically shady sport's ethically scrupulous guiding force. Boxing and documentary, then, aid the intersecting economic and cultural elements that compose HBO's envied industrial status and shed useful light on the vaunted media outlet's history.

Putting the Tuxedo on Boxing

Sports programming drove HBO's November 1972 launch out of Wilkes-Barre, Pennsylvania. The second program HBO aired—after kicking off with Paul Newman's *Sometimes a Great Notion* (1971)—was a live National Hockey League (NHL) game between the New York Rangers and Vancouver Canucks from Madison Square Garden. Live sports broadcasts drew at least modest audiences to the fledgling outlet. HBO's early years included nearly any sporting event to which it could secure rights—professional and college basketball, bowling, gymnastics, wrestling, etc.—as well as some for which it did not have permission. The channel brazenly risked censure by taking the liberty of televising NHL and National Basketball Association (NBA) games that were not otherwise on TV without paying those leagues for rights. "The reaction from the NBA and NHL was a lot of grumbling and grousing," writes media journalist George Mair, "but surprisingly, they decided not to fight with HBO."[4] HBO was presumably too marginal an outlet at the time to arouse enough concern for the sports organizations it was pirating to go to the trouble of filing suit. To be sure, the one constant across HBO's early and eclectic slate of sports programming was that few were watching.

While HBO's early sports programming spanned the athletic spectrum, it soon focused its energies on boxing. At the time, the major TV networks were scaling back their investment in the sport. The reduction in televised boxing created a gap HBO used to identify with prizefighting and distinguish the channel in the budding sports cable TV market. HBO premiered its *World Championship Boxing* programing banner by airing a replay of George Foreman and Joe Frazier's January 1973 "Sunshine Showdown" heavyweight title bout from Kingston, Jamaica. The fight, which Foreman surprisingly won and Cosell immortalized with his "Down goes Frazier!" call on ABC's rebroadcast, was also the first big-ticket match promoted by Don King and marked the beginnings of his intimate and eventually contentious relationship with the premium cable outlet.

HBO amplified its association with boxing when it contracted with Don King Productions to carry Muhammad Ali and Joe Frazier's 1975 "Thrilla in Manila"—their third, final, and most vicious bout. HBO arranged to augment King's closed-circuit broadcasts with a live satellite feed to three of its affiliates. It used the Thrilla in Manila to debut its transition to a continual satellite model. In exchange for the rights, HBO allowed Don King Productions to borrow its New York–area microwave facilities to feed nearby closed-circuit theaters, which generated the bulk of the fight's revenues.[5] HBO unveiled its satellite service with a ceremony that included speeches from executives extolling the channel's unique potential among cable outlets to bring subscribers live content from across the globe.[6] Ali and Frazier's high-profile match provided an ideal vehicle to showcase this new feature—and composed a pivotal moment for the emerging cable industry. HBO's subscribership doubled after the fight—reaching two hundred thousand by the end of 1975 and breaking one million by the end of 1976. Those cable providers that carried HBO showed a roughly 20 percent boost in customers—a spike that prompted most major services to begin offering the channel by the late 1970s. The benefits of boxing, according to Greenburg, convinced HBO to "claim some ownership of the sport" and create exclusive contracts with promising fighters.[7]

HBO's investment in boxing was also aided by the U.S. Court of Appeals' 1977 decision to vacate network-driven antisiphoning rules that prevented cable outlets from carrying certain popular sporting events. The networks argued that cable sports coverage unfairly limited consumers' ability to view events of public interest. The Federal Communications Commission agreed and imposed restrictions on cable sports TV. Spearheaded by HBO, *Home Box Office v. FCC* (1977) overturned the antisiphoning regulations, which opened the door for HBO to expand its sports offerings and laid the foundation for the emergence of cable channels like ESPN. HBO finally turned a profit in 1977—a development this deregulation aided.

Abraham boasted that HBO did not "just do boxing, we do boxing that tells a story." A former ABC Sports employee, Greenburg admitted to "taking the philosophy from ABC Sports and bringing it to HBO" by integrating biographical profiles on participants and using cutting-edge technologies to make its broadcasts more entertaining and widen their viewership.[8] The channel demonstrated this approach with *Boxing Behind Bars*, a 1978 *World Championship Boxing* special televised from Rahway State Prison in Woodbridge, New Jersey (the same prison where former middleweight contender Rubin "Hurricane" Carter was incarcerated).[9] The program featured a light heavyweight match that pitted James Scott—an inmate doing time for a parole

114 • The Boxing Film

violation following an armed robbery conviction—against Eddie Gregory, a title contender who consented to fight his incarcerated opponent within Rahway's sealed walls.

Boxing Behind Bars begins with a short documentary about life inside Rahway that opens with a point-of-view tracking shot entering the prison's imposing gates. "Inside these walls and bars," HBO host Len Berman announces, "Scott works out in his own boxing program. But he cannot leave the walls to box professionally. So for the first time in boxing history, an inmate is fighting a professional fight inside a prison." Berman builds further intrigue for the historic occasion by explaining that the match will occur in an auditorium that "was the site of bloody riots four years ago." HBO and the promoters filled the auditorium with 450 curious customers. Meanwhile, Rahway's roughly 1,100 inmates watched on a closed-circuit feed from the drill hall. The exploitative broadcast, which anticipated the *Penitentiary* franchise of films, periodically cut to the prisoners watching the fight to underscore their enthusiastic support for Scott and to highlight the surveilled sequestration that marks even their leisure time. The introduction suggests *Boxing Behind Bars* will both showcase a live competition and tell a mysterious and illuminating tale about life in prison. It focuses specifically on Rahway's vocational program, which includes boxing training for inmates interested in pursuing the sport professionally upon their release. Cohost Larry Merchant interviews Rahway's warden, who argues that the boxing program fosters self-respect, discipline, and job prospects. HBO, in fact, gained Rahway's cooperation for *Boxing Behind Bars* because the prison sought to promote its vocational programs. "Prison authorities think a Scott win will help boost their funds," Merchant divulges.

The documentary segment focuses most of its attention on the role boxing has played in Scott's life behind bars and his hopes to use the sport to start fresh once he leaves Rahway. "This fight," Merchant explains, "could begin another passage of freedom, and a career [for Scott]." It establishes Scott as a sentimental favorite who, like so many boxing film protagonists, is fighting as much for his own personal and moral redemption as he is for victory in the ring. It also compares Scott to boxers who found success in professional prizefighting after prison stints, such as Sonny Liston and Ron Lyle. HBO Sports' fight coverage clearly prioritizes Scott's narrative and includes frequent cutaways to his fellow prisoners cheering him on from the drill hall, which erupts in applause when Scott is declared the winner by unanimous decision. The coverage, however, also makes note of the deflating fact that despite Scott's great triumph against Gregory, the exhausted boxer will simply return to his cell—albeit with a bit more pride and hope.

With *Boxing Behind Bars*, HBO uses its documentary programming and boxing coverage to contribute to the brand of prison reform Rahway has established. It unsurprisingly does not question the Rahway program's naïve assumption that boxing might provide inmates a realistic or sustainable means for economic betterment. Rather, it uses Scott's story to build interest in an otherwise unimportant pro bout and justifies the gimmicky match through the journalistic treatment it provides the unique prison program. But the documentary-driven experiment paid off. HBO won its first Cable ACE Award for *Boxing Behind Bars*—one of the first industry accolades it gathered. The special demonstrates how HBO Sports' mantra, "boxing that tells a story," helped form the media outlet's quality brand.

Building on the success of *World Championship Boxing*, HBO secured its first exclusive rights to a heavyweight title fight with Larry Holmes and Mike Weaver's June 1979 match. ABC was originally slated to carry the bout, which Don King Productions was promoting. The network, however, refused to pay the $1 million that King demanded. Mostly out of spite, King sold the match to HBO for $125,000.[10] The Holmes-Weaver fight composed an even more visible statement of HBO's connection to prizefighting than did *Boxing Behind Bars*. As *New York Times* sportswriter Red Smith commented, "It was Home Box Office's finest hour—finest three hours, to be exact. The big brains of television's three major networks turned down Friday night's boxing show in Madison Square Garden, so Home Box Office bought it for the cable system's two million subscribers and wound up with the best fight card in recent memory while the networks were regaling their viewers with an eight-year-old movie, a warmed-over soap opera and yet another whodunit."[11] Smith, whose point of view carried considerable industrial weight, suggested that HBO was furnishing boxing fans with programming that the networks were unwilling to offer and establishing itself as a new destination for marquee fights. Soon, HBO consistently began to provide worldwide feeds for championship matches distributed on its main channel and via pay-per-view, which steadily phased out closed-circuit exhibition. "Our theory is that HBO Sports should stand for big events," Abraham said. "We were going to try to create dominance in the sport," Greenburg added.[12]

HBO surrounded its mounting lineup of boxing programming with documentaries. It partnered with Big Fights Inc. to create *Boxing's Greatest Champions* and the *Boxing's Best* series. *Boxing's Greatest Champions* teamed with the Boxing Writers of America to rank the best ever fighters in each weight class, and *Boxing's Best* presented biographical profiles on iconic pugilists. The documentaries presented a mutually beneficial arrangement for Big Fights and HBO. They gave Big Fights an opportunity to repackage its footage, much of which it had used in theatrically released documentaries like *Legendary Champions*, *Jack Johnson*, and *A.K.A. Cassius Clay*. The programs also accentuate Big Fights Inc.'s role as boxing's primary visual archive. *Boxing's Greatest Champions* host Curt Gowdy, for instance, calls attention to the documentary's inclusion of "some of the rarest film in all of sports," and a *Boxing's Best*

116 • The Boxing Film

segment on Jack Johnson describes Big Fights' Jim Jacobs as "boxing's preeminent historian" when he appears on camera as an interviewee. Beyond buttressing Big Fights' authority, the documentaries cast HBO as an arbiter of sport history.

HBO Sports' boxing documentaries also use the genre's enriching repute to distance the media outlet from the sport's stereotypical seediness. "The politics of boxing are as close to 17th century buccaneering as anything that exists on the planet today," Abraham acknowledged. But HBO, according to Greenburg, possessed integrity that its business associates and competitors lacked. "I think over the years we've been able to professionally handle this sport, conduct business the right way, and really create big events for television and kind of stay above the fray," he explained. "I think just there's a certain responsibility that comes with HBO boxing and to carry on that legacy you have to stay on the straight and narrow, so that's always been our kind of way of doing business here." HBO's documentaries helped to construct this scrupulous identity—an image that Showtime's Jay Larkin claims "put the tuxedo on boxing"—and gave the sport renewed acceptability among mainstream audiences.[13]

"A Cash Register in Short Pants"

By 1985, the *New York Times* recognized HBO Sports as television's leading producer of boxing broadcasts. While HBO's documentary-driven practices drew critical acclaim, the network's contracts with star prizefighters drove its steadily bulging ratings and subscribership. The middleweight "Marvelous" Marvin Hagler became what *Sports Illustrated*'s Richard Hoffer called HBO's "original meal ticket" during the early 1980s. He was the cable channel's biggest attraction, and his fights generated larger audiences than even HBO's most popular movies.[14] But the bruising young heavyweight "Iron" Mike Tyson soon eclipsed even Hagler's ratings. HBO signed Tyson, who was managed by Big Fights Inc.'s Cayton and Jacobs, to a limited deal shortly after the undefeated nineteen-year-old registered his nineteenth consecutive knockout in March 1986 by flooring Steve Zouski in the third round. Big Fights' established relationship with HBO helped get Tyson on TV; but the young heavyweight's string of explosive knockouts made his star status imminent.[15]

Around the time Tyson joined HBO, Don King began collaborating with fellow promoter Butch Lewis to pitch the channel on a heavyweight unification tournament that would produce a single, undisputed champion recognized across the often-bickering International Boxing Federation, World Boxing Association, and World Boxing Council. HBO paid eighteen million dollars for rights to televise the eighteen-month tournament that would straddle 1986 and 1987. Abraham believed the event would cement HBO's position atop boxing's TV hierarchy and reinforce its role as a virtuous entity set on bringing some order to the messy sport. "The three networks have a presence in boxing," Abraham explained, "but they don't have the big fights. We'd like to be the home of boxing's big fights, and I thought the heavyweights were an interesting way to go."[16] Although Tyson was still establishing his professional credentials, his rapidly escalating celebrity as a merciless knockout artist made him a must for the tournament, which he cruised through to become the youngest ever heavyweight champion and the first undisputed champ since Leon Spinks in 1978.

HBO signed Tyson to a $26.5 million seven-fight deal shortly after the tournament. The contract, according to biographer Peter Heller, helped the boxer to earn more in 1988 than Jack Dempsey, Joe Louis, Rocky Marciano, and Muhammad Ali made in their entire careers combined. *Wall Street Journal's* Mark Robichaux described Tyson as "a phenomenon like none other in boxing television history."[17] He was the sport's biggest star since Ali and had the benefit of a more robust sports media landscape seeking to turn his image into profits. The boxer signed endorsement deals with Pepsi, Kodak, and Nintendo, which made him the focal point of the 1987 video game *Mike Tyson's Punch-Out!!* The popular game marketed Tyson to Nintendo's typically younger consumers and traded on his superhuman image by making him the nearly invincible final obstacle who knocked opponents down with a single punch. Two years later, the hip-hop duo DJ Jazzy Jeff and the Fresh Prince released the single "I Think I Can Beat Mike Tyson," a comic track that fishes for laughs by pointing out the absurdity of anyone—let alone the then-scrawny Fresh Prince (Will Smith)—believing they could possibly go toe-to-toe with the unbeatable boxer. These combined factors made HBO home to the biggest star in sports. HBO president Michael Fuchs called Tyson "a cash register in short pants," and Abraham referred to him as the media outlet's "most important employee" and a "walking billboard in black shorts."[18] As *USA Today* succinctly put it, "Mike Tyson made HBO the place for boxing."[19] A 1987 survey found that 40 percent of the men who subscribed to the channel for the first time were doing so to watch Tyson's fights, which were attracting a 35 share of HBO subscribers.

While Tyson's popular matches gained much of their value through their live and "video-proof" status, HBO deepened its investment in its "walking billboard" by making a deal with Big Fights Inc. to create a series of home video documentaries that highlighted his most thrilling moments. Titles like *Mike Tyson and History's Greatest Knockouts* (1989) and *Tyson and the Heavyweights*—extensions of HBO Sports and Big Fights' *Boxing's Best* documentary series—installed Tyson in the pantheon of historic fighters. They also, of course, advertised HBO's place as the boxer's home. HBO Sports bolstered further its association with Tyson in the 1989 special *Boxing's Greatest Hits*, which offered a history of boxing on the channel since its launch. As host Jim Lampley announces, the program covers "seventeen years of great boxing memories on HBO." *Boxing's Greatest Hits* conflates the recent history of boxing with HBO's past and emphasizes the media outlet's centrality to the sport's most important recent moments. The special ends with the emotional soft-rock song "Born to Be Champions" alongside an image of Tyson raising his arms triumphantly, which the HBO Sports logo eventually replaces. The special builds a historical narrative that aligns Tyson and HBO Sports with boxing's peak.

Tyson became so important to HBO that the channel tried to negotiate a lifetime deal with him—an unprecedented arrangement in sports. But the boxer's once-cozy relationship with HBO Sports began to fray shortly after he lost his first match—against James "Buster" Douglas in February 1990—and faced a variety of legal and personal troubles. He also severed ties with Cayton shortly after Jacobs died in 1988 and hired Don King to serve as his new manager. King sold Tyson on the importance of having African American management to look after his affairs, like Ali had after forming Main Bout. The promoter largely employed this strategy to break into the sport in the 1970s. Critics, however, charged that King simply used race as an exploitative wedge to gain access to Tyson before swindling the fighter in ways that make *Body and Soul*'s Roberts and *The Harder They Fall*'s Benko look like tenderhearted altruists.[20]

To combat the increasingly negative publicity he and King were facing, Tyson demanded that HBO run a Spike Lee–directed documentary profile prior to his December 1990 fight against Alex Stewart. Lee also hailed from Tyson's hometown of Brooklyn, New York, and had emerged as a leading voice in African American culture since the release of his breakout hit *Do the Right Thing* (1989), a film set in Brooklyn that features prominently shots of a Mike Tyson mural that celebrates the boxer's status as a local hero. HBO Sports had no involvement in the segment's production and worried that the documentary's overt bias would compromise the journalistic principles on which its boxing coverage and documentaries trade. In this case, however, it sacrificed editorial control to pacify its disgruntled "cash register." Lampley emphasized that the production was Lee's creation—not a product of HBO Sports—in an interview with the director before it ran. When he asked Lee whether the documentary was "journalism or advocacy," Lee shrugged and called it "a little bit of both." He contended that Tyson and King had been unfairly "pummeled in the press" and claimed he wanted to show a different side of the misunderstood sports celebrities. "We want to make clear that this was Spike's baby," Lampley said. "We interfered in no way, shape, or form after we gave Spike the opportunity to bring a 35mm camera here and to Brooklyn for this profile of Mike Tyson." A title card emerged with an image of Lee that reads "Spike Lee Presents Mike Tyson." The project, which marked the beginning of a long-standing relationship between the filmmaker and HBO, both took advantage of Lee's auteur persona and distanced HBO Sports from the incendiary perspective it presents.

The profile opens with the same Brooklyn-based mural of Tyson that Lee includes in *Do the Right Thing* and, harkening back to *Raging Bull*, is shot in black-and-white to accentuate its unflinching tone. In particular, the documentary charges the mainstream sports establishment with racism and attributes Tyson and King's infamy to this prejudice. King proclaims Tyson a Black hero whose success in the ring has profound social import for Black Americans. "When he strikes a blow," King says of Tyson with his famous bombast, "he strikes a blow for all those who are discriminated against, all those who are segregated, all those who are downtrodden, the underprivileged, and denied." King bluntly continues to explain how Tyson's racial identity makes him suspicious regardless of his many athletic, economic, and personal successes. "If you're a nigger, you're a nigger until you die. You're either a poor nigger or a rich nigger. But you never get to stop being a nigger. And if you get to be educated, you're just an educated nigger." Tyson and King, the profile suggests, have banded together to fight against this bigoted system, which HBO Sports belongs to and supports. "They always change the rules when black folks come into success," King argues. "Black success is unacceptable."

Lee's documentary came under immediate fire for its language and divisiveness. HBO Sports boxing analyst Larry Merchant responded directly after it aired by calling King a "snake-oil salesman" who made his way in the boxing business by "wrapping himself in the emotional flags of race and injustice." Former professional tennis player and Civil Rights activist Arthur Ashe published a critique in the *Washington Post* that accused Lee of "simplifying, compartmentalizing, and unofficially amplifying what is already a social mine field" with his treatment of race.[21] Lee, Ashe charged, fanned racial tensions without offering any inkling as to how they might be improved. But the confrontational documentary skillfully built excitement for Tyson's match against Stewart, which he easily won in the first round, strengthening his salable reputation as the "Baddest Man on the Planet." It also showed the editorial compromises HBO would make to stay in business with its "most important employee" and the role documentary played in their important but precarious relationship.

King eventually steered Tyson away from HBO and toward a deal with its main competitor, Showtime. Tyson attributed the divorce primarily to his distaste for Larry Merchant, who had repeatedly criticized King and the boxer. "I didn't want [Merchant] commenting on my fights," Tyson told ESPN's Roy Firestone, "[HBO] didn't back down so I left." But more than Tyson's enmity toward Merchant, King wanted the deal to include a provision that made him the exclusive promoter for Tyson's television partner. HBO would not make

120 • The Boxing Film

such a concession—not even for Tyson—so King took his boxer to Showtime in late 1991 with an agreement that guaranteed roughly $120 million for eight to ten fights.[22] King immediately created the pay-per-view service KingVision PPV, to compete with the TVKO pay-per-view outlet HBO launched in 1991. Despite TVKO's promise, HBO lost its biggest star. Tyson, however, was soon forced out of boxing after being convicted of rape in 1992 and spending the next three years in prison.

Docu-Branding Boxing

Tyson returned to the ring—still under contract with Showtime—almost immediately after his March 1995 release from prison. Though Tyson and King had severed ties with HBO, the cable channel's film production unit, HBO Pictures, capitalized on the company's association with the infamous sports celebrities through producing unauthorized biographical docudramas on each that did not necessitate TV rights. Like most "based on a true story" productions, docudramas anchor their tales in the real world and trade on audiences' familiarity with the people and events they depict. They are also routinely subject to the critiques historical films garner. "Commercial imperatives most often fuel cinematic rewrites of history," explains film critic Frank Sanello. "Complex economic and social issues are pureed into easily digestible bits of information intended for consumption by Hollywood's most sought-after demographic: the lowest common denominator." Despite these frequent gripes, film scholar Robert Rosenstone defends historical films by contending that they can offer "a new form of history, what we might call history as vision."[23] Derek Paget distinguishes docudramas from other historical films by suggesting they maintain a closer relationship to reality by reproducing events and sometimes even incorporating indexical footage. Docudramas, Steven Lipkin contends, furnish a useful, if imperfect, documentary function "when actual documentary materials either do not exist or by themselves are incomplete or insufficient to treat the subject matter adequately." As the historical worlds docudramas build, according to Lipkin, "contribute to a culture's vision of itself," HBO's Tyson and King films build a past that contributes to the channel's identification as an authority in boxing.[24]

HBO premiered *Tyson* (1995), based in part on José Torres's book *Fire and Fear: The Inside Story of Mike Tyson* (1989), just after the boxer's release from prison. Directed by Uli Edel and starring Michael Jai White, the production depicts Tyson as a tragic figure who lost his way after the passing of Jim Jacobs (Tony Lo Bianco) as well as his trainer and adoptive father Cus D'Amato (George C. Scott). These guardians' absence, the film suggests, left a vulnerable hollowness that Don King (Paul Winfield) and Tyson's ex-wife Robin Givens (Kristen Wilson) preyed upon. The film begins with Tyson in a courtroom

FIG. 6 HBO Pictures released Uli Edel's *Tyson* (1995) shortly after the former heavyweight champion's release from prison. The biopic periodically emphasizes the role HBO Sports played in Tyson's career.

standing trial for rape and reflecting on how he went from a poor kid in Brooklyn to one of the world's most famous athletes to a convicted rapist. The film proceeds from this flashback to chronicle his rise and fall.

As communications scholar Jack Lule observes, popular press depictions of Tyson amid his arrest, trial, and conviction commonly depicted him through two similarly dehumanizing tropes. He was either a simple-minded victim of his dire upbringing and malicious crooks like King or a beastly savage who could not abide by society's mores.[25] Both depictions, Lule contends, reinforce white supremacist racial hierarchies. HBO's *Tyson* reinforces these tropes by portraying the boxer as a dangerous and pitiful man-child who cannot resist turning to violence to solve his problems, has a history of abusing women, and is too naïve to see through King and Givens's different but equally blatant forms of malevolence. Moreover, the docudrama suggests Tyson functioned productively only when under the direction of compassionate White custodians like Jacobs and D'Amato. The docudrama contrasts the critique of boxing's racial politics that Spike Lee offered in his prefight documentary.

The film concludes by returning to the courtroom for the announcement of Tyson's rape conviction and, like many docudramas, ends with text that explains the disgraced boxer's eventual fate: "Mike Tyson was found guilty on charges of rape and criminal deviant conduct and sentenced to six years in the Indiana Youth Center." Police escort the handcuffed Tyson to prison as the text appears on screen. The final shot depicts the boxer looking up to the sky—and to a freedom the onetime champ can no longer enjoy—before being corralled into a police cruiser. The conclusion then notes Tyson's release in March 1995, a little more than three years into his six-year sentence, and his intention to continue boxing before explaining that "Don King will retain his role as Mike Tyson's manager" and adding that "King is scheduled to stand trial for insurance fraud in May of 1995," just one month after the film premiered. The production positions King as a shady villain who contributed to Tyson's demise and will likely continue taking advantage of the boxer after his release. King's impending trial for insurance fraud is hardly relevant to the tragic tale *Tyson* weaves; however, including the point helps HBO to characterize him as a snake. By extension, it distances the media outlet from King's devious machinations and suggests Tyson was better off before he left for Showtime.

HBO extended this vilification of the promoter in *Don King: Only in America* (1997), a biopic starring Ving Rhames and based on Jack Newfield's exposé *Only in America: The Life and Crimes of Don King* (1995), which at one point likens the promoter to Hitler.[26] The production—which opens by blaring the O'Jays song "For the Love of Money"—traces King's transformation from a Cleveland numbers runner who once did four years in prison for manslaughter into a wealthy boxing impresario. It repeatedly evokes King's insistence that his remarkable story is possible "only in America," but presents his tale as a perverse version of the American Dream that single-mindedly pursues fortune regardless of the wreckage it leaves behind. The docudrama's distinguishing aesthetic feature is a series of fourth-wall-breaking soliloquies King delivers from a boxing ring—his preferred stage—that share his perspective on sport, race, and money. "I'm the American dream," King hollers from the ring with a smoldering cigar in hand. "I am entertainment. If you didn't have Don King, you'd have to invent him." The docudrama, which won a Peabody Award on the strength of Rhames's performance, presents King as the manifestly unethical ringmaster of a blatantly corrupt sport.

Tyson and *Only in America* build realism by reproducing familiar moments in their subjects' careers and including cameos from recognizable members of the fight world. In particular, they frequently include references to HBO. *Tyson* re-creates matches that originally appeared on the channel with HBO Sports personalities calling the action and the organization's cameras and microphones capturing it. The scenes use HBO Sports to lend the fictionalized depictions authenticity while emphasizing the prominent role that the media outlet played in Tyson's tumultuous career. Similarly, *Only in America* uses HBO's contentious relationship with King as a plot point. Two of the promoter's profanity-laced rants single out HBO as an adversary. "HBO? I made those motherfuckers a fortune," King exclaims while venting about his many skirmishes with the channel. As with *Tyson*, the scene accentuates HBO's role in King's career while distancing it from his questionable values. HBO Pictures, in fact, promised that HBO Sports' rift with King did not inform the docudrama's production. "They were uninvolved and I had a clear path," HBO Pictures' president John Matoian said of HBO Sports. Abraham claimed that HBO Sports provided only a few minor notes and that HBO Pictures had final say over the production's ultimate shape. While HBO Sports was not directly involved in *Tyson* or *Only in America*, both docudramas mark HBO's continued efforts to profit on the former business partners while emphasizing the media outlet's importance to their careers and separating it from their faults.

HBO Sports continued making boxing documentaries through the 1990s, such as *Sonny Liston: The Mysterious Life and Death of a Champion* (1995) and *Sugar Ray Robinson: The Bright Lights and Dark Shadows of a Champion* (1998). The Liston and Robinson documentaries reflect *Tyson* by offering comparable stories of tortured boxers. But the process of creating these films became more challenging in 1998, when ESPN outbid HBO, Fox, the NBA, and Madison Square Garden to purchase the Big Fights Inc. library for eighty million dollars. HBO continued to produce boxing documentaries, but the prospect of licensing historical footage from a competitor that was attempting to break into the sports documentary genre made the task more arduous.

HBO Sports skirted these challenges with *Legendary Nights* (2003), a historical documentary series made entirely of HBO-owned footage. Branded as part of HBO Sports' *Sports of the 20th Century* series of historical documentaries, *Legendary Nights* commemorated HBO's thirtieth anniversary by creating twelve segments that offer the stories behind the greatest fights the channel covered. As Greenburg commented, "Fifty or 60 years from now when people wonder what boxing was like from 1973–2002, they can pull out these 12

124 • The Boxing Film

documentaries and see that HBO was there in the middle of the ring documenting history." Lampley plugged the documentary series as "testimony to how rich our heritage is and how many great fights and stories we've had."[27] Anticipating ESPN's *30 for 30* series, a documentary project launched in 2009 to memorialize the network's thirtieth anniversary, *Legendary Nights* conflates boxing's recent past with HBO—points it reinforces by using its own footage as the primary historical record and relying mostly on its personalities to serve as expert interviewees. *Legendary Nights* also continues HBO's insistence that it remains a rare force for good in the sport. The segment on Meldrick Taylor and Julio César Chávez's 1990 light welterweight championship fight—a bout the documentary says "had it all" and that *Ring* magazine named the match of the decade—was particularly telling. After recounting their historic brawl, the episode ends by commenting on Taylor's ill-advised decision to continue boxing even though he is obviously suffering from dementia pugilistica (now commonly known as chronic traumatic encephalopathy [CTE]) and by critiquing the boxing establishment that enables the fighter to persist despite his cognitive impairment. *Legendary Nights* casts HBO Sports as a principal player in boxing's recent history and an advocate for reform that looks after the legends it helped to create once they leave the spotlight.

Aside from its own films, HBO makes frequent arrangements to incorporate HBO Sports trademarks and personalities into fictional Hollywood productions. Nearly every big-budget film since the late 1990s that depicts a prominent televised boxing match has marked the bout as an HBO event. The movies integrate HBO Sports' fight broadcast aesthetics to suggest the matches they create for the screen appear precisely as they would were they actually occurring and being produced for TV by HBO. HBO Sports, in turn, benefits from the brand placements' suggestion that it is the first stop for big-time boxing matches. This practice marks a broader shift from boxing films building realism by simply mimicking TV conventions to branding those practices as the work of an actual sports media entity. For instance, Ron Shelton's *Play It to the Bone* (1999) stars Antonio Banderas and Woody Harrelson as Cesar Dominguez and Vince Boudreau, two aging boxers and best pals who get the unexpected opportunity to compete on the undercard of a Mike Tyson bout that HBO is carrying via TVKO. The rub is that the friends must fight each other. The formulaic comedy follows their harried road trip from Los Angeles to Las Vegas for the bout along with Grace (Lolita Davidovich)—Vince's exgirlfriend and Cesar's current flame. The movie's combination of the road film, buddy comedy, and love triangle reflects Shelton's earlier (and far more successful) sports film *Bull Durham* (1988).

Play It to the Bone presents the HBO Sports bout as a vehicle through which Cesar and Vince hope to restart their languishing careers. Accordingly,

Shelton uses HBO and its personalities to stress the match's profile. He also references HBO's credibility in a scene where the promoter—a stereotypically scheming businessman named Joe Domino (Tom Sizemore)—confronts Lampley before Cesar and Vince's fight. He apologizes for the substitute match's seemingly shoddy quality and asks the sportscaster if HBO Sports can "put the best face" on it for the audience. Lampley refuses and begins to ask probing questions about Cesar and Vince's fitness, potentially damaging queries the slippery promoter dodges. The scene buttresses HBO Sports' journalistic reputation preceding its coverage of Cesar and Vince's match. Their bloody slugfest concludes in a draw, and Lampley dubs the surprisingly engaging bout "an instant classic" and an "epic battle." "Years from now," Lampley continues in his effusive postmatch summary, "the real fight fans will be telling each other they were here to see this bout." It was the kind of match, he implies, that might eventually wind up on *Legendary Nights*.

David O. Russell's *The Fighter* (2010), an inspirational biopic about light welterweight boxer "Irish" Micky Ward, similarly uses HBO to accent its subject matter's importance and to build realism. The film presents Ward (Mark Wahlberg) through a familiar underdog narrative à la *Rocky* (1976) in which the White fighter out of Lowell, Massachusetts, overcomes economic hardship and past failures to find success in the ring and redeem his brother Dicky Eklund (Christian Bale), a onetime pro boxer who became a drug addict. HBO's *America Undercover* documentary series, in fact, used Eklund's transformation from promising boxer to down-and-out junky as the topic of a 1995 episode titled *High on Crack Street: Lost Lives in Lowell. The Fighter* shows the *America Undercover* crew following Eklund and uses the poignant but embarrassing documentary to highlight Ward's long shot status.

As HBO explained Eklund's struggles with *High on Crack Street*, it helped to make Ward a star through televising a series of three fights against Arturo Gatti—matches that eventually appeared on a *Legendary Nights* segment that Wahlberg narrated. Like *Play It to the Bone*, *The Fighter* showcases Ward's matches through HBO Sports' visual aesthetic and with some of the same talent that commented on his original bouts. But Russell took this quest to build realism even further by using the same cameras HBO Sports employed to broadcast Ward's matches. This televisual and branded aesthetic—which included HBO Sports graphics and shots of the division's equipment—composed a key quality that critics identified in the mostly positive reviews the Academy Award–nominated film gathered. "We had HBO come and shoot the fights for us, use the same cameras that they shot the great Micky Ward–Arturo Gatti fights with," said Wahlberg, who served as a producer on the film. "HBO does such a great job of capturing all the action and suspense and drama in a fight. As long as it's there in the ring, they never miss anything."[28] Wahlberg's endorsement cites HBO Sports as the standard bearer for televised boxing—a perspective *The Fighter* reinforces by mimicking the division's coverage. It also, although indirectly, supported Wahlberg's interest in *Entourage* (2004–2011), a comedic HBO series he produced at the time that shared the channel's mostly male boxing audience.

The 2000 Acclaim Sports video game *HBO Boxing* channeled the brand placements' efforts to advertise HBO Sports' association with boxing toward a younger crowd. Like many sports video games, *HBO Boxing* has participants adopt the avatar of actual fighters and climb the ranks to compete for a championship. Although ostensibly based on reality, the game includes only those contemporary fighters under contract with HBO Sports and excludes its competitors' boxers. Moreover, and like the films, its fights occur as if they are being televised by HBO Sports with the channel's graphics packages and announcers. "The video game accurately reflects the electricity and excitement of what it's really like to fight on HBO," enthused HBO fighter and eventual ringside commentator Roy Jones Jr. while promoting the game.[29] Extending the Hollywood brand placements, the game creates a reality in which HBO Sports is not simply the leader in television boxing but the only perceptible presence.

HBO Boxing's "career mode" most conspicuously markets HBO Sports by having players graduate through the media outlet's increasingly prominent boxing shows. Fighters begin on *KO Nation* (2000–2001), a short-lived Saturday afternoon program geared toward younger viewers that featured less polished professionals. They then work their way up to *Boxing After Dark* (1996–2018), *World Championship Boxing,* and ultimately a TVKO championship bout. "If you work hard," the game's booklet reads, "you can beef up your boxer as you rise to the pinnacle of your career: a chance to have the world watch you fight in a TVKO Pay-Per-View from HBO." The game advertises HBO Sports' varied boxing programs, which inflect its fights with televisual realism while branding HBO's TVKO pay-per-view events as the sport's apex.

The documentary/reality series *24/7*, which debuted in 2007 to provide viewers an inside view of fighters' preparations leading up to an appearance on pay-per-view, composed HBO Sports' most consistent effort to docu-brand its association with boxing. Narrator Liev Schreiber described the first installment—a four-episode primer to Oscar De La Hoya and Floyd Mayweather's 2007 championship bout—as "an unprecedented, unfiltered look at the lives of two champions as they prepare for an historic showdown." The program continued HBO Sports' commitment to producing "boxing that tells a story" by building narratives that might expand the fight's eventual pay-per-view audience. "The programs we present," Greenburg promised, "will appeal far beyond the hardcore boxing fan."[30] The first season framed the featured combatants as opposites. Mayweather is a trash-talking playboy who resides in Las Vegas and parties with rappers. De La Hoya is a soft-spoken family man. But both are steadfast competitors who train unrelentingly in preparation for their fight. *24/7* also emphasizes the tensions between Mayweather and his estranged father, Floyd Sr., who previously served as De La Hoya's trainer. Worried that Mayweather Sr. would not be able to coach him properly for a fight against his son, De La Hoya replaced the trainer. As a result, Mayweather Sr. attempts to reconnect with his son, who is coached by his uncle Roger, and become part of his team. The family drama added another layer of intrigue to the prefight buildup.

Depending on the situation, HBO Sports marketed *24/7* as a documentary series and reality program to take advantage of the overlapping genres' different cultural meanings and audiences. "In order to court a particular type of audience identification and set of expectations," writes television scholar Susan Murray, "television networks can take a program that has somewhat liminal textual generic identifiers and set it as either a documentary or a reality program by packaging it in such a way as to appear either more educational/informative or more entertaining/sensational, or in some cases both."[31] When asked whether *24/7* was a reality program, for instance, Greenburg curtly claimed to "hate that word. 'Reality' shows to me are manufactured reality," he huffed. "This is dramatic documentary filmmaking." In a separate interview conducted the same year, Greenburg praised Mayweather—whose legal troubles and sometimes-contentious relationship with HBO recalled Tyson—as a "reality superstar" on par with the cast of *American Idol* and *Survivor.*[32] Greenburg's selective branding practices indicated that *24/7* both participated in trends in reality television and bolstered the "quality" status that HBO's documentaries helped to build.

Regardless of *24/7*'s precise generic designation, the program continued HBO Sports' multipronged docu-branding efforts to place the media outlet at the center of boxing while publicizing its coverage of the sport. The series, as *New York Times* sports media critic Richard Sandomir points out, "served a dual function as a documentary and infomercial" for an HBO Sports pay-per-view event coursing with the drama *24/7* brought out.[33] HBO Sports even self-reflexively made the *24/7* series into a plot point in its documentation of the lead-up to De La Hoya and Mayweather's match. The second episode shows Mayweather and his team watching the series' first installment. Mayweather is so motivated by the sight of his adversary training that he immediately leaves to do some road work of his own. Later in the series, Mayweather critiques De La Hoya's *24/7* performance as boring—another indication that he was watching the show carefully and that its production enhanced the fight's stakes. The scenes suggest that HBO Sports does not simply cover boxing matches but also composes a cultural hub for the sport and a resource that boxers use to learn about their trade, survey their competition, and even taunt their opponents.

24/7's first three episodes aired on Sunday evenings after *The Sopranos* and *Entourage*—the most coveted spot on HBO's weekly schedule at the time—and

128 • The Boxing Film

replayed twelve times a week. "It's the first time an HBO Sports product has broken through the get the kind of space," a satisfied Greenburg said of *24/7*'s scheduling. "If we can perform, it takes the stature of HBO Sports up a notch within the building."[34] The final episode aired on the Thursday before the Saturday evening fight and ended with shots of HBO Sports banners at the event site to call attention to the media spectacle that was about to unfold—a sort of fifth installment of *24/7* that HBO subscribers would have to pay an extra fifty-five dollars to see.

HBO's pay-per-view coverage of the Mayweather–De La Hoya match, which Mayweather won by a split decision, gathered 2.5 million purchases to become the biggest selling non-heavyweight title fight ever and the most lucrative prize-fight of all time. *24/7* expanded the fight's reach. The series "exposed a lot of young viewers to Oscar and Floyd," remarked HBO Sports spokesperson Ray Stallone. "That's what boxing needs." *24/7* quickly became a standard ingredient of HBO Sports' marquee fights and extended into other sporting events that sought to benefit from its ability to grow their audience.

Like the documentaries, docudramas, product placements, and video games, *24/7* fashions a reality for boxing that asserts the sport could not exist—or would at least be dramatically different—without HBO Sports while publicizing the premium cable channel's fight coverage. These docu-branding efforts perform cultural work that helped to turn HBO into what *SportsBusiness Journal* described as boxing's "economic engine" and "de facto custodian."[35] They also expand on HBO Sports' long-standing combination of boxing and documentary to show the crucial—but mostly overlooked—roles these intersecting genres play in HBO's history.

7

Protecting Boxing with the Boxing Film

Predictions of boxing's death accompanied the sport throughout its history, with rationales ranging from its violence and corruption to the invasion of new media. But these prophesies gained unprecedented traction during the 1990s. Ali was long retired, and the excitement Tyson generated dimmed along with his rape conviction and continued legal trouble after his release from prison. Moreover, mixed martial arts (MMA)—which combines boxing, wrestling, and various types of martial arts—emerged to offer a controversial and dynamic competitor that began tapping into boxing's shrinking fan base. Critically and commercially unsuccessful boxing films like *Diggstown* (1992), *Gladiator* (1992), and *The Great White Hype* (1996) did little to alleviate the sport's struggles. But as boxing dipped, a swell of films worked to argue for its continued relevance within the rapidly changing circumstances surrounding it. "It's interesting at a time when there's a historic low point of interest in boxing, that you suddenly have this creative burst," observed HBO Sports' Larry Merchant.[1] These films often defended boxing by working to expand its demographic scope and by appealing to the sport's rich cultural and filmic heritage.

Mainstreaming Boxing History

Muhammad Ali was diagnosed with Parkinson's disease three years after his 1981 retirement, though he had shown signs of the illness's early stages years prior. The ailment slowed the garrulous fighter's speech and stiffened his famous

130 • The Boxing Film

fluidity. As a result, Ali, perhaps ashamed by his drastic physical decline, largely faded from public view. Looking to provide a climax for its presentation of the 1996 Summer Olympic Games' opening ceremonies, NBC arranged for Ali to light the torch in Atlanta's Centennial Olympics Stadium. The network kept the decision secret—and even had Ali sign a nondisclosure agreement—to ensure his surprise appearance would achieve maximum dramatic effect. A procession of famous athletes, many with connections to Atlanta, passed the torch while heading into the packed stadium. Swimmer Janet Evans jogged the final stretch to the podium, where Ali emerged to rapturous applause. The retired fighter's arm quaked as Evans handed him the torch and his feet tightly shuffled while he walked the few steps to set the cauldron ablaze and officially open the event. As NBC's Bob Costas announced, "Once the most dynamic figure in sports, a gregarious man, now trapped inside that mask created by Parkinson's syndrome. So, in one sense a poignant figure, but look at him, still a great, great presence. Still exuding nobility and stature. And the response he evokes is part affection, part excitement, but especially respect."

International Olympic Committee president Juan Antonio Samaranch later presented Ali with a gold medal to replace the one he earned in 1960 and claimed to have thrown into the Ohio River after being denied service at a racially segregated Louisville restaurant.[2] Ali's appearance was praised as an inspirational highlight of the 1996 Olympics that recast the once rebellious and polarizing figure—who, in fact, helped to inspire African American protests at the 1968 Summer Games—into a universally admired symbol of tolerance and unity. The torch lighting, as Ali biographer Michael Ezra puts it, "translated into a sign of his transcendent moral authority, his ability to bring the races together, and his symbolizing the infinite possibilities of life." Ali's Olympics cameo, the *Washington Post*'s Frank Ahrens added, "framed the former fighter as an almost holy figure, no longer pitiable but somehow heroic and certainly beloved."[3]

Ali's involvement in the Olympics primed audiences for Leon Gast's *When We Were Kings*, a documentary on the 1974 Rumble in the Jungle that debuted at the Sundance Film Festival in January 1996 and was released theatrically shortly after the Atlanta games. *Kings* explores how the Rumble in the Jungle built connections between African American and African culture and demonstrates how the fight cemented Ali's place as a Black global icon. In particular, Gast zeroes in on a six-week delay that occurred when Foreman sustained a cut above his right eye while training. The fighters stayed in Zaire as Foreman healed up. Ali used the intermission to mingle with the locals and establish himself as a man of the people. Foreman, by contrast, was prickly in public and did not conceal his distaste for Africa. The Zaireans expressed their overwhelming preference for Ali by developing the chant, "Ali bomaye!" (Ali, kill him!) to support the extroverted underdog as he sought to regain the title.

Kings culminates by exploring Ali's famous "Rope-a-Dope" strategy—in which he went on the defensive against the more powerful Foreman, leaned against the ropes while the heavyweight champion punched himself to exhaustion, and then surged to knock out his fatigued rival in the eighth round. The documentary marvels at Ali's strategic genius in developing the risky tactic, predicting Foreman's gullible response to it, and keeping his plan hidden from the press and his trainers. Even sophisticated fight fans like the writers Norman Mailer and George Plimpton, both of whom attended the fight and served as two of Gast's primary interviewees, confess to having dismissed Ali's chances. "You suddenly realized there must be some design in this madness," Plimpton recalls in amazement at finally identifying the fighter's unorthodox plot to outfox his stronger and younger opponent. *Kings* suggests that Ali's politics, like the Rope-a-Dope, were inspired and ahead of their time. Mirroring the 1996 Olympics, *Kings* designates Ali as a singular idol who prompted increased tolerance within the United States and across the globe. "Kids today will be missing a whole lot if they don't know about the legacy of Muhammad Ali," says Spike Lee toward the end of the film. "Because no matter what era you live in, you see very few true heroes."

The borderline-hagiographic documentary gathered a slew of accolades, including the Academy Award for Best Documentary Feature. Actors Tommy Lee Jones and Will Smith—the former Fresh Prince who once rapped about Tyson and eventually gained an Oscar nomination for playing Ali in Michael Mann's biopic—presented the accolade to Gast and producer David Sonenberg. During their acceptance speech the filmmakers thanked Ali, who was seated alongside Foreman in the audience. Rigid tremors nearly prevented Ali from participating in the applause his acknowledgment inspired, which cascaded into a standing ovation and call for him to join Gast and Sonenberg on stage. He slowly approached the dais with assistance from Foreman, the same "dope" he humiliated in the documentary, as Hollywood's elite honored him. Ali's appearance contrasted dramatically with his cameo at the same event twenty years prior, when he pranced onto the stage to dance and jaw with Stallone. But it sought to reproduce the dramatic recipe NBC used so successfully with the Olympic opening ceremonies.

Productions like the opening ceremonies, *When We Were Kings*, and the Academy Awards contributed to what Ezra calls "a full-blown movement to canonize [Ali] as a standard-bearer of American values and embodiment of the best things this country has to offer." They "triggered a renaissance," wrote *USA Today*'s Jon Saraceno, that "reignited the world's smoldering adoration for him, resulting in a sweeping brushfire of new-found popularity."[4] After spending most of the previous decade outside of the public eye, Ali was "back and ready to be marketed." His lawyer Ron DiNicola acknowledged "a synergy right now between who he is as an activist and what he is as a businessman."[5] This

132 • The Boxing Film

marketability, however, worked through rounding off Ali's once sharp political edges. Ali represented conventional values with which politically cautious organizations like the Olympics and major television networks were comfortable aligning.

A surge of productions surfaced to profit on Ali's renewed popularity and participate in his political neutralization. In January 2000 ABC released the TV movie *King of the World* (John Sacret Young), an adaptation of David Remnick's biography of the fighter's early life starring Terrence Howard. The following month, Fox debuted the telefilm *Ali: An American Hero* (Leon Ichaso), a similarly celebratory docudrama that tells Ali's life story through the Rumble in the Jungle. Later that year, HBO Sports premiered the documentary *Ali-Frazier I: One Nation . . . Divisible*. Although they have different points of emphasis, each production shows Ali's transformation from divisive to unifying—a figure who draws near comprehensive praise in twenty-first-century America. They use Ali to celebrate the progress he inspired and to intimate that the obstacles against which he battled during his career have largely been resolved, or at least improved. Ali's individual suffering, the productions suggest, prompted crucial cultural growth.

Michael Mann's *Ali* (2001) composed the highest profile and most acclaimed effort to remember the former champion and capitalize on his revived marketability. The biopic builds on *When We Were Kings* by presenting a similarly triumphant story of Ali's life and by using the Rumble in the Jungle as its dramatic climax, a timeframe that allows the film to offer a tidy narrative of struggle, achievement, and redemption without addressing the boxer's eventual athletic decline and illness. *Ali* dramatically reproduces several of the moments *Kings* includes through archive footage and devotes its third act to retelling the documentary's celebratory tale about the Rumble in the Jungle. It similarly depicts the boxer as a tactical savant who devised the Rope-a-Dope independently and in defiance of his trainers' advice. The fight scene, for instance, cuts out the diegetic sound between rounds when Ali's exasperated corner men desperately urge him to dance around the ring rather than absorb Foreman's powerful slugs against the ropes. By muting Ali's frustrated trainers, the film plays up the fighter's unusual focus and resolve—an assured intransigence that mirrors his broader courage to stand up for his beliefs. *Ali* ends with a rainstorm that erupts almost immediately after the fighter beats Foreman to regain the title. The film closes with Ali hollering victoriously to the adoring African crowd as the rain beats down. It presents the storm as a sort of divine intervention conjured by a quasi-messianic figure whose unexpected conquest signals a new beginning. As with *Kings*, Mann's uplifting production depicts Ali as a unifying force. It similarly rode this mainstream-friendly representation to critical and commercial success.

The Ali renaissance spawned other redemptive films about Black boxers whose unusual bravery taught valuable cultural lessons. Norman Jewison's *Hurricane* (1999) stars Denzel Washington as Rubin "Hurricane" Carter, a one-time contender from Patterson, New Jersey, who was wrongly convicted of murder. A victim of rampant institutionalized racism, Carter spent nearly twenty years in prison. Like Ali, Carter is a militant and outspoken African American who will not compromise his principles despite the injustices he faces. Insisting on his innocence, Carter refuses to wear the prison's standard-issue uniform and defies its normal daily patterns, which lands him in solitary confinement. He also pens a memoir that tells his life story and outlines the racist conspiracy that put him behind bars. The injustice Carter suffered prompted widespread outrage and inspired both Bob Dylan's "Hurricane" (1976) and Nelson Algren's *The Devil's Stocking* (1981).

Lesra Martin (Vicellous Reon Shannon), a young Black man from Brooklyn who has been taken in by a group of White Canadian activists, stumbles upon Carter's tome at a book fair and is profoundly moved. After corresponding with and befriending Carter, Martin persuades his guardians to commit themselves to exonerating the boxer. The group of pure-hearted idealists band together and eventually get Carter's conviction overturned—a task at which others had previously failed. The film ends with the tear-jerking verdict that secures Carter's release. Although based on a true story, *Hurricane* was widely critiqued as taking dramatic liberties with Carter's biography. It provided what the *New Yorker*'s David Denby called "a liberal fairytale" in which clever and benevolent White people combat and correct racial injustice that Carter cannot solve alone.[6] It also, again much like *Ali*, assigns the injustice Carter endured to a lamentable cultural past that is no longer as relevant thanks to the courage of the falsely convicted fighter and his activist allies.

Ken Burns's *Unforgivable Blackness: The Rise and Fall of Jack Johnson* (2005) similarly probes racism in the United States through the provocative figure of Jack Johnson. Extending *Legendary Champions*, *The Great White Hope*, and *Jack Johnson*, *Unforgivable Blackness* remembers Johnson as an outspoken and disobedient figure like Ali and Carter whom a racist society targeted and punished. As narrator Keith David says during the film's opening moments, "When whites ran everything, Jack Johnson took orders from no one. While most African Americans struggled merely to survive, Jack Johnson reveled in his riches and his fame. When Black Americans were expected to defer to whites, Jack Johnson battered them to the ground. And at a time when the mere suspicion that a Black man had flirted with a white woman could cost him his life, Jack Johnson slept with whomever he pleased." Burns uses a combination of archival footage and talking head interviews to remember Johnson as a brave iconoclast who rejected oppressive social mores and suffered unjustly for his

134 • The Boxing Film

unrepentant recalcitrance. But like *Ali* and *Hurricane*, *Unforgivable Blackness* closes on an optimistic note by stressing how Johnson's rebelliousness, when read retrospectively, illustrates the United States' capacity for change and ultimately helped to nurture greater tolerance. The documentary finishes with cultural critic Stanley Crouch praising Johnson as "the kind of person who could have only come about in the United States. Because America, whatever its problems," Crouch continues, "still has a certain elasticity, a certain latitude that allows the person to dream a big enough dream that can be achieved if the person is as big as the dream." The documentary uses Johnson's story to praise the United States as a flawed meritocracy, but a meritocracy nonetheless.

Ali, *Hurricane*, and *Unforgivable Blackness* extend the cultural and economic logic informing Muhammad Ali's commercialized rebirth after the 1996 Olympics. They celebrate courageous Black boxers who defied and helped to transform cruel social protocols. But they do so from a temporal distance that assigns this oppression to the past. As a result, they designate Ali, Carter, and Johnson as sporting heroes who fit neatly within contemporary social institutions. These films, of course, all could have been produced in ways that connect their subjects to the persistence of racism and inequality in the United States, particularly the legal system that unjustly punished all three of these figures and continues to disproportionately oppress people of color. But they elide these relevant connections in favor of narratives that affirm the status quo.

A concurrent pair of biographical docudramas focusing on White boxers offers similarly redemptive tales about the sport's history. Showtime's *Marciano* (Charles Winkler, 1999) details Rocky Marciano's (Jon Favreau) rise to become the only undefeated heavyweight champion. The biopic situates Marciano's 1951 fight against Joe Louis as a turning point in his career that solidified his racialized identity as a beloved champion—a contrast to how *The Joe Louis Story* uses the fight to mark the Brown Bomber's downfall. "So I finally get to meet the Great White Hope," Louis (Duane Davis) smugly cracks when he first encounters Marciano before their match. Although the public and press celebrated Marciano as a symbol of racial pride, Showtime's film presents the fighter as resentful of the racism that drives his celebrity. Marciano, for instance, rebukes and threatens a reporter who makes a bigoted comment about Louis. And he is bittersweet after beating the aging former champ, whom he idolizes. The film ends by cross-cutting between Marciano visiting Louis's dressing room after their 1951 bout and a trip Marciano made to check on Louis after he was briefly admitted to a Colorado mental hospital years later. As Marciano leaves the hospital, he gives an administrator a wad of cash to look after his friend and hero—a gesture of kindness the film punctuates by stressing the boxer's famous stinginess earlier on. The movie explains that while Marciano was exalted as a White Hope, he did not identify with this role and detested the politics that informed it.

Steve James's *Joe and Max* (2002), produced by the premium cable channel Starz, provides a similar portrait of Max Schmeling (Til Schweiger) through focusing on his unlikely friendship with Louis (Leonard Roberts) after their 1936 and 1938 matches. The film explores how the Nazi Party repeatedly tried to get Schmeling to participate in and support its platform of Aryan superiority. Schmeling, who had Jewish friends and a Jewish manager (David Paymer), initially wanted no part of the hateful agenda. But he relented upon discovering that the German government would permit him to fight Louis only if he publicly endorsed the Nazis. Although he never officially joined the party—and even hid a Jewish neighbor in his apartment during the Holocaust—Schmeling was eventually ostracized for his identification with it, an association films like *The Negro Soldier* and *The Joe Louis Story* emphasized. Louis, on the other hand, went on to become a national hero. Despite their wildly divergent images, the rivals eventually grew to be friends. Like Marciano, Schmeling regretted the ideological ends to which his image was put and helped Louis when he faced economic hardship in retirement. *Joe and Max* provides a recuperative and sympathetic take on this villainized German fighter. "I want people to know that Schmeling really isn't who the American public believes he was," explained executive producer Mike Kerz. "He's not a Nazi. He actually saved Jews from the Nazis. He refused to join the Nazi party and he was a true friend to a man who needed a true friend, Joe Louis."[7]

Marciano and *Joe and Max* insist that their subjects were antiracist models of tolerance far ahead of their times. But—and as with *Ali*, *Hurricane*, and *Unforgivable Blackness*—these tales could have been told very differently. While they may not have been bigots, Marciano and Schmeling certainly benefitted from the prejudice that powered their images, and they opted to safeguard their own careers rather than speak out against this intolerance. The films, however, present them as proponents of open-mindedness in ways that enhance their marketability within the moment when they were produced. They filter boxing's past through a salable framework at a time when the sport's relevance was dwindling.

New Protagonists, Old Tales

Aside from building politically pasteurized versions of boxing's past, boxing films began to broaden the genre's traditionally masculine parameters. The low-budget productions *Girlfight* (Karyn Kusama, 2000), *The Opponent* (Eugene Jarecki, 2000), and *Knockout* (Lorenzo Doumani, 2000) all concern women who use the sport to cope with and battle against difficult domestic circumstances. Karyn Kusama's *Girlfight* was the most renowned of the bunch and the first boxing film to both be directed by and star women of color. It centers on Diana Guzman (Michelle Rodriguez), an angsty teen from Brooklyn's Red Hook neighborhood. Diana's mother committed suicide, and she is left with her abusive father Sandro (Paul Calderón) and sensitive brother Tiny (Ray Santiago). Her father encourages Tiny to box and pays for him to take lessons at a local gym even though the boy is more interested in pursuing art. When Sandro refuses to support Diana's interest in fighting, she begins stealing money to take lessons and finally convinces the local trainer (Jaime Tirelli)—who initially does not believe girls should box—to coach her.

Diana excels at boxing and gains the begrudging respect of several men—including her father, whom she beats up at one point when he drunkenly confronts her at home. While training she develops a relationship with the fellow boxer Adrian (Santiago Douglas), a boy whose name evokes *Rocky* and showcases the gender politics *Girlfight* contests. But she and Adrian eventually have to compete in an amateur tournament—an encounter in which Adrian is reluctant to participate. He ultimately fights and loses to Diana by decision. Emasculated by the defeat, Adrian assumes Diana will no longer be romantically interested in him. "So now I lose your respect, huh?," he asks shortly after the match. "You boxed with me like I was any other guy," Diana tenderly responds. "You boxed with me and you showed me respect." Diana is heartened by the fact that Adrian will not use traditional gender norms to subordinate her, either in their athletic competition or in their budding relationship.

While *Girlfight* won the Grand Jury and Best Director awards at Sundance, the independent film secured only a limited release and was almost never made. Its obstacles were largely attributed to Kusama's insistence that her main character be Latina. Producers urged Kusama to reconsider her vision and suggested that a Latina protagonist—despite boxing's long-standing connection to the Latinx community—would be "unappealing" and "unbelievable" to audiences accustomed to White protagonists in sports films.[8] Although far from a commercial blockbuster, *Girlfight*'s critical accolades provided a foundation on which Clint Eastwood's Hollywood production *Million Dollar Baby* (2004) built. An adaptation of F. X. Toole's short story of the same title, *Million Dollar Baby* took the racial advice Kusama rejected by casting the up-and-coming White actress Hilary Swank to play the lead.

Million Dollar Baby centers on Maggie Fitzgerald (Swank), a poor woman from rural Missouri who, like Diana, pursues boxing after struggling with an abusive home life. She persuades the curmudgeonly trainer Frankie Dunn (Eastwood)—who initially rebuffs her entreaty by gruffly insisting "I don't train girls"—to coach her. As Fitzgerald's career blossoms, she and Frankie, who is estranged from his biological daughter for undisclosed reasons, build a surrogate family to replace their broken relationships. Frankie, who studies Gaelic in his spare time, gives Maggie the nickname "Mo Cuishle"—which translates to "my blood"—to reinforce their kinship. He also has her fight under the name "Irish" Maggie Fitzgerald. Both monikers connect her to the Irish community, which enthusiastically accepts her as one of its own and provides ethnically

Protecting Boxing with the Boxing Film • 137

motivated support that propels the White fighter's status. Maggie eventually secures a title bout against Billie "The Blue Bear" Osterman, a vicious Black German who worked as a prostitute before turning to boxing. Maggie dominates the match early, which prompts her adversary to take a cheap shot between rounds. In a freakish and tragic turn, the illegal hit causes Maggie to break her neck on a stool in the corner, which leaves her paralyzed from the neck down. Frankie becomes Maggie's primary caretaker after the accident and watches in agony as the newly disabled fighter descends into depression while her once-chiseled body erodes. She twice attempts suicide and begs Frankie to euthanize her. Frankie eventually carries out her request and mercifully destroys the family he managed to build—a controversial ending that religious groups attacked as an endorsement of assisted suicide.

Eastwood's melodrama won the Academy Award for Best Picture and became the most critically acclaimed boxing film since *Rocky* and *Raging Bull*. The accolades indicate that the boxing film could productively accommodate new types of protagonists beyond White men. But it also secures many of the genre's most entrenched norms. Toole's original story, for instance, coded the Blue Bear as White by making her a Russian—"a big-busted, masculine looking Russian girl living in Hamburg, who grew a faint mustache and dated fashion models." Eastwood, however, turned her into a Black former sex worker to punctuate her treachery. The film also, as Ellexis Boyle, Brad Millington, and Patricia Vertinsky point out, ultimately subordinates and marginalizes Maggie's tragic story in favor of centering on Frankie as "the white male patriarch and primary protagonist."[9] *Million Dollar Baby*, they argue, is more a film about a tortured White male trainer than a female boxer.

Charles S. Dutton's *Against the Ropes* (2004) premiered the same year as *Million Dollar Baby* and had a similarly wide release. The critical and commercial flop stars Meg Ryan as Jackie Kallen, boxing's first influential female manager and promoter. It celebrates Kallen's tenacity in working her way up from a lowly administrative assistant to a power player in a business dominated by men. The Hollywood production shares *Million Dollar Baby*'s racial and gender politics. Kallen's career begins when she tells a promoter that she believes she could salvage a washed-up former champion's (Tory Kittles) career. As a lark, the promoter sells Kallen the fighter's contract for a dollar. Kallen is quickly deflated to find her boxer destitute and hooked on crack. But she identifies a new opportunity when the drug dealer Luther Shaw (Omar Epps) comes to collect payment from her boxer and easily pummels him when he protests. Kallen convinces Shaw to begin boxing and turns him into a contender. The film suggests that the criminal and Black Shaw needs the guidance of the shrewd and White Kallen to channel his brutishness into a productive direction.

But Shaw becomes disillusioned at the charismatic manager's tendency to steal the spotlight and overshadow him—publicity that is a consequence of

Kallen's novelty as a rare woman in boxing. Meanwhile, Kallen had so irked fellow promoters—again, largely because of her outsider status—that they refused to give Shaw a title shot. She eventually decides Shaw's career will be best served if she steps aside and sells his contract. Although Kallen and Shaw reunite as the film climaxes—a reconciliation that unsurprisingly helps him finally win the title—*Against the Ropes'* plot resolves by humbling the disobedient woman until she dials down her outspokenness. Along with *Million Dollar Baby*, *Against the Ropes* suggests that there is room for women in mainstream Hollywood boxing films so long as they do not disturb too severely its traditional gender and racial hierarchies.

Mixed Martial Arts and the Boxing Film Boxing Film

MMA emerged as a niche spectator sport while boxing continued to sag in the 1990s. The budding sport was at once celebrated and condemned for its lawless reputation. Senator John McCain denounced it as "ugliness and rule-less brutality" and the bloody competitions were banned in most states.[10] Led by charismatic executive Dana White, the Ultimate Fighting Championship (UFC) formed in 1993. The organization instituted safety regulations and launched aggressive public relations efforts—some of which borrowed from prizefighting and boxing films—to change MMA's image without sacrificing its edginess.

Chief among the UFC's efforts was *Ultimate Fighter*, a competition-based reality TV program that launched in January 2005 on Spike TV—a cable channel whose macho demographic overlapped with the UFC's mostly young male fan base. *Ultimate Fighter* put sixteen MMA hopefuls in a house and had them compete in an elimination tournament to win a UFC contract. Beyond showing the matches, the program created dramatic narratives surrounding the competitors and their weekly bouts. "What appealed to us most was the character-driven aspect," said Spike TV executive Brian Diamond. "You were going to love these guys or hate them, but you were going to feel something." The reality program devoted more time to the human-interest stories it told—a fighter battling for redemption after facing obscurity, an athlete seeking to improve his family's financial circumstances, a loudmouth who could stand to get knocked down a peg or two—than to the matches they preceded and fueled. *Ultimate Fighter'*s narrative-driven approach broadened the UFC's audience and helped to save the fledgling organization from bankruptcy.[11] By 2006, the UFC's marquee events were regularly outperforming HBO's pay-per-view boxing packages. Emboldened by this success, Spike scheduled an *Ultimate Fighter* finale against HBO's broadcast of Ricky Hatton and Jose Luis Castillo's June 2007 welterweight title bout. One month before the fight, *Sports*

Illustrated featured a cover story on the UFC. *Ultimate Fighter* accelerated this legitimization by using the narratives upon which boxing films had been relying for decades to normalize the unfamiliar sport spectacle and, in so doing, to turn those narratives into competitive weapons to batter the very sport that had so successfully employed them in the past.

As UFC began to thrive, sports films started engaging MMA in ways that adapted boxing movies. Walter Hill's *Undisputed* (2002), his second boxing film after *Hard Times*, cribs from Mike Tyson's biography to tell the tale of championship boxer George "Iceman" Chambers (Ving Rhames). Iceman is convicted of rape and sentenced to Sweetwater Prison, a state-of-the-art facility that houses only the most hardened criminals. Sweetwater also has an underground boxing league and gambling ring. The prison's taciturn and cerebral champion, Monroe Hutchens (Wesley Snipes), is a former contender who was sentenced to life after killing someone with his bare hands, which the courts deemed deadly weapons. The pompous Iceman, who is eager to assert his status within Sweetwater, and the Zen-like Hutchens eventually fight. The prison champ beats the world's champ—although the film reveals that Iceman maintained that the underground bout never happened after he was released from Sweetwater and regained the title.

While *Undisputed* did not attract critical plaudits, it gained enough commercial success to prompt three direct-to-video sequels—without Hill, Rhames, and Snipes. The sequels shifted their focus to MMA. *Undisputed II: Last Man Standing* (Isaac Florentine, 2006) stars Michael Jai White as Iceman. The fighter is framed for possession of cocaine while in Russia and ends up in a violent prison that, like Sweetwater, houses a fighting ring. This penitentiary, however, specializes in MMA fighting and features the ruthless champion Boyka (Scott Adkins). The gangsters and corrupt warden (Valentin Ganev) who run the fights offer to release Iceman if he beats Boyka, who gamely agrees to accommodate his opponent by following boxing's rules. Boyka, however, quickly switches to MMA fighting when Iceman gains an early upper hand. The prison champ dominates and beats Iceman as soon as he changes styles.

Iceman demands a rematch and begins learning MMA while training. He adopts the new style in the rematch, beats Boyka, and secures his release. In no uncertain terms, *Undisputed II* depicts MMA as a superior form of fighting. While *Undisputed II* began with a boxer and transitioned to MMA, the direct-to-video franchise's subsequent installments—*Undisputed III: Redemption* (Isaac Florentine, 2010) and *Boyka: Undisputed* (Todor Chapkanov, 2016)—abandon boxing entirely in favor of MMA. The franchise's metamorphosis indicates that MMA is not simply superior to boxing, but also more marketable than the archaic sport.

David Mamet's 2008 thriller *Redbelt* centers on Mike Terry (Chiwetel Eji-ofor), a principled jiujitsu instructor who believes that competing for money cheapens the honorable sport to which he has devoted his ascetic life. Ironi-cally, Terry has married into a family of Brazilian jiujitsu fighters who are thrilled to cash in on MMA's growing audience. *Redbelt* depicts an MMA industry that is as crooked as the boxing business represented in *The Set-Up* and *Requiem for a Heavyweight*. For instance, after Terry refuses to compete in a professional tournament put on by an organization like the UFC, the shady promoters steal a game he uses to train students and make it the backdrop for a televised tournament, in which the bouts are all fixed to ensure additional fights and the profits they will deliver. An unfortunate and tightly wound series of circumstances forces Terry to compromise his values and compete in the tournament—which he manages to expose as a fraud and salvage his threat-ened integrity. As it tells Terry's heroic story, *Redbelt* repeatedly stresses MMA's ascendance and boxing's simultaneous decline. One reporter (Mike Goldberg) covering the tournament marvels that "the explosion of mixed martial arts is unbelievable," and another commentator—played by the real-life MMA fighter Randy Couture—declares boxing as "dead as Woodrow Wilson." "I've become fascinated by the art and science of jiujitsu and the death of boxing," Mamet explained while promoting the film. "Anybody who's observed it for several years knows that boxing is over and it's time to be replaced."[12] Mamet, an ardent student of jiujitsu himself, used *Redbelt* to comment on these shifts in sports culture and to suggest that MMA offers a more exciting filmic vehicle than boxing.

Gavin O'Connor's MMA melodrama *Warrior* (2011) tells the story of two estranged brothers who enter the same tournament to address their separate economic hardships. Brendan Conlon (Joel Edgerton) is a high school physics teacher facing potential foreclosure on his home after being overwhelmed with his daughter's hospital bills. His brother Tommy (Tom Hardy), a war veteran who deserted the military after his unit was slaughtered by friendly fire, wants to give the winnings to a platoon mate's widow. Both Brendan and Tommy are estranged from their father Paddy (Nick Nolte), a recently sober alcoholic who taught them how to fight but ruined their family with his vio-lent drunkenness. The brothers predictably wind up battling each other in the tournament's championship and achieve some reconciliation through the gru-eling competition. Although *Warrior* concerns MMA fighting, O'Connor admitted that he followed the boxing film template. "I guess I could have made a boxing movie," he says, "but this was enticing since we hadn't seen it in cin-ema."[13] O'Connor, like Mamet, viewed MMA as a more relevant and market-able backdrop for his sports film. Even *Joe Palooka* participated in the migration to MMA by rebooting in 2012 and transforming its eponymous boxer into an MMA fighter.

Productions that maintained a focus on boxing defended the sport against MMA's incursion. Mark Burnett's NBC reality program *The Contender* debuted two months after *Ultimate Fighter* to apply the successful formula he developed with *Survivor* and *The Apprentice* to boxing.[14] Like *Ultimate Fighter*, *The Contender* put aspiring boxers in a house and had them compete for a cash prize. Burnett suggested *The Contender*—which boasted the tagline "The next great human drama"—would offer stories and personalities engaging enough to revive the waning interest in boxing. "To be a star, you've got to be a great boxer, but you've also got to have charisma," he said. "What's wrong with boxing today? There are not enough great characters!"[15] *The Contender* nurtured this charisma by relying on the boxing film's dramatic tropes. The reality show's title references Terry Malloy's famous lines in *On the Waterfront*. More specifically, it evokes *Rocky* by giving previously unknown fighters a chance at glory—a connection it emphasized by hiring Stallone to cohost the first season alongside retired champion Sugar Ray Leonard. Stallone helped Burnett develop the program and align it with his classic boxing film. "Sly told me to go back and watch *Rocky* again, and this time, as a writer, watch it through the eyes of Adrian, which I did, and I understood immediately how *The Contender* should be made," Burnett explained. "The men are boxers by profession," Stallone added, "but the majority of their life obviously is lived outside the ring and that's what we come to know and understand and can identify with." *New York Times* sports media critic Richard Sandomir asserted that boxing might alleviate its struggles by adapting some of the *Rocky*-inspired practices *The Contender* implemented. But not even the *Rocky* connection could save Burnett's project, which NBC canceled after its underwhelming first season.[16]

Stallone began work on *Rocky Balboa* (2006)—which he wrote, directed, and starred in—as he was hosting *The Contender*. The franchise's sixth film, *Rocky Balboa* premiered almost exactly thirty years after *Rocky*. In a 1977 *Variety* interview, the young and cocksure Stallone asserted that he "would like to do Rocky at age 40, when I'm 40, at age 50, when I'm 50. Nobody has ever followed the same character like that."[17] He was sixty when he dusted off the boxer for *Rocky Balboa*. The film begins with HBO pay-per-view coverage of a heavyweight title match in which champion Mason "The Line" Dixon (Antonio Tarver) effortlessly beats another palooka in a long line of outclassed opponents. Bored by the lack of competition at boxing's apex, fans boo and heckle the victorious champion. "They seem to be blaming Dixon for the decline not only of the heavyweight division, but for the entire sport," HBO's Lampley comments. "All of boxing is hoping for a boxer who thrills us with his passion," adds Merchant. *Rocky Balboa*'s opening scene comments on prizefighting's lamentable tedium—the very situation that motivated Mamet and O'Connor to create MMA movies instead of boxing films—and hints that Balboa might resuscitate the sport.

142 • The Boxing Film

The film immediately cuts to inner-city Philadelphia along with the acapella song "Take You Back," which the first *Rocky* used to introduce Balboa's worn-down neighborhood. The retired fighter is living a subdued and lonesome life. He owns an Italian restaurant called Adrian's, named after his recently deceased wife, and struggles to nurture a relationship with his son (Milo Ventimiglia), who is intent on escaping his legendary father's colossal shadow. The film suggests that Balboa lives in the past to escape the pain he faces in the present—a situation its opening moments emphasize by packing in references to the first film. For instance, Balboa lets the down-and-out Spider Rico eat for free at his restaurant, grabs a beer at the Lucky 7 Tavern, and reconnects with Marie (Geraldine Hughes), a once-rambunctious neighborhood kid whom he tried to give advice to in the inaugural *Rocky*. Along these nostalgic lines, Balboa's eatery is a veritable museum to his career whose patrons come to hear the fighter recite tired old stories about battling Creed and training with Mickey. His first lines in the film, in fact, are "time goes by too fast" as he and Paulie somberly leave Adrian's gravesite and a mournful rendition of the Rocky theme plays. To honor his deceased wife, the aggrieved widow takes Paulie on a tour of landmarks from happier times that includes Mickey's gym, the pet shop where Adrian worked, and his old apartment—all of which have since been boarded up. Balboa is yet another relic whose best days have passed.

But Rocky's mundane and joyless life is jostled by an ESPN *SportsCenter* segment titled "Then vs. Now." Adapting and updating the *Super Fight*, "Then vs. Now" uses video-game-inspired graphics to stage a statistically driven imaginary bout between Balboa and Dixon. Like Marciano in the *Super Fight*, the retired Balboa knocks Dixon out in the thirteenth round. Invigorated by the special, Balboa decides he wants to begin fighting again and believes doing so will give his dreary life some purpose. He passes the requisite physical tests and convinces the Pennsylvania Athletic Commission—which was understandably concerned about his advanced age—to let him fight. Balboa intends to participate in low-profile and local matches. But Dixon's management views the provocative ESPN special and Balboa's return as opportunities to elicit some interest in their unpopular champ. They challenge Balboa to an exhibition. Much like Apollo Creed in *Rocky*, Dixon's team needs a gimmick to attract an audience. The promoters market the fight as "Skill vs. Will"—Balboa is once again the determined White fighter who battles against a more technically talented and heavily favored Black opponent.

The match is presented through HBO Sports coverage complete with the division's graphics and Lampley, Merchant, and Max Kellerman calling the fight. *Rocky Balboa* amplifies this realism by including the real-life ring announcer Michael Buffer and referee Joe Cortez and by shooting the bout at Las Vegas's MGM Grand Garden Arena during Bernard Hopkins and Jermain Taylor's actual July 2005 middleweight title fight, which HBO broadcast live on pay-per-view. Stallone claimed these efforts resulted in "the truest of all the fights [in the *Rocky* franchise] because at this point HBO had become the template for how boxing is watched." HBO opened its coverage with a short documentary segment that introduces Dixon through actual footage from Tarver's professional fights and presents Balboa with snippets from the *Rocky* series' earlier installments. Beyond simulating HBO Sports' broadcasting style and integrating actual figures from the world of boxing, the docudramatic scene ironically builds realism by using footage from Balboa's fictional past.

Balboa performs surprisingly well against Dixon, who underestimates his aging but fearless opponent. As with his first match against Creed, Rocky goes the distance but loses by a split decision. He is once again the moral victor and is again indifferent to the result's announcement, which the crowd's wild cheers for the courageous underdog nearly drown out. As Dixon's promoters wagered, Balboa's return gave boxing a needed lift. Lampley and Merchant's enthusiastic commentary on the Balboa-Dixon match contrasts their unimpressed response to the Dixon bout that opened the film—and the spectators' riotous applause for Balboa diverges from the taunts Dixon received after the introductory fight. *Rocky Balboa* implies that boxing requires a mythic character like Balboa to reawaken interest in the sport and furnish the "passion" Merchant complains is lacking.

Peter Segal's boxing comedy *Grudge Match* (2013) expands on *Rocky Balboa* by having Sylvester Stallone and Robert De Niro respectively play the aging Pittsburgh-based rivals Henry "Razor" Sharp and Bill "Kid" McDonnen. The film works through relying on viewers' familiarity with Stallone and De Niro's famous roles as Balboa and Jake LaMotta. Melding the Rocky Balboa and Terry Malloy archetypes, Sharp is a humble retired fighter who works in a shipyard. McDonnen, similar to LaMotta, is a short-fused and fast-talking playboy who owns a nightclub and car dealership. Sharp and McDonnen fought twice during their careers—with each winning one match. Intensifying their rivalry, Sharp's girlfriend Sally (Kim Basinger) had a brief affair with McDonnen that resulted in a son whom the pathologically irresponsible fighter never met.

Like *Rocky Balboa*, *Grudge Match* is set in motion by HBO Sports coverage that laments contemporary boxing's dullness. A documentary segment on Lampley's sports talk show *The Fight Game* reflects on Sharp and McDonnen's classic matches, which the host calls boxing's "fiercest rivalry." The nostalgic program argues that boxing has lost the vivacity it had when Sharp and McDonnen were facing off and speculates about how a third match between them might have turned out. The *Fight Game* segment uses footage from Stallone training for *Rocky* and De Niro preparing for *Raging Bull* to document the characters' earlier days.[18] Reflecting *Rocky Balboa*, *Grudge Match* integrates fictional content from the boxing film's history to help its docudramatic scenes make realistic claims about the sport's past.

144 • The Boxing Film

The HBO special prompts a video game manufacturer to hire Sharp and McDonnen to model in motion capture suits so its designers can create authentic avatars that—extending the hypothetical logic of the *Super Fight* and ESPN's "Then vs. Now" special in *Rocky Balboa*—would allow gamers to pit the long-retired rivals against each other. The old enemies quickly get into a brawl while wearing the comically skin-tight suits. A video of the scuffle goes viral and compels the ambitious promoter Dante Slate Jr. (Kevin Hart) to convince the boxers to fight one last time to settle their score and capitalize on their renewed popularity. Slate publicizes the match as "Grudgement Day," and the film spends much of the buildup to the bout combining jokes about the fighters' age with references to *Rocky* and *Raging Bull*. Sharp, for instance, guzzles eggs and performs a bunch of outdated training techniques like Balboa. At one point, his trainer Lightning Conlon (Alan Arkin) brings him to a meat locker. Sharp prepares to punch the meat until a befuddled Conlon stops him and explains they were just buying a steak for dinner. The gag works only if viewers are intimately familiar with *Rocky*—an assumption that is baked into *Grudge Match*'s premise.

Despite their mutual loathing, Sharp and McDonnen must team up for a series of publicity stunts to peddle Grudgement Day. In one instance they give an interview at a UFC event between its various matches. Their shared disdain for MMA is about the only point on which Sharp and McDonnen find common ground. When asked what they think about MMA, both fighters dismiss it as an unimportant fad. Sharp chides it as effeminate, and McDonnen compares it to professional wrestling. Their jabs prompt UFC fighter Chael Sonnen, who plays himself, to confront the boxers in defense of MMA's legitimacy. The argument escalates and Sonnen eventually slaps Sharp, who responds by punching the younger MMA fighter out. The scene makes an argument for boxing's grittiness in the face of MMA's ascendance. MMA might be more popular, but boxing—as Sharp's ability to floor Sonnen with a single punch suggests—harbors greater masculine toughness and authenticity. These qualities, however, are assigned not only to boxing's past but to its legacy on film.

As with *Rocky Balboa*, HBO covers *Grudge Match*'s final fight on pay-per-view. Although Sharp wins the decision, the rivals finally bury their decades-long enmity. Like *Rocky Balboa*, *Grudge Match* is a nostalgic sports film that expresses dissatisfaction with boxing's present and a longing for the past that Sharp and McDonnen represent. Again, the crowd Grudgement Day attracts and the HBO Sports announcers' laudatory response to the bout show that the return of Sharp and McDonnen infused boxing with the excitement it had been lacking and that MMA could not supply.

While *The Contender*, *Rocky Balboa*, and *Grudge Match* argue for boxing's legitimacy amid the cultural and economic challenges it faces, they do so through appealing to the boxing film's heritage. The genre, these productions suggest, composes a legacy that overshadows and is perhaps more enduring than the sport it depicts. They complement the films that reimagine boxing's past and expand its scope to demonstrate the sport's relevance in mainstream media culture. But they assign this relevance to the already invented mythology boxing films have established and popularized. These fictions are perhaps the best hope for boxing's reality as it struggles to maintain a place in a sports landscape that seems to have passed it by.

Conclusion

••••••••••••••••••••••

Handling the Rules

Boxing continued waning and MMA steadily grew as the twenty-first century wore on. Only intermittent blockbuster matches—distributed via pay-per-view broadcasts and featuring celebrity fighters like Floyd Mayweather Jr. and Manny Pacquiao—managed to attract interest beyond die-hard boxing fans. But the sustained production of boxing movies during this time gives the faulty impression that the increasingly fringe sport still stands at the center of U.S. popular culture. Antoine Fuqua's *Southpaw* (2015) and Ryan Coogler's *Creed* (2015) demonstrated signs of change and continuity in the boxing film. They were the first mainstream boxing films made by Black directors since Charles S. Dutton's *Against the Ropes* and Reginald Hudlin's *The Great White Hype*. But *Southpaw* and *Creed* handle the boxing film's generic characteristics and racial politics very differently.

Southpaw stars Jake Gyllenhaal as Billy "The Great" Hope—an aging White champion whose impoverished background, slurred speech, tendency to block punches with this face, and Whiteness all evoke Rocky Balboa. The film begins with HBO pay-per-view coverage of a Hope title defense from Madison Square Garden. The broadcasters provide much of the film's initial exposition by explaining that Hope grew up in a Hell's Kitchen orphanage, where he met his wife Maureen (Rachel McAdams). As Jim Lampley announces after Hope successfully defends his title, "From an orphanage in Hell's Kitchen to a professional fighting career in Madison Square Garden is a distance of only a few blocks and a million miles. It's a journey Billy Hope has made in his lifetime." Hope, Lampley explains, is the American Dream personified who rose from poverty to become a rich and famous champion with a beautiful family.

148 • The Boxing Film

Like most cinematic pugilists, Hope's macho toughness is premised upon his ability to deliver and endure punishment—qualities that transform his fights into gory but crowd-pleasing spectacles. His comparatively level-headed wife, however, worries that the abuse that accompanies her husband's lucrative job will leave Hope in physical and mental tatters. Maureen urges him to retire and warns that his friends and manager—the Don King–like Jordan Mains (Curtis "50 Cent" Jackson)—will "scatter like roaches" once he inevitably stops winning. "The more you get hit the harder you fight, I get it," Maureen says after Hope's initial victory leaves him oozing blood and barely able to walk. "But you're going to be punch drunk in two years if you keep this up." She wants Billy to be able to enjoy raising their daughter Leila (Oona Laurence). Hope seems persuaded by Maureen's plea when tragedy rips his family apart.

While leaving a charity event the easily riled Hope gets into a scuffle with Miguel "Magic" Escobar (Miguel Gomez), a contender who had been hectoring the champion to give him a title shot. During the melee one of Escobar's cronies accidentally discharges his firearm. The errant bullet strikes Maureen, who dies in her husband's arms. Her tragic passing leaves Hope in disarray. Beyond the emotional turmoil, the boxer has little sense of how to manage his finances or take care of their daughter—responsibilities his wife handled. Mains advises the champ to sign a new contract with HBO for a series of pay-per-view fights and take a match only eight weeks after he is widowed. Feigning concern for his distraught client, Mains suggests the bout will both improve Hope's finances and help him grieve. "When you're in the ring you're gonna feel different," the self-interested manager tells Hope.

The champion, however, has a self-destructive breakdown in the ring. At one point Hope lowers his hands and lets his opponent pummel him unimpeded. When Hope's befuddled trainer finally throws in the towel and the referee steps in to end the match, the boxer flattens the official with a headbutt. Hope loses the title and is suspended, which puts him in breach of his contract with HBO and extinguishes his sole source of income. As Maureen predicted, Hope's friends and business associates disperse immediately. The disturbed boxer continues spiraling downward and winds up crashing his car while intoxicated in what appears like a suicide attempt. He finally goes bankrupt and the state takes custody of Leila, who ends up in the same institutionalized setting in which Hope was raised. The struggling former champ can see his child only on supervised visits until he demonstrates financial stability and takes anger management courses. The melodrama punctuates Hope's despair in a scene where he visits Leila and helps with her spelling homework. The words she is learning—"dismantle" and "hopelessness"—gesture toward their family's dissolution.

Needless to say, Hope—who goes from a wealthy family man to a penniless loner—is ripe for a comeback. The down-and-out former champ seeks the guidance of Tick Wills (Forrest Whittaker), a temperamental Black trainer who owns a rundown urban gym. Not unlike Charley Davis's alliance with Ben Chaplin in *Body & Soul*, Hope pursues Tick because he knows the trainer has unusual integrity in the fight game. The monastic trainer initially refuses to coach Hope on the grounds that he does not believe the troubled fighter can "handle the rules" he demands of fighters, which include not drinking or swearing. Hope eventually convinces Tick he can abide by the trainer's strict protocols, which require changing both his fighting style and his boorish attitude. He further humbles himself by taking a part-time custodial job in the gym—a plot point that evokes Balboa's nadir in *Rocky II*—to satisfy the court's requirement that he demonstrate gainful employment.

Tick teaches Hope a more protective approach that will help the fighter absorb fewer punches. "I'm going to introduce you to something you never knew before," the trainer says unironically. "It's called defense." This new style requires Hope to control his signature rage and operate with patience and purpose. These rules eventually bleed over into the boxer's personal life. He initially had outbursts in the courtroom and was surly with the social worker (Naomie Harris) who coordinates his supervised parental visits. Once he accepts the court's orders, his relationship with Leila improves and he begins to convince the state that he can take care of her. Hope's life slowly begins falling back into place after he puts his trust in these rules and the authorities who administer them. He wins an exhibition match, regains his boxing license, and gets custody of Leila.

Hope is offered a fight against Escobar, who went on to win the title Hope once held, immediately after the boxing commission reinstates him. The opportunistic Mains, who abandoned Hope for Escobar, turns the match into a pay-per-view bonanza by promoting it as an occasion for Hope to avenge Maureen's murder. While Tick is skeptical of the shameless publicity, he eventually agrees to aid Hope, who desperately needs the money. The training sequences leading up to the match demonstrate Hope's newly disciplined style and his tenacious contrast to the ostentatious, self-absorbed, and wealthy Escobar. As in *Rocky*, Hope trains with old-school methods in dimly lit gyms while Escobar works out in bright and modern settings.

HBO Sports, following up on Mains's promotion, presents the fight as an epic revenge story. "In his heart," Lampley says when introducing Hope before the match, "he believes he is avenging the death of his wife in a bizarre incident in which Escobar was involved." Hope debuts his new and defensive approach, which surprises both the HBO commentators and Escobar. "I've never seen Billy Hope block a punch," remarks HBO's incredulous Roy Jones Jr. Beyond the changed style, Tick concocted a strategy for Hope to fight orthodox for most of the match and then surprise Escobar by switching to southpaw—a game plan that requires a degree of patience the notoriously impetuous boxer has never before exhibited. Hope almost ruins the plot after Escobar insults his dead wife. But he collects himself and successfully continues to follow the plan, eventually knocking Escobar down and winning the fight by a split decision to regain the title. "We still have Hope," says Jones, who cannot resist the wordplay, after the bout. Hope reunites with Leila, who was watching the match on TV backstage with the social worker—in another cinematic gesture toward the medium's ability to insulate women and children from the sport's brutality. "You guys take care of each other," Tick says as he leaves. The social worker departs immediately after. The authorities who imposed the rules that helped Hope to reorganize his shattered world finally leave him and Leila to resume their lives independently.

Complementing Hope's transformation into a disciplined and obedient fighter, *Southpaw* hews closely to the boxing film's generic norms. The film is derivative almost to the point of novelty. "With a few superficial details adjusted," wrote *Salon*'s Andrew O'Hehir, "*Southpaw*'s mythic tale of fall and redemption could be set in 1965 or 1935." The *Chicago Tribune* panned its "shameless clichés" and pointed out that the film was "made up of massive granite chunks of previous boxing movies."[1] Although critically maligned, *Southpaw* was a commercial hit. Its financial success suggests the predictable boxing film genre can, if nothing else, offer reliable economic returns if followed closely.

As part of its generic conformity, *Southpaw* also followed the boxing film's racial rules. Billy "The Great" Hope overtly references boxing's tradition of White Hopes. His status in the world of the film is clearly premised upon his profitable Whiteness, even though *Southpaw* never explicitly addresses Hope's racial identity aside from briefly showing a newspaper report on his downfall with the headline, "The Great White Dope." *ESPN The Magazine*'s Howard Bryant observes that Antoine Fuqua made a "black film that Hollywood seems to believe couldn't have a black lead." *Southpaw* missed an opportunity, Bryant contends, to create a film with a Black protagonist that actually reflects the sport's racial composition. "It's economics, really," Fuqua candidly explained of the film's predictable racial dynamics. "It comes down to what the people with the money think they can sell. The thinking is, 'Why take the risk when you can do it with formula?'"[2] *Southpaw* found itself in the same situation as *The Set-Up* nearly sixty years after Robert Wise's film was produced. As Billy Hope began following the rules to achieve success, *Southpaw* conforms to the boxing film's protocols, including its racial norms, to gather an audience. Ryan Coogler's *Creed*—released four months after *Southpaw*—issued some challenges to these firmly entrenched rubrics.

Creed rebooted the Rocky franchise with a Black director, writers, and star. Coogler describes the film as a "millennial generation hand-off" that updates the series.[3] Scripted by Coogler and Aaron Covington, it is the only Rocky movie Stallone did not have a hand in writing. Coogler, who grew up watching the Rocky films, developed an idea to reinvent the series through the lens of Apollo Creed's son, a character that did not appear in the earlier films. Coogler's road to directing *Creed* was not unlike Stallone's struggles to get *Rocky* made. Stallone initially rebuffed Coogler's pitches. But the independent filmmaker continued pestering Stallone and finally secured his consideration after directing *Fruitvale Station* (2013), a historical drama about police violence against African Americans that won the Sundance Film Festival's Grand Jury Prize. "I just dismissed Ryan's idea," Stallone later admitted, "and then I thought: 'You know, my story is told, but there's a whole other generation out there—two generations since *Rocky* started—and their story has not been told.'"[4] In particular, Coogler's reinvention courted a younger and less White audience—viewers like the director, who loved *Rocky* but could never fully identify with its main character.

Creed introduces Adonis "Donnie" Johnson (Michael B. Jordan)—the product of Apollo Creed's extramarital affair. Adonis was born after Ivan Drago (Dolph Lundgren) killed Apollo in the ring—the tragedy that sets *Rocky IV* into motion. Similar to Billy Hope, Donnie grew up in a combination of foster care and juvenile detention centers after his mother died. But Apollo Creed's widow Mary Anne (Phylicia Rashad) adopts Donnie and raises him in the Los Angeles mansion her deceased husband left behind. Donnie gravitates toward boxing despite his comfortable upbringing—a sport the film suggests both is in his blood and offers him a way to connect with the father he idolizes but never met. He insists on fighting as Donnie Johnson to build his own identity and resorts to underground matches in Tijuana when the trainers at Apollo's old gym refuse to coach him. Donnie eventually quits his cushy job in finance and moves to Philadelphia in hopes of training with Balboa, who is running his restaurant in relative seclusion. Adrian, Mickey, and Paulie have died, and the retired fight legend has not spoken to his son in years. Despite his loneliness, Rocky, like Apollo's old coaches, has no interest in coaching Donnie. But he is eventually worn down by a combination of the young fighter's persistence and his respect for Apollo.

Balboa leads Donnie to a surprising victory over a promising local fighter—a result that prompts boxing reporters to learn more about the mysterious boxer who attracted Rocky's guidance. They soon discover that he is Creed's son. The story catches the attention of those who manage the light heavyweight champion "Pretty" Ricky Conlan (Tony Bellew). Conlan is about to serve a prison sentence for gun possession and needs a quick payday before he is put away. The champ's manager believes that fighting Donnie—despite his lack of experience—would draw the kind of crowd Conlan needs to secure his family's financial future. Their one condition is that Donnie fight under the more bankable name of Creed. The headline-grabbing fight is not unlike the hype-fueled match Apollo Creed orchestrated against Balboa in 1976. Although suspicious of the bout's contrivances and the fact that Conlan's team is proposing the match only because they believe it will be a surefire win, Balboa supports Donnie's decision to take the fight.

Rocky is diagnosed with cancer during preparations for the Conlan bout. The old and lonesome boxer-turned-trainer initially refuses treatment—which did not work for Adrian before she perished from the same disease. Donnie, however, convinces him to receive chemotherapy. "If I fight, you fight," he tells his battle-worn coach. Inspiring each other to face their respective challenges, Rocky successfully undergoes cancer treatment and Donnie shockingly goes the distance against Conlan and loses the decision—the same result Rocky achieved in his first match against Apollo. And like the first Rocky fight, the match transforms Donnie from a curiosity into a viable boxer who deserves his famous name. "He is no longer the namesake of Apollo Creed," says HBO's Max Kellerman when summing up the fight. "He is the living embodiment of him."

Creed became the *Rocky* franchise's most critically lauded installment since its Academy Award–winning debut. Many of the plaudits called attention to its writing and direction. In particular, Coogler and cinematographer Maryse Alberti filmed Donnie's first fight under Balboa's tutelage with a single shot—a "oner" in industry jargon—that covered the entire two-round match by rotating around and weaving between the action to show either boxer's perspective and to convey professional prizefighting's rapid pace. The film also introduces the many boxers it features with graphics that offer their key statistics—a technique it borrows from TV coverage and video games. These practices breathed aesthetic life into a stale genre.

Creed also injected new cultural life into the boxing film. "If you're black," critic Ta-Nehisi Coates said of *Creed*, "it's your *Rocky*"—a point the *Philadelphia Inquirer* reiterated by calling it the "blackest *Rocky* yet."[5] The film

FIG. 7 Ryan Coogler's *Creed* (2015) borrows graphic practices from television and video games to introduce boxers. (Screengrab by author)

Conclusion • 153

showcases a Black version of Philadelphia that its predecessors largely ignored in favor of stressing the White ethnic community Rocky represents. When Donnie reprises Balboa's iconic runs through Philly, he is surrounded by a group of Black motorcyclists popping wheelies as a hip-hop-infused adaptation of Bill Conti's theme song plays. Along these lines, *Creed* features a hip-hop soundtrack that includes songs by Philadelphia artists the Roots and Meek Mill, and Donnie's love interest Bianca (Tessa Thompson) is a musician who works in the fertile cultural scene out of which these acts emerged. *Creed* combines its integration of Black culture into the *Rocky* universe with updated gender politics. Bianca, a motivated artist just as driven as Donnie, has no interest in putting aside her professional goals in the service of his boxing career. The "I never asked you to stop being a woman, don't ask me to stop being a man" logic guiding Balboa's relationship with Adrian does not apply to Donnie and Bianca's partnership. To wit, Bianca watches his fights at ringside rather than from the shielded remove TV broadcasts offer.

Creed's skillful and diverse update of *Rocky* garnered Coogler awards from the NAACP and the African American Film Critics Association. But Stallone received most of the mainstream notoriety for his reinvention of Balboa into an avuncular (Donnie affectionately calls him "Unc") and vulnerable supporting character. He received the Golden Globe for Best Supporting Actor and was nominated for an Academy Award in the same category—the only nominations *Creed* attracted from these popular sites of cultural legitimization. While *Creed* shook up the boxing movie's norms, critical reception of the film channeled it back into the genre's traditional conventions by focusing on Stallone's satisfyingly nostalgic portrayal of Balboa. *Creed* may not have entirely followed the rules, but the mainstream praise it attracted made apparent which of its characteristics were most welcome.

Creed's success—which overshadowed *Southpaw* both critically and commercially—made a sequel imminent. But Coogler dropped out for *Creed 2* to direct *Black Panther* (2018)—a landmark in mainstream Black cinema that broadened the superhero film's historically restrictive racial norms. He was replaced by Steven Caple Jr., another African American director with roots in independent film. Stallone returned as a screenwriter, collaborating with Juel Taylor to continue the story Coogler developed. Perhaps reflecting this change in writing duties, *Creed 2* is as much a return to the *Rocky* tradition as a continuation of *Creed*.

Specifically, *Creed 2* builds on *Rocky IV*, in which Rocky avenges Apollo Creed's death by beating Ivan Drago in Moscow as the Cold War raged. The sequel opens with Donnie winning the championship. "This is the first step toward making a legacy of his own," Max Kellerman says when summing up the victory for HBO's coverage. "And I can't hardly wait to see what's next for Adonis Creed." Donnie becomes engaged to Bianca after the fight and settles

154 • The Boxing Film

into adulthood and life as champ. Behind the scenes, the promoter Buddy Marcele (Russell Hornsby) is scheming to have Donnie fight Drago's son Viktor (Florian Munteanu)—a match he knows will attract massive public interest given their fathers' fateful encounter thirty years prior. The fight, Marcele says, will provide "a narrative—something that will stick to the ribs." Adding to the drama, the Dragos have been living in obscurity since Ivan's loss to Balboa, which transformed him from a symbol of national might into a shameful outcast. Ivan has been training Viktor, who is similarly robotic and also seemingly invincible, with hopes of redeeming himself through his son.

Under Marcele's direction, Viktor Drago holds a press conference in Philadelphia to challenge Donnie, who learns of the proposition through an ESPN report on it. Donnie wants to take the fight—an opportunity to both defend his title and honor his father's memory. But Balboa, who was in Apollo's corner for his final match and still harbors guilt about his death, is hesitant to train him. Balboa's reluctance is compounded by the fact that Bianca is pregnant. Were Donnie to die fighting Viktor Drago he would repeat his family's tragic history and leave his own child to grow up fatherless. Despite Balboa's refusal to participate, Donnie insists on fighting Drago. He seeks training from his father's old gym in Los Angeles—the same facility that refused to coach him when he was getting started. The lead-up to the match is littered with references from *Rocky IV*. Ivan Drago applies his most memorable lines from the earlier film—"I must break you"—by repeatedly directing his son to "break" Donnie, and clips from *Rocky IV* offer historical context for the upcoming fight and its stakes. "It all feels so Shakespearean," Jim Lampley says when introducing the bout for HBO's pay-per-view broadcast. "Two sons raised worlds apart, inexorably linked by tragedy." Echoing but not replicating Apollo Creed and Ivan Drago's match, Donnie takes a horrific beating. He survives the manhandling but ends up hospitalized and retains the title only because the brutal Viktor hit him after the bell. Donnie is still champ; but the fight leaves no doubt that Viktor is the superior fighter.

Donnie slowly recovers from the humiliation and acclimates to fatherhood while pondering how, if at all, he will continue his career. He struggles with this decision for so long that he nearly forfeits his title due to inactivity. After some soul searching, and despite the risks, Donnie decides that he must again fight Drago. He secures Balboa's aid, who determines that Donnie is competing for the right reasons and guides him through a punishing training regime in the desert. Although Donnie is still technically champion, he is a twenty-five-to-one underdog coming into the fight, which, like Rocky's match against Drago, is staged in an unfriendly Moscow arena. "It is impossible to forget what happened to [Creed] last time," Lampley says to underscore Donnie's long shot status as the rematch begins. But in true Rocky fashion, Donnie struggles through the early rounds and musters a late comeback. In fact, it seems that

Conclusion • 155

he might kill Viktor, who is beaten into defenselessness but unwilling to go down, until Ivan Drago throws in the towel to save his son in an unexpected display of humanity.

After the match, Balboa embraces Donnie and tells him to enjoy the moment. "It's your time," he says, as Donnie proceeds to celebrate in the ring and Balboa calmly takes a seat outside of it and away from the euphoric frenzy. The film transitions from a triumphant battle score to a wistful soundtrack and cuts to a shot of Balboa's back that slowly pans out as the boxing legend, wearing a sweater with "Creed" spelled across the shoulders, watches his fighter bask in victory. The shot indicates that Balboa is content to fade into the background as his protégé establishes his own legacy that is now on par with those of his legendary father and mentor. The film ends by cross-cutting between Donnie's visit to Apollo Creed's gravesite with his new family and Rocky reconnecting with his estranged son. Donnie and Rocky both reunite their ruptured families and presumably move toward more harmonious and loving futures. The melodramatic and reconciliatory ending moves Balboa back into the foreground as the film's main point of identification. It offers a reminder that Rocky's story remains paramount and the cultural rules of the boxing movie stay more or less in place.

Creed and *Creed 2* did participate in broadening the boxing film's representational norms. They joined productions like *The Fits* (Anna Rose Holmer, 2015), *Blue: The American Dream* (Ryan Miningham, 2016), and the Roberto Durán biopic *Hands of Stone* (Jonathan Jakubowicz, 2016), which also featured non-White protagonists. But the stream of boxing movies centered on White fighters continued as consistently as ever with productions like *The Challenger* (Kent Moran, 2015), *Back in the Day* (Paul Borghese, 2016), *Bleed for This* (Ben Younger, 2016), *The Bronx Bull* (Martin Guigui, 2016), *12 Round Gun* (Sam Upton, 2017), and *Jawbone* (Thomas Q. Napper, 2017). Perhaps informed by the success of *Creed* and *Creed 2*, the Rocky Balboa narrative in particular continued to resonate. The premium cable channel Epix, for instance, rebooted *The Contender* in 2018. Epix banked on the reality program's potential success despite its earlier failures because, as the media outlet's president Michael Wright explained, "every episode is a little *Rocky* episode."[6] Further engaging the *Rocky* universe, *Chuck* (Philippe Falardeau, 2016) and *The Brawler* (Ken Kushner, 2019) dramatized Chuck Wepner's story as the gutsy inspiration for Stallone's boxing film franchise.

Aside from capitalizing on *Creed*, the spiking interest in *Rocky* coincided with the ascendance of Trump-style conservatism, which reflects the reactionary politics that drove *Rocky*'s popularity and iconic status. In particular, Trumpism often laments the alleged softening and disenfranchisement of White American men as the United States grows more diverse. Reflecting the moment when *Rocky* debuted, this political movement condemns government

156 • The Boxing Film

intervention in favor of praising self-reliant individuals who will restore order to these imperiled traditions, or, to use the political movement's rallying cry, "Make America Great Again." Who better exemplifies this motto than a White, hard-nosed, and patriotic boxer who rises to the top of his sport during a time when it is becoming ever Blacker and browner?

Trump and his political comrades demonstrate a special attachment to *Rocky*. At a September 2016 campaign stop in the Philadelphia suburb of Chester Township, Conti's *Rocky* theme blasted through the public address system as Trump took the stage. The soundtrack both pandered to Philadelphia cultural traditions and emphasized the presidential candidate's persona as a tough underdog who typifies and seeks to rebuild an American Dream that many of his supporters fear is in jeopardy. The following year, the Republican-led House of Representatives collectively listened to the same anthem to get energized before voting to pass a bill to replace the Affordable Care Act—one of Trump's key campaign promises.

During his second year in office, Trump issued a posthumous pardon to Jack Johnson for his 1913 conviction under the Mann Act. Senator John McCain, a boxing fan and Trump adversary, unsuccessfully lobbied presidents George W. Bush and Barack Obama to pardon Johnson. Trump was finally persuaded— by Sylvester Stallone. The movie star, whose brief work on *The Contender* was modeled in part after Trump's role on *The Apprentice*, contacted the president and told him about the racist injustice Johnson suffered. The White House staged a ceremony with Stallone, several former champions, and Johnson's great-great niece in attendance. "It's incredible that you've done this," said the thankful Stallone. "It's an honor to take a fictional character like Rocky and do something in the world of reality."[7] Trump was motivated by the actor who played Rocky Balboa to exonerate a dissident African American athlete whose rebelliousness gave rise to the reactionary tradition of White Hopes that Rocky embodies.

The Johnson pardon also occurred while Trump was receiving widespread backlash for his admonishment of Black athletes—whom he called "sons of bitches" at one rally—protesting against racism and police brutality by kneeling during the national anthem. Critics suggested Trump's condemnations were bigoted efforts to keep these noncompliant Black Americans in line. Ironically, the protesting athletes continue a heritage of sporting insurgence that can be traced directly back to Jack Johnson—whose defiance was not overtly political but certainly gave no truck to White authorities who attempted to dictate his actions. The pardon allowed Trump to deflect charges that he is racist with a low-stakes and symbolic move that did not require him to alter any of his political positions. As *The Undefeated*'s Jesse Washington points out, Trump pardoned Johnson while his administration was "reviving policies on criminal charges that disastrously and disproportionately packed American prisons with blacks and Latinos."[8] Similar to *Creed* and *Creed 2*, the pardon at once gestures toward racial equality and works to sustain the nostalgic brand of institutionalized Whiteness that Trump and *Rocky* represent.

As boxing's popularity diminishes, the sport increasingly relies on a blockbuster model imported from cinema that banks on irregularly scheduled big fights featuring the small handful of stars who can convince casual fans to purchase a pay-per-view feed. These big fights, as HBO's *24/7* demonstrates, need the help of compelling narratives that will, to borrow Buddy Marcele's phrase, "stick to the ribs." In 2017, the undefeated Floyd Mayweather—boxing's biggest name at the time—came out of retirement to box Conor McGregor, who made his name in MMA. McGregor had never boxed professionally, but he is famous, media savvy, and White. The promoters correctly wagered that many would pay $99.95 to see whether McGregor could finally take out the similarly cocky, and Black, Mayweather. The *New York Times* dismissed the match as "a farce," a cynical money-making ploy with little sporting merit.[9] Mayweather and McGregor, as much promotional partners as athletic adversaries, went on a four-city publicity tour to hype the bout. The fighters traded semiscripted taunts throughout the tour—many of which played on the racial tensions informing the match. At one point, McGregor commanded Mayweather to "Dance for me, boy!" The fight was powered by the same White Hope narrative that had coursed through boxing since the late 1900s. And the durable strategy worked remarkably well. The match attracted so much interest that promoters decided to release it both via Showtime's pay-per-view service and through live closed-circuit broadcasts in 534 North American theaters. "The buzz that my fight against Conor McGregor is getting has been great," Mayweather said during the publicity blitz, "so what better way to watch this larger-than-life event than on the big screen?"[10] The bout became one of the most watched fights ever and earned Mayweather $275 million—the largest single payday an athlete has ever received. McGregor gathered a reported $85 million. Driven by racial animosity, the Mayweather-McGregor match was such a monumental spectacle that it warranted cinematic exhibition on par with film blockbusters.

While Showtime provided the pay-per-view feed for Mayweather and McGregor's big fight, HBO maintained its grip on boxing movies. The media outlet figured prominently in *Southpaw*, *Creed*, and *Creed 2*, all of which included scenes from the perspective of its boxing coverage. But HBO suspended its investment in prizefighting—and the authoritative status in the sport that its film brand placements advertise—in November 2018, the same month that *Creed 2* premiered. "We've seen audience research that indicates boxing is no longer a determining factor for our subscribers," explained HBO Sports executive vice president Peter Nelson.[11] Live boxing helped to establish the infrastructure from which HBO built its prestigious brand. But the prizefights outlived their utility to the media outlet now primarily known for its original series.

As HBO separated from live boxing, emergent live and on-demand streaming services used the sport to establish themselves. The U.K.-based company DAZN, a streaming service known as the "Netflix of Sport," paired its 2018 expansion into the United States with a commitment to boxing. It signed Canelo Álvarez to an eleven-fight, $365 million deal—the biggest sports contract an individual athlete had ever received at the time—and inked a billion-dollar agreement with the promotions company Matchroom boxing. DAZN moved away from the blockbuster pay-per-view model that HBO and Showtime popularized in favor of a monthly subscription format that it claims better serves fans by offering more consistent and less expensive content. ESPN followed suit with ESPN+, a premium live-streaming add-on for subscribers that launched in 2018. Like DAZN, ESPN+ made boxing one of its featured properties while getting off the ground.

Unlike most other major sporting events, boxing matches can be secured on an à la carte basis that does not require lengthy contracts with sports leagues. Prizefighting, then, is one of the only popular sports that can accommodate new entrants in the sports media market. Echoing boxing's role in film, radio, and network and cable TV, DAZN and ESPN+ show prizefighting participating in the foundation of yet another new phase in sports media. But beyond the technological and economic convenience driving boxing's alliance with emergent media since the late nineteenth century, the sport offers the basis for these commercial media to deliver dramatic tales that will gather a reliable audience—purehearted underdogs overcoming the odds, seedy scenes where corrupt gangsters and idealistic sportsmen face off, White men triumphing in worlds that no longer seem set up to guarantee their success. These sturdy stories are built, sustained, and sometimes even challenged and reinvented through boxing films.

Filmography

The Boxing Cats (1894), William K. L. Dickson and William Heise
Corbett and Courtney Before a Kinetograph (1894), William Kennedy Dickson and William Heise
Leonard-Cushing Fight (1894), William K. L. Dickson
Corbett-Fitzsimmons Fight (1897), Enoch J. Rector
The Gordon Sisters Boxing (1901), Thomas Edison
Johnson-Jeffries Fight (1910), J. Stuart Blackton
The Knockout (1914), Charles Avery
The Champion (1915), Charlie Chaplin
The Challenge of Chance (1919), Harry Revier
The Egg Crate Wallop (1919), Jerome Storm
The Best Mouse Loses (1920), Vernon Stallings
The Brute (1920), Oscar Micheaux
Daredevil Jack (1920), W. S. Van Dyke
As the World Rolls In (1921), W. A. Andlauer
Black Thunderbolt (1921), A. A. Millman
For His Mother's Sake (1922), Blackburn Velde Productions
Fight and Win (1924), Erle C. Kenton
The Great White Way (1924), E. Mason Hopper
Manhattan Madness (1925), Allan Dwan
Battling Butler (1926), Buster Keaton
The Fighting Marine (1926), Spencer Gordon Bennet
Battle of the Century (1927), Clyde Bruckman
Tunney-Dempsey Fight (1927), Goodart Pictures
Night Parade (1929), Malcolm St. Clair
The Young Man of Manhattan (1930), Monta Bell
The Champ (1931), King Vidor
Iron Man (1931), Tod Browning
They Never Come Back (1932), Fred C. Newmeyer
Winner Take All (1932), Roy Del Ruth
The Big Chance (1933), Albert Herman

160 • Filmography

The Life of Jimmy Dolan (1933), Archie Mayo
The Prizefighter and the Lady (1933), W. S. Van Dyke
The Blonde Bomber (1936), Lloyd French
Cain and Mabel (1936), Lloyd Bacon
Kid Galahad (1937), Michael Curtiz
The Crowd Roars (1938), Richard Thorpe
The Kid Comes Back (1938), B. Reeves Eason
Spirit of Youth (1938), Harry L. Fraser
Golden Boy (1939), Rouben Mamoulian
Keep Punching (1939), John Clein
They Made Me a Criminal (1939), Busby Berkeley
The Brown Bomber (1940), Torch Films
City for Conquest (1940), Anatole Litvak
The Notorious Elinor Lee (1940), Oscar Micheaux
The Great American Broadcast (1941), Archie Mayo
The Pittsburgh Kid (1941), Jack Townley
Gentleman Jim (1942), Raoul Walsh
This Is the Army (1943), Michael Curtiz
The Negro Soldier (1944), Stuart Heisler
The Great John L. (1945), Frank Tuttle
Joe Palooka, Champ (1946), Reginald Le Borg
Body and Soul (1947), Robert Rossen
The Fight Never Ends (1948), Joseph Lerner
Champion (1949), Mark Robson
The Set-Up (1949), Robert Wise
Right Cross (1950), John Sturges
The Ring (1952), Kurt Neumann
The Joe Louis Story (1953), Robert Gordon
On the Waterfront (1954), Elia Kazan
The Battler (1955), Arthur Penn
The Harder They Fall (1956), Mark Robson
The Leather Saint (1956), Alvin Ganzer
Requiem for a Heavyweight (1956), Ralph Nelson
Somebody Up There Likes Me (1956), Robert Wise
World in My Corner (1956), Jesse Hibbs
Kid Galahad (1962), Phil Karlson
Requiem for a Heavyweight (1962), Ralph Nelson
Legendary Champions (1968), Harry Chapin
A.K.A. Cassius Clay (1970), Jim Jacobs
The Great White Hope (1970), Martin Ritt
Jack Johnson (1970), Jim Jacobs
The Super Fight (1970), Murray Woroner
Fat City (1972), John Huston
Hammer (1972), Bruce Clark
The All-American Boy (1973), Charles K. Eastman
Ali, the Fighter (1974), William Greaves
Muhammad Ali: The Greatest (1974), William Klein
Hard Times (1975), Walter Hill
Mandingo (1975), Richard Fleischer

Filmography • 161

Drum (1976), Steve Carver
Rocky (1976), John Avildsen
Bare Knuckles (1977), Don Edmonds
The Greatest (1977), Tom Gries and Monte Hellman
Every Which Way but Loose (1978), James Fargo
Matilda (1978), Daniel Mann
Movie Movie (1978), Stanley Donen
The Champ (1979), Franco Zeffirelli
Goldie and the Boxer (1979), David Miller
The Main Event (1979), Howard Zieff
Penitentiary (1979), Jamaa Fanaka
The Prize Fighter (1979), Michael Preece
Rocky II (1979), Sylvester Stallone
Raging Bull (1980), Martin Scorsese
Body and Soul (1981), George Bowers
Penitentiary II (1982), Jamaa Fanaka
Rocky III (1982), Sylvester Stallone
Dempsey (1983), Gus Trikonis
Tough Enough (1983), Richard Fleischer
Terrible Joe Moran (1984), Joseph Sargent
Rocky IV (1985), Sylvester Stallone
Last Man Standing (1987), Damian Lee
Penitentiary III (1987), Jamaa Fanaka
Homeboy (1988), Michael Seresin
The Opponent (1988), Sergio Martino
Split Decisions (1988), David Drury
Thunderground (1989), David Mitchell
The Big Man (1990), David Leland
Rocky V (1990), John Avildsen
Diggstown (1992), Michael Ritchie
Gladiator (1992), Rowdy Herrington
Sonny Liston: The Mysterious Life and Death of a Champion (1995), HBO Sports
Tyson (1995), Uli Edel
The Great White Hype (1996), Reginald Hudlin
When We Were Kings (1996), Leon Gast
Don King: Only in America (1997), John Herzfeld
Sugar Ray Robinson: The Bright Lights and Dark Shadows of a Champion (1998),
     HBO Sports
Hurricane (1999), Norman Jewison
Marciano (1999), Charles Winkler
Play It to the Bone (1999), Ron Shelton
Ali: An American Hero (2000), Leon Ichaso
Ali-Frazier I: One Nation . . . Divisible (2000), HBO Sports
Girlfight (2000), Karyn Kusama
King of the World (2000), John Sacret Young
Knockout (2000), Lorenzo Doumani
The Opponent (2000), Eugene Jarecki
Ali (2001), Michael Mann
Joe and Max (2002), Steve James

162 • Filmography

Undisputed (2002), Walter Hill
Against the Ropes (2004), Charles S. Dutton
Million Dollar Baby (2004), Clint Eastwood
Unforgivable Blackness: The Rise and Fall of Jack Johnson (2005), Ken Burns
Rocky Balboa (2006), Sylvester Stallone
Undisputed II: Last Man Standing (2006), Isaac Florentine
Resurrecting the Champ (2007), Rod Lurie
Redbelt (2008), David Mamet
The Fighter (2010), David O. Russell
Undisputed III: Redemption (2010), Isaac Florentine
Warrior (2011), Gavin O'Connor
Grudge Match (2013), Peter Segal
The Challenger (2015), Kent Moran
Creed (2015), Ryan Coogler
The Fits (2015), Anna Rose Holmer
Southpaw (2015), Antoine Fuqua
Back in the Day (2016), Paul Borghese
Bleed for This (2016), Ben Younger
Blue: The American Dream (2016), Ryan Miningham
Boyka: Undisputed (2016), Todor Chapkanov
The Bronx Bull (2016), Martin Guigui
Chuck (2016), Philippe Falardeau
Hands of Stone (2016), Jonathan Jakubowicz
12 Round Gun (2017), Sam Upton
Jawbone (2017), Thomas Q. Napper
Creed 2 (2018), Steven Caple Jr.
The Brawler (2019), Ken Kushner

Acknowledgments

First of all, I would like to thank Aaron Baker and Les Friedman for the opportunity to be part of this exciting book series. Aaron and Les also provided immensely helpful guidance, feedback, and encouragement along the way. Leslie Mitchner and Nicole Solano generously fielded my questions and shepherded the book through the early stages. Thanks to the rest of the good folks at Rutgers University Press for assisting in the book's production.

University of Iowa graduate student Aja Witt briefly served as my research assistant and helped me to secure a variety of source material. The Indiana Black Film Archive granted me access to a copy of Oscar Micheaux's *Notorious Elinor Lee*—a rare film that will remain a part of scholarly discourse because of the important work the Black Film Archive performs. My University of Iowa colleague Corey Creekmur educated me on the alleged censorship of Classical Hollywood musicals. I also received helpful feedback from audiences at the University of Amsterdam, University of California, Santa Cruz, Northwestern University, the Society for Cinema and Media Studies, and the North American Society of Sport History. An early version of chapter 4 was published in *Film History* and benefitted from Julie Lavelle and Greg Waller's feedback. An earlier version of chapter 6 appears in *Sporting Realities: Critical Readings of the Sports Documentary* and was aided by comments from the anthology's anonymous readers.

I had the benefit of a University of Iowa Career Development Award while writing this book that helped move things along. I also have the great benefit of being around a bunch of eminently decent colleagues, staff, and students at UI who help to make my working life a mostly pleasant one.

Notes

Introduction

The Bert Sugar quotation is from Mark Emmons, "Sports Might Be on the Ropes, but Boxing Plays Well on Screen," Knight Ridder Tribune News Services, June 13, 2005, 1.

1   Ian Christie and David Thompson, eds., *Scorsese on Scorsese* (New York: Farrar, Straus & Giroux, 2004), 77; Red Smith, "Rocky Fights It Over," *New York Times*, June 13, 1979, D21.
2   Leger Grindon, *Knockout: The Boxer and Boxing in American Cinema* (Oxford: University of Mississippi Press, 2011), 3.
3   See Francesca Borrione, "Rocky Balboa in the Boxing Hall of Fame: When Fiction Becomes Reality," *Celebrity Studies* 3, no. 3 (2012): 340–342.
4   Joyce Carol Oates, *On Boxing* (Garden City, NY: Dolphin/Doubleday, 1987), 72.
5   Norman Mailer, *King of the Hill: Norman Mailer on the Fight of the Century* (New York: Signet, 1971), 29.
6   Aaron Baker, *Contesting Identities: Sports in American Film* (Urbana: University of Illinois Press, 2003); Seán Crosson, *Sport and Film* (London: Routledge, 2013); Lester D. Friedman, *Sports Movies* (New Brunswick, NJ: Rutgers University Press, 2020); Tony Williams, "'I Could Have Been a Contender': The Boxing Movie's Generic Instability," *Quarterly Review of Film and Video* 18, no. 3 (2009): 305–319; Dan Streible, *Fight Pictures: A History of Boxing and Early Cinema* (Berkeley: University of California Press, 2008).
7   Streible, *Fight Pictures*, 287.

Chapter 1   The Boxing Film through the Golden Age of Sports Media

1   Terry Ramsaye, *A Million and One Nights: A History of the Motion Picture through 1925* (London: Frank Cass, 1926), 116.
2   Dan Streible, *Fight Pictures: A History of Boxing and Early Cinema* (Berkeley: University of California Press, 2008), 2. Raymond Fielding observes that prizefighting was among the most common subjects represented in newsreels, which overlapped significantly with nonfiction fight films. See Fielding, *The*

166 • Notes to Pages 9–16

American Newsreel: A Complete History, 1911–1967, 2nd ed. (Jefferson, NC: McFarland, 2006), 12; Luke McKernan, "Sport and the First Films," in *Cinema: The Beginnings and the Future*, ed. Christopher Williams (London: British Film Institute, 1996), 107–116, 107.

3 Streible, *Fight Pictures*, 18.

4 "The Kinetograph," *New York Sun*, May 28, 1891, 1–2.

5 Randall E. Stross, *The Wizard of Menlo Park: How Thomas Alva Edison Invented the Modern World* (New York: Broadway Books, 2008), 202; Charles Musser, *The Emergence of Cinema: The American Screen to 1907* (Berkeley: University of California Press, 1994), 82–83.

6 Matthew Josephson, *Edison: A Biography* (New York: McGraw-Hill, 1959), 395.

7 Tom Gunning, "The Cinema of Attractions: Early Film, Its Spectator and the Avant Garde," *Wide Angle* 8, no. 3 (Fall 1986): 63–70.

8 Ramsaye, *Million and One Nights*, 109–110; Kasia Boddy, *Boxing: A Cultural History* (London: Reaktion Books, 2008), 152.

9 Fielding, *American Newsreel*, 10; Streible, *Fight Pictures*, 35.

10 Musser, *Emergence of Cinema*, 200–203.

11 Streible, *Fight Pictures*, 18; Boddy, *Boxing*, 152; Musser, *Emergence of Cinema*, 195.

12 Ramsaye, *Million and One Nights*, 282, Streible, *Fight Pictures*, 73.

13 "The Record by the Veriscope of the Corbett-Fitzsimmons Fight," *New York World*, May 22, 1897, 3–4.

14 Musser, *Emergence of Cinema*, 208.

15 "The Veriscope," *New York Times*, May 26, 1897, 6.

16 Ramsaye, *Million and One Nights*, 195; Musser, *Emergence of Cinema*, 200; Boddy, *Boxing*, 154.

17 Streible, *Fight Pictures*, 193.

18 Al-Tony Gilmore, *Bad Nigger! The National Impact of Jack Johnson* (Port Washington, NY: Kennikat Press, 1975), 9.

19 "Champion Jeffries Sees No Logical Opponent," *National Police Gazette*, October 8, 1904, 10.

20 Geoffrey Ward, *Unforgivable Blackness: The Rise and Fall of Jack Johnson* (New York: Vintage, 2004), 118.

21 "Johnson Has Would-Be Champions on the Run," *National Police Gazette*, December 8, 1906, 10; Streible, *Fight Pictures*, 202; Ward, *Unforgivable Blackness*, 127.

22 Jack London, "Jack London Describes the Fight and Jack Johnson's Golden Smile," *New York Herald*, December 27, 1908, 1.

23 "Three Judges for Boxing Matches," *New York Times*, June 15, 1913, S4.

24 "Johnson-Burns Prizefight Here," *New York Times*, April 13, 1909, 11.

25 Streible, *Fight Pictures*, 195.

26 Jeffrey T. Sammons, *Beyond the Ring: The Role of Boxing in American Society* (Urbana: University of Illinois Press, 1988), 37; David Remnick, *King of the World: Muhammad Ali and the Rise of an American Hero* (New York: Vintage, 1998), 222.

27 Rex E. Beach, "Reno Now Center of the Universe," *Chicago Tribune*, July 2, 1910, 1; Streible, *Fight Pictures*, 220; Eileen Bowser, *The Transformation of American Cinema, 1907–1915* (New York: Charles Scribner's Sons, 1990), 202.

28 *Moving Picture World*, July 9, 1910, 80–81.

29 Gilmore, *Bad Nigger!*, 61; Tim Brooks, *Lost Sounds: Blacks and the Birth of the Recording Industry* (Urbana: University of Illinois Press, 2005), 241; "Sad Crowd at Ringside," *New York Times*, July 5, 1910, 2.

Notes to Pages 16–23 • 167

30 "Fight Pictures Prohibited Here by Mayor," *San Francisco Examiner*, July 5, 1910, 1; Theodore Roosevelt, "The Recent Prize Fight," *Outlook*, July 16, 1910, 550.

31 "'Man about Town' on the Jeffries-Johnson Fight," *Moving Picture World*, July 16, 1910, 190; Travis Vogan, "Irrational Power: Jack Johnson, Prizefighting Films, and Documentary Affect," *Journal of Sport History* 37, no. 3 (Fall 2010): 397–413.

32 U.S. Congress, House of Representatives, Seaborn A. Roddenbery (Georgia), "Transportation of Prize-Fight Pictures," *Congressional Record* 48, pt. 9 (July 19, 1912): 9305.

33 Streible, *Fight Pictures*, 262–263; Ramsaye, *Million and One Nights*, 695. See also Lee Grieveson, "Fighting Films: Race, Morality, and the Governing of Cinema, 1912–1915," *Cinema Journal* 38, no. 1 (1998): 40–72.

34 Randy Roberts, *Jack Dempsey: The Manassa Mauler* (Urbana: University of Illinois Press, 2003), 263.

35 Ward, *Unforgivable Blackness*, 231; Streible, *Fight Pictures*, 256–257; Randy Roberts, *Joe Louis: Hard Times Man* (New Haven, CT: Yale University Press, 2010), 8–9.

36 Bruce J. Evensen, *When Dempsey Fought Tunney: Heroes, Hokum, and Storytelling in the Jazz Age* (Knoxville: University of Tennessee Press, 1996), xiv.

37 Evensen, *When Dempsey Fought Tunney*, 16.

38 "The Challenge of Chance," *Billboard*, June 28, 1919, 31.

39 Evensen, *When Dempsey Fought Tunney*, xiii, 17.

40 Benjamin G. Rader, "Compensatory Sport Heroes: Ruth, Grange, and Dempsey," *Journal of Popular Culture* 16 (Spring 1983): 11–22, 11.

41 Evensen, *When Dempsey Fought Tunney*, xiv; Roger Kahn, *A Flame of Pure Fire: Jack Dempsey and the Roaring '20s* (New York: Harcourt, 1999), 101.

42 Ira Berkow, *Red: A Biography of Red Smith* (New York: Times Books, 1986), 105.

43 Grantland Rice, "The Dempsey-Willard Fight," *New York Tribune*, July 5, 1919, 1; Damon Runyon, "Jack Dempsey Wins in Three Rounds," *New York American*, July 5, 1919, 1.

44 Evensen, *When Dempsey Fought Tunney*, xv.

45 Robert Lipsyte, *Sportsworld: An American Dreamland* (New York: Quadrangle, 1975), 170.

46 "In the Wake of the News," *Chicago Daily Tribune*, February 12, 1920, 11.

47 "Comet Releases Jack Johnson Picture," *Billboard*, October 8, 1921, 95; "Ohio Bars Johnson Film," *Billboard*, April 8, 1922, 97.

48 Kenneth Bilby, *The General: David Sarnoff and the Rise of the Communications Industry* (New York: Harper & Row, 1986), 56; "Voice-Broadcasting the Stirring Progress of the 'Battle of the Century,'" *Wireless Age*, August 1921, 11–21.

49 Bilby, *General*, 56; David Sarnoff, *Looking Ahead: The Papers of David Sarnoff* (New York: McGraw-Hill, 1968), 36; "Voice-Broadcasting."

50 Eugene Lyons, *David Sarnoff* (New York: Pyramid Books, 1967), 123; "Voice-Broadcasting."

51 Streible, *Fight Pictures*, 266.

52 Evensen, *When Dempsey Fought Tunney*, xvi; Kahn, *Flame of Pure Fire*, 45.

53 Kahn, *Flame of Pure Fire*, 354.

54 "Mrs. Jack Dempsey Needs Actor for Lead," *Variety*, November 18, 1925, 11.

55 Rickard initially wanted to stage the fight at New York City's Yankee Stadium. But the New York state licensing committee refused to let Dempsey fight unless he faced the African American Harry Wills, whom it deemed the top contender.

168 • Notes to Pages 23–37

Rickard moved the match to Philadelphia so Dempsey could fight Tunney instead. "New York Boxing Control Insists on Wills Battle," *St. Petersburg Times*, August 17, 1926, 8.

56 Evensen, *When Dempsey Fought Tunney*, 42.

57 Evensen, xiv; Grantland Rice, "The Golden Fleece," *Collier's*, September 17, 1927, 9, 44.

58 Evensen, 89.

59 "Dempsey-Tunney," *Dayton Herald*, September 23, 1926, 13.

60 Evensen, *When Dempsey Fought Tunney*, 116; Streible, *Fight Pictures*, 277.

61 Cagney appeared as an aging former boxer in the made-for-TV *Terrible Joe Moran* (1984). The production used clips from *Winner Take All* to reflect on the character's life as a fighter.

62 "Newspaper Makes Masquerade as Film Stars as the Rialto," *Washington Post*, March 31, 1924, 5; "Too Much Hearst," *Variety*, February 28, 1924, 16.

63 *The Prizefighter and the Lady* also attracted a big international audience given its inclusion of the well-known heavyweight fighters. Joseph Goebbels, however, banned the film in Germany. The Nazi minister of propaganda claimed that he prohibited the film because Baer had beaten the German fighter Max Schmeling. But most critics and historians suspect that he barred the production because of Baer's Jewish heritage. "It doesn't make much difference to me," the charismatic Baer said in a taunting response to the Nazi ban. "But I'm sorry for the women and children of Germany. Too bad they won't get a chance to see the world's greatest lover and the world's greatest fighter in action." See "Baer Sorry for German Woman," *New York Times*, March 30, 1934, 26.

Chapter 2   St. Joe Louis, Surrounded by Films

1 Martin Luther King Jr., *Why We Can't Wait* (New York: Harper & Row, 1964), 119–120.

2 Jeffrey T. Sammons, *Beyond the Ring: The Role of Boxing in American Society* (Urbana: University of Illinois Press, 1988), 96; Leger Grindon, *Knockout: The Boxer and Boxing in American Cinema* (Oxford: University of Mississippi Press, 2009), 40.

3 Jack Johnson offered to replace Blackburn as Louis's trainer. After Louis denied his entreaty, Johnson took to denigrating Louis and pointing out his shortcomings to journalists eager to stoke any animosity that existed between the two. See Randy Roberts, *Joe Louis: Hard Times Man* (New Haven, CT: Yale University Press, 2010), 70, 83.

4 Roberts, *Joe Louis*, 51.

5 Sammons, *Beyond the Ring*, 96–98.

6 "Dempsey to Conduct 'White Hope' Tourney," *Los Angeles Times*, December 24, 1935, A9.

7 Roberts, *Joe Louis*, 72–73; Grantland Rice, "Baer's Career Ends with Setback," *Atlanta Constitution*, September 25, 1935, 15.

8 Edward Van Every, *Joe Louis, Man and Super-Fighter* (New York: Frederick A. Stokes, 1936), 1–2; Roberts, *Joe Louis*, 97.

9 Sammons, *Beyond the Ring*, 107.

10 "Fight Excitement Causes 12 Deaths," *New York Times*, June 21, 1936, S11; Marvel Cooke, "Death and Sadness Mark Louis Defeat," *New York Amsterdam News*, June 27, 1936, 1.

Notes to Pages 37-47 • 169

11 "German Censor Praises Films," *Los Angeles Times*, July 9, 1936, A15; "Austrians Heil Schmeling," *New York Times*, July 5, 1936, 7.

12 "Braddock-Louis," *Variety*, June 30, 1937, 21.

13 Luther Carmichael, "Nashville Theaters Snub Fight Films," *Chicago Defender*, July 17, 1937, 6.

14 Ben Davis Jr., "Harlem's Victory Cheers Echo Will of People to Crush Fascism," *Daily Worker*, June 24, 1938, 1, 6; William L. Van de Burg, *Black Camelot: African American Culture Heroes in Their Times, 1960–1980* (Chicago: University of Chicago Press, 1999), 95. For more on the Louis-Schmeling rematch, see Lewis Erenberg, *The Greatest Fight of Our Generation: Louis vs. Schmeling* (Oxford: Oxford University Press, 2006); David Magolick, *Beyond Glory: Joe Louis vs. Max Schmeling and a World on the Brink* (New York: Vintage, 2006).

15 "Hitler Bars Film Showing Max Schmeling's Defeat," *Chicago Defender*, July 16, 1938, 19; "Nazis Deny Faking Louis Fight Films," *New York Times*, July 31, 1938, 28.

16 Fay M. Jackson, "Louis Signs Contract for Movie Roles," *Chicago Defender*, October 16, 1937, 21.

17 "Spirit of Youth," *Variety*, January 5, 1938, 16.

18 Dan Burley, "'I'll Keep Punching to Defend American Way'—Henry Armstrong," *New York Amsterdam News*, September 21, 1940, 18.

19 Frederick V. Romano, *The Boxing Filmography: American Features, 1920–2003* (Jefferson, NC: McFarland, 2004), 187; "Ban on Negro Artists, Says Columnist," *Atlanta Daily World*, November 6, 1939, 1.

20 See Steven A. Riess, *City Games: The Evolution of American Urban Society and the Rise of Sports* (Urbana: University of Illinois Press, 1989); Robert Sklar, *City Boys: Cagney, Bogart, Garfield* (Princeton, NJ: Princeton University Press, 1992).

21 Grindon, *Knockout*, 41.

22 Frank S. Nugent, "The Screen," *New York Times*, May 27, 1937, 21.

23 "Dempsey Asks for Removal of Fight Film Ban," *Chicago Daily Tribune*, May 26, 1939, 34; "Television Angle Up in D.C. Move to Repeal Old Fight Film Law," *Variety*, May 31, 1939, 12.

24 "On Capitol Hill: Senator Barbour Urges Repeal of Ban on Interstate Shipping of Fight Films," *Washington Post*, April 4, 1939, 2. "Legalizing Transportation of Prizefight Films," *Congressional Record*, 76th Cong., 1st Sess. (May 25–26, 1939). Individual states maintained the right to ban films after the federal restriction was overturned.

25 "This Is the Army," *Variety*, August 4, 1943, 8. Roberts claims that southern exhibitors took advantage of *This Is the Army*'s episodic structure by cutting segments that included African Americans. Indeed, aside from two brief shots of Louis during montages, none of the scenes in *This Is the Army*—many of which include dozens of performers—features African Americans aside from "Well-Dressed Man." Moreover, the musical includes a song that adopts the style of a minstrel show with White actors in blackface. *This Is the Army* could have potentially been excised in favor of a version that included only White soldiers, including some in blackface. While these racist alterations were certainly possible, there is little evidence to suggest such edits were actually made prior to exhibition of the film. Thomas Cripps disputed this practice as a widely circulated myth about the exhibition of integrated musicals in southern cinema culture. See Cripps, "The Myth of the Southern Box Office: A Factor in Racial Stereotyping in American Movies, 1920–1940," in *The Black Experience in America: Selected*

170 • Notes to Pages 48–61

Essays, ed. James C. Curtis and Lewis L. Gould (Austin: University of Texas Press, 1970), 116–144.

26 "The Negro Soldier," *Time,* March 27, 1944, 94–95.

27 Langston Hughes, "Here's a Film Everyone Should See," *Chicago Defender,* February 26, 1944, 8.

28 Frank Capra, *The Name Above the Title: An Autobiography* (New York: Macmillan, 1971), 358.

29 Al Monroe, "Swinging the News," *Chicago Defender,* March 25, 1944, 8; "Uncle Greggy's Question Box," *Pittsburgh Courier,* April 15, 1944, 14; *New York Amsterdam News,* May 13, 1944, 9B.

30 Thomas Cripps, *Black Film as Genre* (Bloomington: Indiana University Press, 1978), 42.

31 Robert H. Boyle, "A Champ for All Time," *Sports Illustrated,* April 19, 1965, 120–137.

32 Lester D. Friedman, *Sports Movies* (New Brunswick, NJ: Rutgers University Press, 2020), 132.

33 Aaron Baker, *Contesting Identities: Sports in American Film* (Urbana: University of Illinois Press, 2003), 26; Thomas Cripps, *Making Movies Black: The Hollywood Message Movie from World War II to the Civil Rights Era* (Oxford: Oxford University Press, 1993), 212. See also Friedman, *Sports Movies,* 134.

34 Robert Wise, "Dialogue on Film," *American Film* 1, no. 2 (1975): 33–48, 36; Cripps, *Making Movies Black,* 213. Edwards eventually played James Blackburn in *The Joe Louis Story.*

35 Sammons, *Beyond the Ring,* 137.

Chapter 3   TV Fighting and Fighting TV in the 1950s

1 "Radio Men Regard Television as Ally," *New York Times,* January 15, 1928, 5; Rudolf Arnheim, *Film as Art* (Berkeley: University of California Press, 1935), 193.

2 Alva Johnston, "Television's Here," *Saturday Evening Post,* May 6, 1939, 8; Arthur Daley, "Is Boxing On the Ropes?," *New York Times,* January 31, 1954, SM19; Jeff Neal-Lunsford, "Sport in the Land of Television: The Use of Sport in Network Prime-Time Schedules 1946–1950," *Journal of Sport History* 19, no. 1 (Spring 1992): 56–76, 61.

3 "Hot Bidding for Conn-Louis Tele," *Variety,* January 23, 1946, 1, 47; "Theatre Television Held Possible in N.Y. for Louis-Conn Fight," *Variety,* February 6, 1946, 1, 63; Robert K. Richards, "Doubters Kayoed by Fight Telecast," *Broadcasting,* June 24, 1946, 15–16, 93; Nat Kahn, "Television Emerges the Winner in Joe Louis-Billy Conn Title Fight," *Variety,* June 26, 1946, 35.

4 "Theater TV Gets Biggest B.O. Text Via Exclusive on Louis-Savold Fight," *Variety,* June 6, 1951, 1, 39; Murray Rose, "Louis-Savold Expecting Early Kayo," *Washington Post,* June 10, 1951, C3; "Theater TV Fight Showings Sensation at Boxoffice," *BoxOffice,* June 23, 1951, 8–10; James M. Jerauld, "Rush for Television Projectors is On," *BoxOffice,* June 30, 1951, 9; "New York: Big Gate," *New York Times,* September 16, 1951, E2.

5 "Boxing Sponsors Have a Problem," *Advertising Age,* May 4, 1953, 2.

6 Sam Chase, "Joe Louis Film Following Fitecast: A Video Lyric, Point-Counterpoint," *Billboard,* November 3, 1951, 3; "Lotsa Uppercuts & Left Jabs on TV Post-Fight Slots," *Variety,* July 28, 1954, 32.

Notes to Pages 62–74 • 171

7   A. J. Liebling, *The Sweet Science* (New York: North Point Press, 2004), 17, 18, 21.

8   Charles Einstein, "TV Slugs the Boxers," *Harper's*, August 1, 1956, 65–68; Arthur Daley, "Is Boxing on the Ropes?," *New York Times*, January 31, 1954, SM19; "Pennsylvania Board Threatens to Quit NBA if Champion Moore Isn't Suspended," *Washington Post*, January 12, 1954, 18.

9   Liebling, *Sweet Science*, 197.

10 John Lardner, "So You Think You See the Fights on TV!," *Saturday Evening Post*, April 5, 1953, 144–146, 144; Frederick C. Klein, "A Connoisseur of Boxing's Past," *Wall Street Journal*, January 22, 1982, 31; Mike Gray, "What's Wrong with TV Boxing?," *Chicago Tribune*, July 7, 1956, C8.

11 "TV Fans Like Davey to Win Welter Crown but among Ringsiders, It's Galiván, 10 to 1," *Washington Post*, February 5, 1953, 20; David Condon, "What Happened to Boxing?," *Chicago Daily Tribune*, December 15, 1957, G24; Arthur Daley, "Is Boxing on the Ropes?," *New York Times*, January 31, 1954, SM19; Furman Bisher, "Boxing Is a Knockout on TV," *Atlanta Journal and Atlanta Constitution*, May 31, 1953, SM26; Robert Anderson, "Punch," *Chicago Tribune*, June 13, 1959, C23; Einstein, "TV Slugs the Boxers," 68.

12 Lardner, "So You Think You See the Fights on TV!"

13 See Alina Bernstein, "Is It Time for a Victory Lap? Changes in the Media Coverage of Women in Sport," *International Review for the Sociology of Sport* 37, nos. 3–4 (2002): 415–428.

14 Russell Sullivan, *Rocky Marciano: The Rock of His Times* (Urbana: University of Illinois Press, 2002), 86–87; Jeffrey T. Sammons, *Beyond the Ring: The Role of Boxing in American Society* (Urbana: University of Illinois Press, 1988), 150.

15 "TV Bout Shows Seen Crimping H'wood Pug Pix," *Variety*, March 28, 1956, 5.

16 Red Smith, "The Height of Tastelessness," *Boston Globe*, April 8, 1956, C62; "Walcott Fails to Give Grand Jury Proof of Illinois Ring Corruption," *New York Times*, April 17, 1956, 37; "Ring's Corruption Issue Kicks Up Fuss in Chicago," *Variety*, April 18, 1956, 16.

17 *The Harder They Fall* cut a different ending for the version that would appear on TV, which called for a federal investigation into boxing instead of a wholesale elimination of the sport. The softer TV ending was likely taking into account the medium's intimate relationship to boxing and possible backlash for the film version's suggestion that the sport ought to be eradicated altogether. See Philip K. Scheuer, "The Harder They Fall Swings a Haymaker at Fight Game," *Los Angeles Times*, April 15, 1956, E1.

18 Gordon E. Sander, *Serling: The Rise and Twilight of Television's Last Angry Man* (New York: Dutton, 1992), 119; Lawrence Laurent, "Early or Late, Video Scripter's on His Toes," *Washington Post*, October 11, 1956, 70.

19 Jack Gould, "'Requiem for a Heavyweight': Rod Serling's Drama Scores a Knockout," *New York Times*, October 12, 1956, 59.

20 Leger Grindon, *Knockout: The Boxer and Boxing in American Cinema* (Oxford: University of Mississippi Press, 2009), 54, 56.

21 "Heads, Not Headlines," *Sports Illustrated*, December 5, 1960, 14; "Kefauver Seeks Ring Czar," *Chicago Defender*, March 30, 1961, 29.

22 James A. Farley Jr., "My Fight in Defense of Boxing," *Sports Illustrated*, April 23, 1962, 26–27; Truman K. Gibson, *Knocking Down Barriers: My Fight for Black America* (Evanston, IL: Northwestern University Press, 2005), 249.

172 • Notes to Pages 74–79

23 Condon, "What Happened to Boxing?," G24.
24 See Travis Vogan, *ABC Sports: The Rise and Fall of Network Sports Television* (Berkeley: University of California Press, 2018), 19–21.

Chapter 4 Muhammad Ali, *The Super Fight*, and Closed-Circuit Exhibition

1 Anna McCarthy, "'Like the Sound of an Earthquake': Theater Television, Boxing, and the Black Public Sphere," *Quarterly Review of Film and Video* 16, nos. 3–4 (1997): 307–323, 313. McCarthy refers to closed-circuit TV as theater television. I am calling it closed-circuit because these exhibitions, while conducted in the model of theatrical showings, spanned beyond theaters into arenas, convention centers, and other public spaces.
2 "ABC Kayos Friday Fights," *Broadcasting*, December 30, 1963, 40.
3 Eddie Kalish, "Everything Counted in, Liston-Clay Go May Come Close to $3,000,000 Take," *Variety*, March 4, 1964, 25; "Liston-Clay Championship Sets Closed TV Record," *Box Office*, March 2, 1964, 12.
4 Red Smith, "Clay Could Be KO'd in Oslo," *Boston Globe*, February 25, 1964, 15; John Hall, "Plenty of Theater TV Seats Left for Liston-Clay Fight Tuesday," *Los Angeles Times*, February 3, 1964, F10.
5 "Closed Circuit TV and Boxing as 'Perfect' Match," *Independent Film Journal*, October 30, 1970, 24.
6 Kalish, "Everything Counted In," 25; "Cancel 2 TV Casts over Racial Row," *Chicago Tribune*, February 25, 1954, B1.
7 Bill Lane, "The Inside Story," *Los Angeles Sentinel*, September 3, 1964, A7; A. S. "Doc" Young, "Boxing & Private Enterprise," *Los Angeles Sentinel*, February 20, 1964, B2; "Dooto Music Center Carries Title Fight," *Los Angeles Sentinel*, February 6, 1964, A14.
8 Jim Murray, "Ee-yi, Ee-yi, Yo," *Los Angeles Times*, February 21, 1964, B1; Shirley Povich, "This Morning," *Washington Post*, May 21, 1965, D1; "TV Ensures Cassius for $1 Million," *Detroit Free Press*, May 25, 1965, 2C.
9 "Clay's Name Is Mud; Stubs Redeemed," *Variety*, June 2, 1965, 29; Dave Brady, "Clay-Liston Will Be on 'Live' TV Overseas," *Washington Post*, May 13, 1965, C2.
10 Michael Arkush, *The Fight of the Century: Ali vs. Frazier* (Hoboken, NJ: Wiley, 2008), 3; Randy Roberts, "The Wide World of Muhammad Ali: The Politics and Economics of Televised Boxing," in *Muhammad Ali: The People's Champ*, ed. Elliot J. Gorn (Urbana: University of Illinois Press, 1998), 24–53, 44.
11 Michael Ezra, "Main Bout Inc., Black Economic Power, and Professional Boxing: The Cancelled Muhammad Ali/Ernie Terrell Fight," *Journal of Sport History* 29, no. 2 (Fall 2002): 413–427, 414.
12 Doug Gilbert, "Clay-Terrell Package Wrapped in Muslims?," *Chicago's American*, February 5, 1966, 11.
13 Jack Berry, "Clay: He Wouldn't Crawl," *Detroit Free Press*, March 10, 1966, D2.
14 Brad Pye Jr., "Jim Brown Says Bigots Delay Clay-Terrell Bout," *Los Angeles Sentinel*, March 10, 1966, B1; Brad Pye Jr., "Prying Pye," *Los Angeles Sentinel*, March 24, 1966, B1.
15 "Fight Finds Home in Toronto," *Chicago Tribune*, March 9, 1966, C1.
16 Sid Ziff, "Hit or a Flop," *Los Angeles Times*, March 25, 1966, B3; "Clay Fight Ok'd for Toronto," *Detroit Free Press*, March 9, 1966, 2D.

Notes to Pages 79–85 • 173

17 Joe Falls, "Get Red Ink Ready for Fight," *Detroit Free Press*, March 29, 1966, 1D.

18 Brad Pye, "Dooto Carries Clay-Chuvalo Go," *Los Angeles Sentinel*, March 24, 1966, B4.

19 Gilbert Rogin, "A Battle of the Lionhearted," *Sports Illustrated*, April 11, 1966, 32–37, 37.

20 Ezra, "Main Bout Inc.," 427; "Clay-Williams Bout Is Slated for 24 Metropolitan Theaters," *New York Times*, November 1, 1966, 226.

21 "Miami Beach Rejects Clay-Williams TV," *Washington Post*, November 5, 1966, 38; "Pittsburgh," *Box Office*, November 14, 1966, E8; Frank Mastro, "TV Viewers Cheer Clay's TKO Victory," *Chicago Tribune*, November 15, 1966, C2.

22 Brad Pye, "Prying Pye," *Los Angeles Sentinel*, November 17, 1966, B1; "TV Coverage Set for Clay's Fight," *New York Times*, November 5, 1966, 38; Lawrence Casey, "Sports Ledger," *Chicago Defender*, October 27, 1966, 41; "Muhammad Ali Proves Two Points in Williams TKO," *Pittsburgh Courier*, November 19, 1966, 1A; Leigh Montville, *Sting Like a Bee: Muhammad Ali vs. the United States of America* (New York: Doubleday, 2017), 113.

23 "Main Street," *Back Stage*, June 9, 1967, 4. Such uses of film to debate boxers' greatness did not start with Ali. In 1940, exhibitions of the Dempsey-Willard fight film were marketed by suggesting the documents would allow spectators to decide whether Dempsey could have beaten Joe Louis. See *St. Louis Post-Dispatch*, February 8, 1940, 50.

24 Leticia Kent, "A Visit with Muhammad Ali," *Louisville Courier-Journal*, November 23, 1969, D1, D18.

25 William O. Johnson, "And in This Corner . . . NCR-315," *Sports Illustrated*, September 16, 1968, 35–49, 41.

26 Robert L. Harris, "Marciano and Dempsey to Vie for Boxing Title in Ersatz Radio Bout," *Wall Street Journal*, December 15, 1967, 15; Johnson, "And in This Corner," 35.

27 David Remnick, *King of the World: Muhammad Ali and the Rise of an American Hero* (New York: Vintage, 1998), 222.

28 Kenneth Turah, "Computer Stopped Ali 5 Times," *Washington Post*, January 25, 1970, C4.

29 Bud Collins, "Rocky Impressed Even Clay," *Boston Globe*, September 2, 1969, 25.

30 Robert Lipsyte, "The Computer Fight," *Atlanta Constitution*, February 2, 1970, 1C.

31 "Marciano Training for Clay?," *Boston Globe*, September 5, 1966, 74.

32 "Clay-Marciano Super-Fight Set," *Back Stage*, September 26, 1969, 3.

33 "Super Fight," *World Boxing*, May 1970, 16–21, 20.

34 Marciano-Clay Fight in Global One-Shot," *Box Office*, December 15, 1969, 13; "Marciano-Clay: The Computer Knows," *New York Times*, January 18, 1970, 183; "Computer Directing Rocky's Last Fight," *Los Angeles Times*, October 19, 1969, C17; "Rocky-Cassius 'Secret' Bout for Loew's & RKO: One Way to Burb Toll," *Variety*, September 17, 1969, 1, 62.

35 "Marciano vs. Clay: A Computer Makes the Decision," *New York Times*, January 22, 1970, 41; Bob Posen, "Computer Fight Seems Real with Slick Filming," *St. Louis Post-Dispatch*, January 21, 1970, 1E.

36 A. S. "Doc" Young, "News of the World," *Los Angeles Sentinel*, January 29, 1970, A7.

174 • Notes to Pages 86–90

37 "How Ali's Antics Broke Up Rocky," *Detroit Free Press*, January 25, 1970, B1; "Cassius Watches, 'Jabs' at Frazier," *St. Louis Post-Dispatch*, January 21, 1970, 3E. Shortly after the *Super Fight*, Ali guested on ABC's *Dick Cavett Show* and called the match a "Hollywood fake," a charge that provoked Woroner to sue him. "Computer 'Brain' Charges Slander by Cassius Clay," *Los Angeles Times*, September 1, 1970, F7.

38 Jeffrey T. Sammons, *Beyond the Ring: The Role of Boxing in American Society* (Urbana: University of Illinois Press, 1988), 209; Turah, "Computer Stopped Ali 5 Times," C4.

39 "Super Fight," *World Boxing*, May 1970, 16–21, 20.

40 Harold Kaese, "Clay-Rocky: Mystery Gem," *Boston Globe*, January 18, 1970, 69.

41 Turah, "Computer Stopped Ali 5 Times," C4.

42 "Woroner Is Making Return of Clay-Marciano Film," *Box Office*, February 16, 1970, 11.

43 "Not a Oncer Anymore," *Variety*, February 18, 1970, 5. A BBC reshowing reportedly changed the *Super Fight*'s ending to make it appear that Ali had won because of public outcry surrounding the original ending. Woroner denied that this revision took place. "Congenial BBC Shows Clay Beating Marciano," *New York Times*, January 30, 1970, 37.

44 Shirley Povich, "This Morning," *Washington Post*, October 1, 1970, H1.

45 Don Page, "Rams, Vikings and an Ali Fight," *Los Angeles Times*, October 24, 1970, A2.

46 Montville, *Sting Like a Bee*, 275; Arkush, *Fight of the Century*, 53; Muhammad Ali and Richard Durham, *The Greatest: My Own Story* (New York: Ballantine Books, 1975), 332, 389; Budd Schulberg, *The Loser and Still Champion: Muhammad Ali* (New York: Doubleday, 1972), 26.

47 "Miami," *Variety*, February 3, 1971, 46.

48 Robert Lipsyte, "'I Don't Have to Be What You Want Me to Be,' Says Muhammad Ali," *New York Times*, March 7, 1971, SM24.

49 "'AKA Cassius Clay' Film Breaking Records," *Chicago Defender*, November 14, 1970, 16; "Top Hits for the Fall Quarter," *Box Office*, January 25, 1971, 6.

50 "Ali Demands End of TV Blackout," *Washington Post*, November 24, 1970, D3.

51 "Black Marciano Is Tag for Joe," *St. Louis Post-Dispatch*, February 17, 1970, 4B.

52 "Ali-Frazier—World Watches, Barefisted," *Boston Globe*, March 5, 1971, 25, 27; Schulberg, *Loser and Still Champion*, 105.

53 Arkush, *Fight of the Century*, 175; Dave Anderson, "Ali and Frazier Make It Official: They Sign for Title Fight Here March 8," *New York Times*, December 31, 1970, 31.

54 Arkush, *Fight of the Century*, 126–127; "Fight of the Century: Don't Believe It! That's New York Hokum," *Detroit Free Press*, March 7, 1971, 6D; "Neither Cold nor Sleet Chill Mobs at Music Hall," *Variety*, March 10, 1971, 4.

55 "Ali Fight Barred in Oklahoma City," *New York Times*, January 27, 1971, 22; "Telecast a Success Despite Disorders," *St. Louis Post-Dispatch*, March 9, 1971, 3B; "Postmortems to Frazier-Ali Jackpot," *Variety*, March 17, 1971, 2; Francis Ward, "Ali's Goals: Regain Title, Get Elijah's Blessing," *Los Angeles Times*, March 4, 1971, D1.

56 "Neither Cold nor Sleet," 48; "Telecast a Success Despite Disorders," 3B.

Chapter 5 The 1970s, *Rocky*, and the Shadow of Ali

1 Thomas Hauser, *Muhammad Ali: His Life and Times* (New York: Touchstone, 1991), 300.

2 Leger Grindon, *Knockout: The Boxer and Boxing in American Cinema* (Oxford: University of Mississippi Press, 2009), 63.

3 Grindon, *Knockout*, 61.

4 Donald Bogle, *Blacks in American Film and Television: An Encyclopedia* (New York: Garland, 1988), 75.

5 Jonathan Eig, *Ali: A Life* (New York: Houghton Mifflin Harcourt, 2017), 408.

6 For more on these Ali documentaries, see Alexander William McKie Johnston, "'What You Want Me to Be': Documenting Muhammad Ali 1970 to the Present," *Journal of Sport & Social Issues* 43, no. 2 (2019): 106–121.

7 Leonard Gardner, *Fat City* (New York: New York Review of Books, 1969), 81.

8 Michael Durham, "A Short Talk with a First Novelist," *Life*, August 29, 1969, 10.

9 Frank Rich, "*Rocky* Hits a Nerve," *New York Post*, December 4, 1976, 44.

10 David Sterritt, "The Man Behind *Rock*," *Christian Science Monitor*, January 13, 1977, 12; Judy Klemesrud, "'Rocky Isn't Based on Me,' Says Stallone, 'But We Both Went the Distance,'" *New York Times Magazine*, November 28, 1975, 111; Aaron Baker, *Contesting Identities: Sports in American Film* (Urbana: University of Illinois Press, 2003), 130. See also Daniel J. Leab, "The Blue Collar Ethnic in Bicentennial America: *Rocky* (1976)," in *American History/American Film*, ed. John E. O'Connor and Martin A. Jackson (New York: Continuum, 1988), 257–272.

11 John Hall, "The Dreamers," *Los Angeles Times*, May 1, 1980, E3. Eric Lichtenfeld explains several of the embellishments Stallone used to dramatize his underdog narrative in "I, of the Tiger: Self and Self-Obsession in the *Rocky* Series," in *The Ultimate Stallone Reader*, ed. Chris Holmund (London: Wallflower Press, 2014), 75–96.

12 Henry Schipper, "Why Stardom Was a Rocky Road for Stallone," *Boston Globe*, August 16, 1981, A21.

13 Sylvester Stallone, *The Official* Rocky *Scrapbook* (New York: Grosset & Dunlap, 1977).

14 There are conflicting figures surrounding the amount United Artists ultimately offered for the script. Stallone claims it inflated to one million, but other sources suggest it was considerably less. See Stallone, *Official* Rocky *Scrapbook*, 20–21.

15 Andrew Sarris, "Takes," *Village Voice*, November 22, 1976, 61.

16 Michael Ryan and Douglas Kellner, *Camera Politica: The Politics and Ideology of Contemporary Hollywood Film* (Bloomington: Indiana University Press, 1988), 111; "Playboy Interview: Sylvester Stallone," *Playboy*, September 1978, 73–91, 82; Gene Siskel, "Making 'Rocky' a Knockout Down to the Last 'Oomph,'" *Chicago Tribune*, December 13, 1976, A1.

17 John Culhane, "The Man Who Coached Rocky to Victory," *New York Times*, March 27, 1977, 59; Tom Shales, "The Oscars: Top Honors to 'Rocky,' Finch and Dunaway," *Washington Post*, March 29, 1977, B1.

18 Andrew Britton, "Blissing Out: The Politics of Reaganite Entertainment," in *The Complete Film Criticism of Andrew Britton*, ed. Barry Keith Grant (Detroit: Wayne State University Press, 2008), 97–154, 97. See also Robin Wood, *Hollywood from Vietnam to Reagan* (New York: Columbia University Press, 1986), 62.

176 • Notes to Pages 102–111

19 Grindon, *Knockout*, 61.
20 Jim Spence, *Up Close and Personal: The Inside Story of Network Television Sports* (New York: Atheneum, 1988), 232; Roone Arledge, *Roone: A Memoir* (New York: Harper, 2004), 170; Jack Newfield, *Only in America: The Life and Crimes of Don King* (New York: William Morrow, 1995), 107.
21 Ryan and Kellner, *Camera Politica*, 111. For a different take on *Rocky*'s cultural politics, see Grant Wiedenfeld, "The Conservative Backlash Argument Controverted: Carnivalesque, Comedy, and Respect in *Rocky*," *Critical Studies in Media Communication* 33, no. 2 (2016): 168–180.
22 Quoted in David Thompson and Ian Christie, eds., *Scorsese on Scorsese* (London: Faber and Faber, 1989), 80.
23 Scorsese's decision to shoot in black and white was also shaped by the filmmaker's concerns about the shoddy color film stock available at the time. Thompson and Christie, *Scorsese on Scorsese*, 79–84.
24 Grindon, *Knockout*, 249.
25 Roger Ebert, "Watching *Rocky II* with Muhammad Ali," *Chicago Sun-Times*, July 31, 1979, 2B.
26 Dave Brady, "His Movie Draws Both Raves, Jabs from Fight Crowd," *Washington Post*, March 13, 1977, 44; William Sluis, "Ali to Give Rocky His Chance," *Chicago Tribune*, March 31, 1977, B4; "Ode to Sly from Ali," *Los Angeles Times*, February 23, 1977, F18.
27 "Ali: I'm the Black Gable," *Variety*, May 31, 1978, 6; Robert Lipsyte, "Muhammad Ali Tries for a Knockout as a Movie Star," *New York Times*, November 7, 1976, D1.
28 Bruce McCabe, "Rocky and Ali—in Opposite Corners," *Boston Globe*, May 29, 1977, A8.
29 "Cannon Aims to Boost Budgets and Quality of Its Pic Product," *Variety*, October 14, 1981, 82; Roderick Mann, "Actress Has Soul in New Body," *Los Angeles Times*, February 16, 1982, G1. For more on the *Penitentiary* franchise, see Keith Corson, *Trying to Get Over: African American Directors after Blaxploitation, 1977–1986* (Austin: University of Texas Press, 2016), 124–137.
30 Gene Siskel, "New 'Body' Entertaining, But Script Is Down for the Count," *Chicago Tribune*, October 15, 1981, C1.
31 James H. Cleaver, "Jayne Kennedy's Husband Answers 'Girlie' Mag Critics," *Los Angeles Sentinel*, June 25, 1981, A1.
32 John A. Meyers, "A Letter from the Publisher," *Time*, June 14, 1982, 3.

Chapter 6   HBO Sports

1 Gary R. Edgerton and Jeffrey P. Jones, eds., *The Essential HBO Reader* (Lexington: University Press of Kentucky, 2008); Marc Leverette, Brian L. Ott, and Cara Louise Buckley, eds., *It's Not TV: Watching HBO in the Post-Television Era* (New York: Routledge, 2008).
2 Tom Umstead and Ross Greenburg, interview, Cable Center Oral History Collection, May 2003.
3 See Michael Curtin, *Redeeming the Wasteland: Television, Documentary, and Cold War Politics* (New Brunswick, NJ: Rutgers University Press, 1995); Travis Vogan, "ESPN Films and the Creation of Prestige in Contemporary Sports Television," *International Journal of Sport Communication* 5, no. 2 (2012): 137–152; Susan Murray, "'I Think We Need a New Name for It': The Meeting of

Notes to Pages 112–120 • 177

Documentary and Reality TV," in *Remaking Television Culture*, ed. Susan Murray and Laurie Ouellette (New York: New York University Press, 2004), 40–56.

4 George Mair, *Inside HBO: The Billion Dollar War between HBO, Hollywood, and the Home Video Revolution* (New York: Dodd, Mead, 1988), 16.

5 "Bird Is in Hand for Pay Cable," *Broadcasting*, October 6, 1975, 26.

6 Mair, *Inside HBO*, 25.

7 Toby Miller and Linda J. Kim, "It Isn't TV, It's the 'Real King of the Ring,'" in Edgerton and Jones, *Essential HBO Reader*, 217–236, 228; Dean J. DeFino, *The HBO Effect* (New York: Bloomsbury, 2014), 52.

8 Umstead and Greenburg interview.

9 Rahway was also the site where Arnold Shapiro's infamous 1978 documentary *Scared Straight!* was filmed.

10 Hoffer, "A Fistful of Dollars," *Sports Illustrated*, January 15, 1990, 102.

11 Red Smith, "The Big One That Got Away," *New York Times*, June 24, 1979, S3.

12 Neil Amdur, "For Cable, a Week of Prime Coverage," *New York Times*, February 15, 1983, B9; Umstead and Greenburg interview.

13 Hal Lancaster, "Despite Big Obstacles, HBO Sports Chief Has Grand Plans for the Cable Network," *Wall Street Journal*, October 15, 1987, 35; Umstead and Greenburg interview; Hoffer, "Fistful of Dollars," 102.

14 Hoffer, "Fistful of Dollars," 99.

15 See José Torres, *Fire and Fear: The Inside Story of Mike Tyson* (New York: Warner Books, 1989), 203; Richard Hoffer, *A Savage Business: The Comeback and Comedown of Mike Tyson* (New York: Simon & Schuster, 1998), 148.

16 Skip Myslenski, "HBO Series Tries Cleaning Boxing Mess," *Chicago Tribune*, April 15, 1986, C3.

17 Peter Heller, *Bad Intentions: The Mike Tyson Story* (Boston: Da Capo Press, 1995), 189; Mark Robichaux, "Cable TV Promotes Holyfield-Holmes as It Faces Life after Mike Tyson," *Wall Street Journal*, June 19, 1992, A7.

18 Mike Tyson with Larry Sloman, *Undisputed Truth* (New York: Penguin, 2013), 168; Rudy Martzke, "HBO's Multi-Million Dollar Deal with Tyson Pays Off," *USA Today*, February 24, 1989, 3C; Norman Chad, "HBO and Tyson: Trying Another Combination," *Washington Post*, July 21, 1989, B3.

19 Brian Donlon, "Increased Options Made Cable a Live Wire," *USA Today*, November 30, 1989, 3D.

20 In James Toback's documentary *Tyson* (2008), Mike Tyson called King "a wretched, slimy, reptilian motherfucker. This is supposed to be my 'black brother,' right? He's just a bad man, a real bad man. He would kill his own mother for a dollar."

21 Arthur Ashe, "Spike Lee Can't Have It Both Ways," *Washington Post*, December 15, 1990, D3. Kristen Fuhs explains how several documentaries—including the HBO and Spike Lee production *Undisputed Truth* (2013)—brokered Tyson's reintegration into popular culture after his legal troubles and brief suspension from boxing for biting Evander Holyfield's ear in 1997. See Fuhs, "How Documentary Remade Mike Tyson," *Journal of Sport & Social Issues* 41, no. 6 (2017): 478–492.

22 Larry Stewart, "A Sad L.A. Story: KCBS Last Again for NCAA Field," *Los Angeles Times*, March 8, 1991, C3; Phil Berger "A Tyson HBO Deal That Wasn't," *New York Times*, December 12, 1990, D23; "HBO and Showtime Climb into the PPV Ring," *Broadcasting*, December 24, 1990, 28.

178 • Notes to Pages 120–133

23 Frank Sanello, *Reel v. Real: How Hollywood Turns Fact into Fiction* (Lanham, MD: Taylor Trade, 2002), xiii; Robert A. Rosenstone, *History on Film/Film on History* (New York: Routledge, 2013), 160.

24 Derek Paget, *No Other Way to Tell It: Docudrama on Film and Television* (Manchester, UK: Manchester University Press, 1998); Steven Lipkin, "Defining Docudrama: *In The Name of the Father, Schindler's List*, and *JFK*," in *Why Docudrama? Fact-Fiction on Film and TV*, ed. Allan Rosenthal (Carbondale: Southern Illinois University Press, 1999), 370–384, 372; Steven Lipkin, *Docudrama Performs the Past: Arenas of Argument in Films Based on True Stories* (Newcastle, UK: Cambridge Scholars, 2011), 91.

25 Jack Lule, "The Rape of Mike Tyson: Race, the Press, and Symbolic Types," *Critical Studies in Mass Communication* 12, no. 2 (1995): 176–195.

26 Jack Newfield, *Only in America: The Life and Crimes of Don King* (New York: William Morrow, 1995), 289.

27 Dan Rafael, "HBO Honors Its Bouts of Class; Legendary Nights Highlights 12 Fights over 30-Year Period," *USA Today*, March 13, 2004, C14.

28 Mark Wahlberg, "Interview with Terry Gross," *Fresh Air*, National Public Radio, January 6, 2011; "The Fighter: Why Movies and Boxing Go Together," *Wall Street Journal*, November 18, 2010, D2.

29 "Acclaim Sports' HBO Boxing Shits to Retailers," *Business Wire*, November 15, 2000, 1.

30 Chuck Johnson, "HBO to Air Four-Part Prelude to De La Hoya-Mayweather Jr.," *USA Today*, January 29, 2007, C9.

31 Murray, "'I Think We Need a New Name for It,'" 44, 49.

32 "Quotable," *USA Today*, January 26, 2007, C3; Chuck Johnson, "Dancing with Success," *USA Today*, December 6, 2007, C1.

33 Richard Sandomir, "Worshipping at the Altar of Pay-Per-View," *New York Times*, May 6, 2007, 15; Richard Sandomir, "With '24/7' HBO Refines Winning Formula," *New York Times*, January 2, 2012, D7.

34 Ben Grossman, "HBO Sports Increases Its Reach," *Broadcasting & Cable*, March 5, 2007, 4.

35 Bill King, "From Russia with Glove: Who Will Step Up?," *SportsBusiness Journal*, October 9, 2006, 22–23.

Chapter 7   Protecting Boxing with the Boxing Film

1 Mark Emmons, "Sports Might Be on the Ropes, but Boxing Plays Well on Screen," Knight Ridder Tribune News Services, June 13, 2005, 1.

2 For more on the myth surrounding Ali's medal, see Jonathan Eig, *Ali: A Life* (New York: Houghton Mifflin Harcourt, 2017), 421–422.

3 Michael Ezra, *Muhammad Ali: The Making of an Icon* (Philadelphia: Temple University Press, 2009), 180, 177; Frank Ahrens, "Director Gast Goes the Distance," *Washington Post*, March 2, 1997, G1.

4 Ezra, *Muhammad Ali*, 137; Jon Saraceno, "Ali's Return Not Met with Pity, But with Affection," *USA Today*, October 11, 1996, A1.

5 Ezra, *Muhammad Ali*, 177; Bruce Horovitz, "Authentic Ali: Many Fans, New and Old, Drawn to Spiritual Side," *USA Today*, June 8, 1999, A1.

6 David Denby, "On the Battlefield," *New Yorker*, January 10, 2000, 90–92, 92.

Notes to Pages 135–150 • 179

7 Wenty Bowen, "'Joe and Max' Depicts Real-Life Friendship of Legendary Foes," *Bay State Banner*, March 7, 2002, 15.

8 Dinita Smith, "Now It's Women's Turn to Make It in the Ring," *New York Times*, October 1, 2000, AR13.

9 F. X. Toole, *Million Dollar Baby: Stories from the Corner* (New York: Ecco, 2005), 80; Ellexis Boyle, Brad Millington, and Patricia Vertinsky, "Representing the Female Pugilist: Narratives of Race, Gender, and Disability in *Million Dollar Baby*," *Sociology of Sport Journal* 23 (2006): 99–116, 101.

10 Clyde Gentry III, *No Holds Barred: The Complete History of Mixed Martial Arts in America* (Chicago: Triumph Books, 2011), 116.

11 Walker Childs, "UFC Fights to Be Ring Leader," *McClatchy Tribune Business News*, July 30, 2006, 1; Stuart Miller, "UFC: Two Decades of Eventual Growth," *Broadcasting & Cable*, November 11, 2013, 3A. See also Jennifer McClearen, "'We Are All Fighters': The Transmedia Marketing of Difference in the Ultimate Fighting Championship (UFC)," *International Journal of Communication* 11 (2007): 3224–3241.

12 Richard Sandomir, "Mixed Martial Arts: From the Edge of Madness to Fighting's Mainstream," *New York Times*, May 25, 2007, D2.

13 Scott Bowles, "Mixed Martial Arts Elbows Way into Hollywood," Gannett News Services, September 7, 2011, 1.

14 Fox premiered the very similar and short-lived program *The Next Great Champ* in fall 2004. The program, hosted by Oscar De La Hoya, failed to find a consistent audience and was canceled after its first season. NBC sued Fox for allegedly stealing its concept and rushing it to air before *The Contender* was ready to debut.

15 Frazier Moore, "Will NBC and Fox Shows Turn Boxers into Stars?," *St. Louis Post-Dispatch*, May 24, 2004, C6.

16 Daniel Fienberg, "The 'Adrian Factor' Fuels NBC's Contender," Knight Ridder News Service, March 6, 2005; Richard Sandomir, "There Are Fighters and There Are Contenders," *New York Times*, May 11, 2005, D6. Stallone left the program after the NBC cancellation. ESPN carried *The Contender* for its next two seasons with Leonard serving as the sole host. The program then moved to the upstart sports channel Versus in 2008 for one season before ceasing production.

17 James Harwood, "Stallone Visualizes Himself as 'Rocky' Reaching Ages 40 and 50," *Variety*, April 6, 1977, 32.

18 Scott Bowles, "A Cinematic Heavyweight Bout," *USA Today*, September 11, 2013, D1.

Conclusion

1 Andrew O'Hehir, "Southpaw: A Gripping, Conflicted Fable of a White Champ in an Imagined America," *Salon*, July 24, 2015, www.salon.com/2015/07/23 /southpaw_a_gripping_conflicted_fable_of_a_white_champ_in_an_imagined _america/; Michael Phillips, "Jake Gyllenhaal's Boxer Fights through Shameless Clichés," *Chicago Tribune*, July 23, 2015, www.chicagotribune.com/entertainment /movies/ct-southpaw-movie-review-jake-gyllenhaal-20150723-column.html.

2 Howard Bryant, "With 'Southpaw' Hollywood Ignores Reality of Today's Boxing Champions," *ESPN.com*, July 16, 2015, www.espn.com/boxing/story/_/id /13179950/boxing-black-champions-made-leap-hollywood.

180 • Notes to Pages 150–157

3 Bob Thompson, "Underdog Tale Still a Champ," *Regina Leader-Post*, November 27, 2015, C2.
4 Steven Rea, "'Creed' Filmmakers, Stars on Philly, Boxing, Time," *Philadelphia Inquirer*, November 22, 2015, H10–H11.
5 Bill Simmons Podcast, November 15, 2017; Clark DeLeon, "'Creed' Shows There Are Still More Rocky Tales to Tell," *Philadelphia Inquirer*, January 24, 2016, C2.
6 R. Thomas Umstead, "What Epix Wants You to Know about 'The Contender,'" *Multichannel News*, August 24, 2018, www.multichannel.com/blog/what-epix-wants-you-to-know-about-the-contender.
7 "Remarks by President Trump at Pardoning of John Arthur 'Jack' Johnson," *WhiteHouse.gov*, May 24, 2018, www.whitehouse.gov/briefings-statements/remarks-president-trump-pardoning-john-arthur-jack-johnson/.
8 Jesse Washington, "The Irony of Trump's Jack Johnson Pardon," *The Undefeated*, May 24, 2018, https://theundefeated.com/whhw/the-irony-of-trumps-jack-johnson-pardon/. Apparently invigorated by the Jack Johnson pardon, Trump claimed that he was exploring the possibility of pardoning Muhammad Ali as well. But Ali's conviction for refusing to report for induction into the military was overturned by the Supreme Court in 1971. Ali's lawyer politely reminded Trump that a pardon was unnecessary. See Eileen Sullivan, "Trump Jabs at a Pardon, but Ali Is Beyond Reach," *New York Times*, June 8, 2018, A12.
9 Kevin Draper, "Checking in on ESPN's Big Bet on Boxing (Yes, Boxing)," *New York Times*, December 17, 2017, D1.
10 Seth Kelley, "Mayweather-McGregor Fight Is a Box-Office Hit," *Variety*, August 27, 2017, https://variety.com/2017/film/news/mayweather-mcgregor-box-office-1202539950/.
11 Wallace Matthews, "HBO Says It Is Leaving the Boxing Business," *New York Times*, September 27, 2018, B8.

Index

ABC (American Broadcasting Company), 3, 61, 76, 77–78, 115, 132
ABC Sports, 3, 103, 113
Abraham, Seth, 113, 115, 116–117, 123
Academy Awards, 82, 125, 153; *Body and Soul* (1947), 108; *Million Dollar Baby* (2004), 137; *Raging Bull* (1980), 105; *Rocky* (1976), 92, 102, 106, 152; *When We Were Kings* (1996), 131
Adkins, Scott, 139
Admiral company, 60
African American Film Critics Association, 153
African Americans, 42, 47, 48, 51, 70, 77; audiences for Ali fights, 80; blaxploitation films and, 92; economic downturn of 1970s and, 97; hero status of Joe Louis, 33–34, 36, 38, 44; Johnson's victory as "second emancipation," 15; opportunities in Hollywood, 108–109; opportunities offered by closed-circuit TV, 81; promoters, 94; protests at Olympic Games (1968), 130; as stars in boxing films, 54, 56; U.S. World War II effort and, 49, 169n25; White working-class resentment toward, 104–105
Against the Ropes (Dutton, 2004), 137–138, 147
Ahrens, Frank, 130
A.K.A. Cassius Clay (Jacobs, 1970), 88, 115
Alberti, Maryse, 152

Aldrick, William F., 12, 13
Algren, Nelson, 133
Ali (Mann, 2001), 132, 134
Ali, John, 78
Ali, Muhammad, 2–3, 93, 101, 117; biopic based on memoir of, 105–107; as Black global icon, 130; in *Body and Soul* remake (1981), 107; Chuvalo match, 79–80, 86; closed-circuit exhibition and, 6, 76–81; conversion to Islam, 75; conviction for refusal of military induction, 81, 180n8; documentaries about, 94–95, 97; Foreman match ["Rumble in the Jungle"] (1974), 94, 130–131, 132; Frazier match ["Fight of the Century"] (1971), 87–90; Frazier match ["Thrilla in Manila"] (1975), 113; *Legendary Champions* (1968) and, 81–82; Liston match (1964), 76–77, 88, 94; Olympic Games and, 130; opposition to Vietnam War, 75, 78, 87; Parkinson's syndrome diagnosis, 129–130; Quarry match, 87–88, 90; renaissance of interest in, 132–133, 134; retirement of, 129; "Rope-a-Dope" strategy, 131, 132; status as undefeated heavyweight champion, 83; *Super Fight* (1970) and, 4, 83–87, 174n37, 174n43; suspension from boxing, 75–76, 81, 87; Wepner match (1975), 91. *See also* Clay, Cassius
Ali: An American Hero (Ichaso, 2000), 132

181

182 • Index

Ali-Frazier I: One Nation . . . Divisible
(HBO Sports, 2000), 132
Ali, the Fighter (Greaves, 1974), 94
All-American Boy, The (Eastman, 1973), 102
All-Time Heavyweight Tournament
(Woroner, 1967), 82–83
Álvarez, Canelo, 158
American Cinephone Company, 16
American Dream, 122, 147, 156; Louis and,
34; *Rocky* (1976) and, 98, 102
Anspaugh, David, 1
antisiphoning regulations, 113
Any Given Sunday (Stone, 1999), 1
Arbuckle, Fatty, 17, 24
Arkin, Alan, 144
Arkush, Michael, 75
Armstrong, Henry, 40–41, 51
Arnheim, Rudolf, 59
Arum, Bob, 78, 80
Ashe, Arthur, 119
Associated Press, 23
As the World Rolls In (1921), 20–21
Avildsen, John, 99, 109

Back in the Day (Borghese, 2016), 155
Baer, Buddy, 46
Baer, Max, 29, 30, 31, 36–37, 66, 168n63; in
The Harder They Fall, 65, 67; in *The Joe
Louis Story*, 56
Baker, Aaron, 4
Bale, Christian, 125
Banderas, Antonio, 124
Barbour, Ralph, 45
Bare Knuckles (Edmonds, 1977), 102
Barnes, T. Roy, 27
Barrow, Joe Louis. *See* Louis, Joe
Barrow, Lillie, 35
Barry, Dave, 24
Basinger, Kim, 143
Basquiat, Jean-Michel, 34
Battle of the Century (Laurel and Hardy,
1927), 25–26
"Battler, The" (Hemingway), 70
Battler, The (Penn, 1955), 70–71, 72
Battling Butler (Keaton, 1926), 25
Bellew, Tony, 151
Bellows, George, 99
Bend It Like Beckham (Chadha, 2002), 1
Berkeley, Busby, 1, 27, 44

Berlin, Irving, 46
Berman, Len, 114
Best Mouse Loses, The (Bray Productions,
1920), 18
Big Chance, The (1933), 26, 27, 29, 30
Big Fight, The (Broadway play, 1928), 25
Big Fights Inc., 81, 88, 115, 116, 123
Big Man, The (Leland, 1990), 109
Birth of a Nation, The (Griffith, 1915), 18
Bisher, Furman, 63
Black, Julian, 35
Blackboard Jungle (Brooks, 1955), 67
Blackburn, Jack, 35, 168n3
Black fighters, 5, 37, 53; Ali renaissance and,
133; boxers as African American heroes,
52; television and, 64
Black Journal (National Educational
Television, 1968–1977), 94
Blackness, 16, 35, 45, 49
Black Panther (Coogler, 2018), 153
Black Thunderbolt (1921), 21
blaxploitation films, 6, 94, 95, 97, 102, 111;
Ali and, 106, 109; race film tradition
and, 92; remake of *Body and
Soul*, 107
Bleed for This (Younger, 2016), 155
Blonde Bomber, The (French, 1936), 51
Blue: The American Dream (Miningham,
2016), 155
Body and Soul (Bowers, 1981), 107–109
Body and Soul (Rossen, 1947), 51–52, 65, 86,
87, 93, 105, 118, 149
Bogart, Humphrey, 65
Bogle, Donald, 93
Bonavena, Oscar, 88–89, 90
Borghese, Paul, 155
Bowers, George, 107
boxing: bareknuckle fights, 4; gender and
racial politics in, 3; hypermasculinity of,
2; interracial bouts, 64; mainstreaming
of boxing history, 129–135; predicted
decline or death of, 7, 129, 140; retired
fighters presented prior to bouts, 31; as
subject of greatest number of sports
movies, 1; television and, 59; theater and,
11. *See also* prizefighting
Boxing After Dark (1996–2018), 126
Boxing Behind Bars (1978), 113–115
Boxing Cats, The (Edison, 1894), 11

Index • 183

boxing films: American Dream narrative and, 34; banned films, 5, 16–17, 20, 21, 22, 24–25, 168n63; ban on interstate transportation of (1912), 3; Black directors of, 7, 94, 147; decline of, 73–74; early films, 10–18; fake films, 84; federal restriction of, 5, 16–17; as first and most popular cinema genre, 9, 165n2; international productions, 4; politics of, 4; put out of business by television, 60; revival of 1970s, 6, 91–92; as sexualized spectacles, 13; on television, 64–73; in transmedia sports culture, 26–32
Boxing's Best series (HBO), 115–116, 117
Boxing's Greatest Champions (HBO), 115, 117–118
Boxing Writers of America, 115
BoxOffice (trade magazine), 60
Boyka: Undisputed (Chapkanov, 2016), 139
Boyle, Ellexis, 137
Braddock, James, 37–38, 42, 45
Brando, Marlon, 67
Brawler, The (Kushner, 2019), 155
Bray Productions, 18
Bridges, Jeff, 95
Britton, Andrew, 102
Broadway plays, 25, 45, 82
Bronson, Charles, 96
Bronx Bull, The (Guigui, 2016), 155
Brooks, Fred, 77
Brooks, Richard, 67
Brown, Jim, 78–79
Brown, Natie, 36
Brown, Phil, 54
Brown, W. L. Lyons, 94–95
Brown Bomber, The (Torch Films, 1940), 45–46
Browning Tod, 1
Bruce, Virginia, 25
Brute, The (Micheaux, 1920), 20, 41
Bryant, Willie, 41
Buffer, Michael, 142
Bull Durham (Shelton, 1988), 124
Burnett, Mark, 141
Burns, Ken, 133
Burns, Tommy, 13, 14, 15
Bush, George W., 156

Cable ACE Award, 115
cable television, 3, 112, 158
Cagney, James, 25, 168n61
Cain and Mabel (1936), 26–27
Calderón, Paul, 136
Calvert, Fay, 19
Cameron, Lucille, 17
Cannon Films, 107
Canzoneri, Tony, 44
Caple, Steven, Jr., 7, 153
Capra, Frank, 47, 48, 49, 102
Carmichael, Luther, 38
Carnera, Primo, 30, 31, 36, 37; fictional boxer based on, 65; in *The Joe Louis Story*, 56; Schaaf killed by (1933), 66
Carpentier, Georges, 3, 21, 23, 24, 59
Carter, Rubin "Hurricane," 113, 133
Cashel Byron's Profession (play, 1906), 11
Castillo, Jose Luis, 138
Cayton, William, 61, 81, 116
CBS (Columbia Broadcasting System), 59, 61, 71, 73
Chadha, Gurinder, 1
Challenge of Chance, The (Revier, 1919), 18, 19, 21
Challenger, The (Moran, 2015), 155
Champ, The (Vidor, 1931), 25, 102
Champ, The (Zeffirelli, 1979), 102, 103
Champion (Robson, 1949), 4, 86, 87
Champion, The (Chaplin, 1915), 18
Chapkanov, Todor, 139
Chaplin, Charlie, 17, 18, 24
Charles, Ezzard, 54
Chartoff, Robert, 105
Chávez, Julio César, 124
Chicago Defender (newspaper), 38, 48
Chuck (Falardeau, 2016), 155
Chuck Davey's Corner (TV show), 64
Chuvalo, George, 77, 79, 80, 86, 87
City for Conquest (Litvak, 1940), 44
Civil Rights Movement, 92, 97, 119
Clark, Bruce, 92
class, 4, 91, 97, 101, 103, 104–105
Clay, Cassius, 73, 75, 76, 77, 94. *See also* Ali, Muhammad
closed-circuit TV, 60, 64, 76–81, 114; Ali and rise of, 6, 75, 90; phasing out of, 115; as theater television, 172n1
Coates, Ta-Nehisi, 152

184 • Index

Cobb, Lee J., 45, 67
Coburn, James, 96–97
Colasanto, Nicholas, 95
Colbert, Claudette, 26
Cold War, 109, 153
Colicos, John, 94
Collins, Bud, 83
Columbia Pictures, 67, 68, 73
Comiskey, Pat, 65, 67
Condon, David, 63, 74
Conn, Billy, 46, 60
Contender, The (Burnett, reality TV
    program), 141, 155, 156, 179n14, 179n16
Conti, Bill, 103, 104
Coogler, Ryan, 7, 147, 150–151, 152
Cooke, Jack Kent, 89
Cooney, Gerry, 109
Cooper, Henry, 80
Corbett, "Gentleman" Jim, 10–11, 13, 15, 46
Corbett and Courtney Before a Kinetograph
    (Edison, 1894), 10, 11
Corbett-Fitzsimmons Fight (1897), 11–12
corruption, 7, 72–73, 123; government
    investigation of, 73–74; thrown fights,
    73. *See also* gangsters/mobsters
Cortez, Joe, 142
Cosell, Howard, 77, 80, 103, 112
Cosmopolitan Pictures, 26
Costas, Bob, 130
court cases, 83, 113; Ali's draft refusal, 81,
    180n8; *Home Box Office v. FCC* (1977),
    113; IBC and, 73; MMA (mixed martial
    arts) and, 139; Tyson's rape trial and
    conviction, 120–121, 122, 129
Courtney, Peter, 10
Couture, Randy, 140
Covington, Aaron, 150
Creed (Coogler, 2015), 7, 150–153, *152*, 155, 157
Creed 2 (Caple, 2018), 7, 153–155, 157
Cripps, Thomas, 49, 169n25
Crosley company, 60
Crosson, Seán, 4
Crouch, Stanley, 134
Crowd Roars, The (Thorpe, 1938), 44
Curtiz, Michael, 1, 44, 46, 47
Cushing, Jack, 10

Daley, Arthur, 62
D'Amato, Cus, 88, 120, 122

Daredevil Jack (Pathé serial, 1920), 20, 21, 22
Darrow, John, 26
Davey, Chuck, 63, 64, 68, 69, 70
David, Keith, 133
David, Thayer, 100
Davidovich, Lolita, 124
Davis, Duane, 134
DAZN streaming service, 158
death, in the boxing ring, 66, 67
Death Wish (1974), 96
De La Hoya, Oscar, 126–127, 128, 179n14
Dempsey (Trikonis, 1983), 109
Dempsey, Jack, 2–4, 31, 117, 167–168n55;
    All-Time Heavyweight Tournament
    (1967) and, 82; Carpentier match (1921),
    21–22, 23, 24, 59; commercial sports
    media and, 5, 18, 21, 22–26; "Dempsey-
    mania," 22, 32; Firpo match (1923), 61,
    99; in *The Jack Dempsey Revue*, 30;
    Manassa Mauler moniker, 19, 62; in
    Manhattan Madness (1925), 22–23, *23*;
    racial politics and, 26, 36, 56; repeal of
    Sims Act and, 45; retirement of, 5, 34;
    Tunney match (1926), 23–25, 26, 37,
    168n55; Willard match (1919), 18, 19, 46,
    173n23
Dempsey and Firpo (Bellows painting,
    1924), 99
Denby, David, 133
De Niro, Robert, 105, 143
Derek, John, 69
Desmond, Cleo, 39
Devil's Stocking, The (Algren, 1981), 133
Diamond, Brian, 138
Diggstown (Ritchie, 1992), 129
digital streaming, 3
DiNicola, Ron, 131
Dmytryk, Edward, 53
docu-branding, 6, 112, 120–128
docudramas, 6
documentaries, 1, 4, 6, 45; about Ali,
    94–95, 97; HBO's image and, 111, 112;
    home video, 117
Donen, Stanley, 102
Don King: Only in America (Herzfeld,
    1997), 122, 123
Don King Productions, 113, 115
Dooto Music Center (Compton, Calif.),
    77, 79

Do the Right Thing (Lee, 1989), 118, 119
Douglas, James "Buster," 118
Douglas, Santiago, 136
Doumani, Lorenzo, 135
Drum (Carver, 1976), 93–94
Drury, David, 109
DuMont network, 61
Durán, Roberto, 103, 155
Durham, Richard, 105
Dutton, Charles S., 137, 147
Dylan, Bob, 133

Early, Gerald, 18
Eason, B. Reeves, 44
Eastman, Charles K., 102
Eastwood, Clint, 102, 136
Ebert, Roger, 105
Edel, Uli, 120
Edgerton, Joel, 140
Edison, Thomas, 10, 11, 14
Edmonds, Don, 102
Edwards, James, 53
Egg Crate Wallop, The (Storm, 1919), 18
Eig, Jonathan, 94
Einstein, Charles, 62
Ejiofor, Chiwetel, 140
Ellis, Jimmy, 87
Epix cable channel, 155
Epps, Omar, 137
ESPN, 3, 113, 119, 123, 124, 154, 179n16;
    ESPN+ live-streaming add-on,
    158; *ESPN The Magazine,* 150;
    SportsCenter, 142
Evans, Janet, 130
Evensen, Bruce J., 19–23
Every Which Way but Loose (Fargo, 1978), 102
Ezra, Michael, 78, 130, 131

Fairbanks, Douglas, 24, 27
Falardeau, Philippe, 155
Falls, Joe, 79
Fanaka, Jamaa, 107
Fargo, James, 102
Farnsworth, Philo T., 59
fascism, 38, 49
Fat City (Huston, 1972), 95–96, 97, 99,
    100, 104
Favreau, Jon, 134
Federal Communications Commission, 113

Fielding, Raymond, 165n2
Fields, Jackie, 31
Fight and Win serial (Kenton, 1924), 22, 25
Fighter, The (Russell, 2010), 125–126
Fight Game, The (Lampley sports talk
    show), 143
Fighting Marine, The (Bennet, 1926), 23
Fight Never Ends, The (Lerner, 1948), 49, *50*
Fight of the Week (ABC), 76
*Fire and Fear: The Inside Story of Mike
    Tyson* (Torres, 1989), 120
Firestone, Roy, 119
Firpo, Luis, 61, 99
Fisher, Ham, 51
Fits, The (Holmer, 2015), 155
Fitzsimmons, Bob, 11
Fleischer, Nat, 62–63
Fleischer, Richard, 93, 109
Flynn, "Fireman" Jim, 16
Folley, Zora, 81
Ford, Gerald, 94, 95
Ford, John, 87
Foreman, George: Frazier match
    ["Sunshine Showdown"] (1973), 112–113;
    "Rumble in the Jungle" with Ali (1974),
    94, 130–131, 132
For His Mother's Sake (1922), 21
Foster, Norman, 26
Fox, Billy, 73
Fox network, 124, 132, 179n14
Fraser, Harry L., 39
Frazier, Joe, 87, 89, 112, 113
French, Lloyd, 51
Friday Night Fights (TV show), 60, 61, 63,
    70, 72, 74
Friedman, Lester D., 4
Fruitvale Station (Coogler, 2013), 151
Fuchs, Michael, 117
Fuhs, Kristen, 177n21
Fuqua, Antoine, 7, 147

Gallico, Paul, 19, 22
Ganev, Valentin, 139
gangsters/mobsters, 26, 43, 53, 67, 74, 92,
    108, 158. *See also* corruption
Ganzer, Alvin, 69
Gardner, Leonard, 95–96
Garfield, John, 109
Gast, Leon, 130, 131

186 • Index

Gavilán, Kid, 63
gender, 3, 4, 135–138, 153
General Electric, 60
Gentleman Jim (Walsh, 1942), 46
George, Susan, 93
Gibson, Truman, 64
Gilbert, Doug, 78
Gillette Cavalcade of Sports (NBC), 3, 59
Gillette Company, 59, 60, 73, 74
Gilmore, Al-Tony, 13, 15
Girlfight (Kusama, 2000), 2, 135–136
Givens, Robin, 120, 122
Gladiator (Herrington, 1992), 129
Gleason, Jackie, 74
Glick, David, 86
Goebbels, Joseph, 168n63
Golden Age of Sports (1920s), 10, 20
Golden Age of Sports Media, 20, 26, 32
Golden Boy (Mamoulian, 1939), 44–45, 51
Golden Gloves (Dymtryk, 1940), 53
Goldie and the Boxer (Miller, 1979), 103
Gomez, Miguel, 148
Goodart Pictures, 24
Gordon, Robert, 54
Gordon Sisters Boxing, The (Edison, 1901), 11
Gough, Lloyd, 51
Gould, Elliott, 102
Gould, Jack, 72
Gowdy, Curt, 115
Great American Broadcast (1941), 46
Great Depression, 34, 45, 92
Greatest, The (Gries and Hellman, 1977), 105–107, 108, 109
Greatest Fights of the Century series, 61, 81
Great John L., The (Tuttle, 1945), 46
Great White Hope, The (Ritt, 1970), 82, 133, 147
Great White Hype, The (Hudlin, 1996), 129
Great White Way, The (Hopper, 1924), 26, 27
Greaves, William, 94
Green, Alfred E., 54
Greenburg, Ross, 111, 113, 116, 123–124, 126–128
Gregory, Eddie, 114
Grey, Shirley, 27
Griffith, D. W., 18
Grindon, Leger, 2, 4, 45, 73, 92, 105
Grudge Match (Segal, 2013), 143–144

Guigui, Martin, 155
Gunning, Tom, 11
Gyllenhaal, Jake, 147

Hagler, Marvin, 116
Halpern, Nate, 76
Hamilton, Bernie, 93
Hamilton, Kim, 107
Hammer (Clark, 1972), 92–93, 108
Hands of Stone (Jakubowicz, 2016), 155
Harder They Fall, The (Robson, 1956), 65–70, 72, 73, 118, 171n17
Hard Times (Hill, 1975), 4, 96–97, 139
Hardy, Tom, 140
Harlem Globetrotters, The (Brown and Jason, 1951), 54
Harrelson, Woody, 124
Harris, Edna Mae, 39, 43
Harris, Naomie, 149
Hart, Kevin, 144
Hart, Marvin, 14
Hathaway, Henry, 87
Hatton, Ricky, 138
HBO (Home Box Office) and HBO Sports, 3, 6, 111–112, 129, 132, 144, 153; docu-branding and, 120–128; documentaries, 115–116, 123; HBO Pictures, 120, 123; live boxing's role in brand building of, 157–158; pay-per-view, 138, 141, 147, 148, 154; sports programming and launch of, 112; "Thrilla in Manila" match and, 113; TVKO pay-per-view outlet, 120, 124, 126; Tyson's contract with, 116–120
HBO Boxing (video game), 126
Hearst, William Randolph, 26, 27
heavyweight championship, 2, 5, 75; Blacks' control over organization of, 78; early cinema and, 12; first televised bout, 60; race and, 35; racial politics and, 37; unification tournament (1980s), 116–117
Heisler, Stuart, 47
Heller, Peter, 117
Hemingway, Ernest, 70
Hibbs, Jesse, 69
High on Crack Street: Lost Lives in Lowell (HBO *America Undercover* episode), 125
Hill, Walter, 4, 96, 139
Hitchcock, Alfred, 1
Hitler, Adolf, 37, 48

Index • 187

Hoffer, Richard, 116
Holden, William, 44
Hollywood, 1, 17, 46, 70, 103; African Americans in, 108–109; celebrities as boxing fans, 24; classical studio era, 5, 9, 19, 107; "New Hollywood," 70, 92, 102; popularity of Joe Louis and, 34
Holmer, Anna Rose, 155
Holmes, Larry, 109, 115
Holyfield, Evander, 177n21
Home Box Office v. FCC (1977), 113
Homeboy (Seresin, 1988), 109
Hoosiers (Anspaugh, 1986), 1
Hopkins, Bernard, 142
Hopp, Julius, 21
Howard, Terrence, 132
Howe, James Wong, 51, 105
How the West Was Won (Ford, Hathaway, Marshall, 1962), 87
Hudlin, Reginald, 147
Hughes, Geraldine, 142
Hughes, Langston, 48
Hunter, Kim, 72
"Hurricane" (Bob Dylan song, 1976), 133
Hurricane (Jewison, 1999), 133, 134
Huston, John, 1, 95
Huston, Walter, 29

IBC [International Boxing Club] ("the Octopus"), 53–54, 60, 61, 64, 65; government investigation of, 73, 74; *The Harder They Fall* and, 67; televised fights and, 61; TV network programs controlled by, 70
Ichaso, Leon, 132
Independent Film Journal, 76–77
injuries, in the boxing ring, 7
International Boxing Federation, 116
International Boxing Hall of Fame, 2
Ireland, Jill, 97
Iron Man (1931), 25, 26, 27
It's a Wonderful Life (Capra, 1946), 102

Jack Dempsey Revue (vaudeville show), 18, 30
Jackie Robinson Story, The (Green, 1950), 54
Jack Johnson (Jacobs, 1970), 88, 115, 133
Jack Johnson's Own Story of the Big Fight, 16
Jackson, Columbus, 43
Jackson, Curtis "50 Cent," 148

Jacobs, Jim, 81, 116, 118, 122
Jacobs, Mike, 35–36, 37, 53, 54, 59
Jacobs, Raymond, 87
Jakubowicz, Jonathan, 155
James, Steve, 135
James, Willie, 62
Jarecki, Eugene, 135
Jason, Will, 54
Jawbone (Napper, 2017), 155
Jazzy Jeff, 117
Jefferson, Jack, 82
Jeffries, Jim, 13–14, 15, 31, 82, 83
Jewish fighters, 37, 44, 51
Jewison, Norman, 133
Joe and Max (James, 2002), 135
Joe Louis Enterprises, 53
Joe Louis Story, The (Gordon, 1953), 54–55, 55, 61, 105, 134; as first boxing film with Black protagonist, 5, 34, 54, 56; Schmeling's depiction in, 135
Joe Palooka, Champ (Le Borg, 1946), 51, 140
Johnson, Jack, 3, 4, 22, 31, 37, 57; Ali compared with, 78, 81, 82; in *Boxing's Best* series, 115–116; Burns match (1908), 13, 14; Jeffries match (1910), 15–16, 18, 37, 39, 87–88; *Legendary Champions* focus on, 81; Louis's handlers and, 35, 168n3; Mann Act conviction (1913), 17, 20, 156; as outspoken dissident, 13; prison term (1920–1921), 20; in race films, 20–21; racist reactions to, 5; Trump's pardon of, 156–157, 180n8; *Unforgivable Blackness* and, 133–134
Johnson, Mae, 41
Johnson-Jeffries Fight (Blackton, 1910), 15, 16, 18
Jolson, Al, 31
Jones, Bobby, 22
Jones, Robert Earl, 41
Jones, Roy, Jr., 126, 149, 150
Jones, Tommy Lee, 131
Jordan, Michael B., 151
Joyce, Andrian, 21

Kadison, Harry, 41
Kaese, Harold, 86
Karlson, Phil, 44
Kazan, Elia, 67
Keach, Stacey, 95

188 • Index

Kearns, Jack "Doc," 18–19, 28, 36
Keaton, Buster, 24, 25
Keep Punching (Clein, 1939), 40, 41, 49
Kefauver, Estes, 73–74
Kellerman, Max, 142, 152
Kellner, Douglas, 101, 104
Kennedy, Edgar, 17
Kennedy, Jayne, 107, 108
Kennedy, Leon Isaac, 107, 108–109
Kerz, Mike, 133
Ketchel, Stanley, 14
Keystone Studios, 17
Kibbee, Guy, 28
Kid Comes Back, The (Eason, 1938), 44
Kid Galahad (Curtiz, 1937), 44, 45, 51
Kiley, Richard, 88
kinetoscope, 10
Kinetoscope Exhibition Company, 10, 11
King, Don, 94, 103, 112, 148; HBO
    vilification of, 122–123; heavyweight
    unification tournament and, 116; Tyson
    and, 118–120, 177n20
King, Martin Luther, Jr., 33
King, Perry, 93
King of the World (Young, 2000), 132
KingVision PPV, 120
Kirk, Phyllis, 70
Kittles, Tory, 137
Klein, William, 94, 95
Knockout (Doumani, 2000), 135
Knockout, The (Keystone Studios, 1914),
    17–18
K.O. for Cupid (1924), 22
KO Nation (2000–2001), 126
Kotto, Yaphet, 94
Krazy Kat cartoons, 18
Kruger, Otto, 29
Kubrick, Stanley, 1
Ku Klux Klan, 18
Kusama, Karyn, 2, 135, 136
Kushner, Ken, 155

Laemmle, Carl, 22
LaMotta, Jake, 73–74, 105, 143
Lampkin, Charles, 92
Lampley, Jim, 125, 141, 142, 143; *Boxing's
    Greatest Hits* and, 118; in *Creed*, 147, 149;
    in *Creed 2*, 154; *Legendary Nights* and, 124
Lane, Mike, 65

Langford, Sam, 20
Lardner, John, 63
Lardner, Ring, 19, 63
Lardner, Ring, Jr., 106
Larkin, Jay, 116
Last Man Standing (Lee, 1987), 109
Latinx community, boxing connection
    of, 136
Laurel and Hardy, 25–26
Laurence, Oona, 148
Lawford, Peter, 108
Leather Saint, The (Ganzer, 1956), 69–70
Le Borg, Reginald, 51
LeBow, Guy, 82, 83, 85
Lee, Canada, 51
Lee, Damian, 109
Lee, Spike, 118–119, 122, 131, 177n21
Legendary Champions (Chapin, 1968),
    81–82, 85, 88, 115, 133
Legendary Nights (HBO Sports, 2003),
    123–124, 125
Leifer, Neil, 109
Leland, David, 109
Leonard, Mike, 10
Leonard, Sugar Ray, 141, 179n16
Leonard-Cushing Fight (Edison, 1894),
    10, 11
Lerner, Joseph, 49
Lewis, Strangler, 31
Liebling, A. J., 62
Life of Jimmy Dolan, The (Mayo, 1933), 25,
    27–29
Lipkin, Steven, 120
Lipsyte, Robert, 20, 88
Liston, Sonny, 76, 77, 88, 94, 114
Litvak, Anatole, 44
Lo Bianco, Tony, 120
London, Brian, 80
London, Jack, 14
Louis, Joe, 2, 4, 32, 71, 81, 107, 168n3;
    against Braddock, 37–38, 45; earnings,
    117; film boxers modeled after, 41–45;
    hero status among African Americans,
    33–34, 36, 38, 44; International Boxing
    Club (IBC) and, 53–54, 60; life and
    career, 34–39; Marciano match, 54–55,
    56, 60–61, 134; monikers attached to, 36;
    in "race" films, 5; retirement of, 53, 54;
    against Savold, 60; Schmeling's

friendship with, 135; in *Spirit of Youth*, 39–41
Louis–Schmeling bouts, 37–40, 43, 48, 54, 61
Louisville Sponsoring Group, 78, 94, 95
Lovell, Pedro, 99
Loy, Myrna, 29
Lucas, George, 102
Lule, Jack, 121, 122
Lumet, Sidney, 102
Lundgren, Dolph, 151
Lyle, Ron, 114

MacMahon, Aline, 28
made-for-TV movies, 4, 168n61
Mailer, Norman, 2, 13, 131
Main Bout Inc., 78–79, 80, 84, 95, 118
Main Event, The (Zieff, 1979), 102
Malcolm X, 77
Malden, Karl, 67
Malitz, Michael, 78
Mamet, David, 140, 141
Mamoulian, Rouben, 44
Mandingo (Fleischer, 1975), 93–94, 98, 106
Manhattan Madness (1925), 22–23, *23*
Mann, Daniel, 102
Mann, Michael, 131, 132
Mann Act, 17, 20, 156
Marcele, Buddy, 157
March, Joseph Moncure, 53
Marciano (Winkler, 1999), 134, 135
Marciano, Rocky, 4–6, 54, 64, 67, 135;
    All-Time Heavyweight Tournament (1967) and, 82; death in plane crash, 84; depicted in *Marciano* (1999), 134; earnings, 117; evoked by "Rocky Balboa," 91, 92; first title defense (1953), 61; in *The Joe Louis Story*, 56; retirement of, 73, 87; status as undefeated heavyweight champion, 83; in *Super Fight* (1970), 76, 83–87, 101, 142; telecast of fight with Louis (1951), 60–61; White Hope narrative and, 134
Marshall, George, 87
martial arts, 129
Martin, Dewey, 70
Martin, Strother, 97
Martino, Sergio, 109
Mason, James, 93

Matchroom boxing, 158
Matilda (Mann, 1978), 102
Matoian, John, 123
Mayweather, Floyd, Jr., 4, 126–127, 128, 147, 157
McAdams, Rachel, 147
McCabe, Bruce, 106
McCain, Senator John, 138, 156
McCarthy, Anna, 75, 172n1
McCarthy, P. H., 15
McGee, Vonetta, 93
McGeehan, W. O., 19
McGregor, Conor, 157
McIntire, John, 69
McIntosh, Hugh D. "Huge Deal," 14
McKernan, Luke, 9
McNamee, Graham, 24
Meeker, George, 28
Meet John Doe (Capra, 1941), 102
Mein Kampf (Hitler), 48
Merchant, Larry, 114, 119, 129, 141, 142, 143
Meredith, Burgess, 98
Meter, Harry von, 18
Micheaux, Oscar, 1, 20, 41, 43
middleweight championship, 64, 73
Mike Tyson and History's Greatest Knockouts (1989), 117
Mike Tyson's Punch-Out!! (video game), 117
Mildenberger, Karl, 80
Miller, David, 103
Millington, Brad, 137
Million Dollar Baby (Eastwood, 2004), 136–137, 138
Miningham, Ryan, 155
Minx, The (Jacobs, 1969), 87
Mitchell, David, 109
MMA (mixed martial arts), 7, 129, 138–141, 144, 147, 157
Monkey on My Back (Toth, 1957), 44
Moore, Archie, 67
Moore, Dickie, 25
Moran, Frank, 31
Moran, Kent, 155
Moreland, Mantan, 40
Morgan, Anne, 21, 31
Morgan, J. P., 21
Moriarty, Cathy, 105
Morrell, George, 27
Morris, Wayne, 44

190 • Index

Morrow, Jeff, 69
Moss, Carlton, 48–49
Most Valuable Boxers, 40
Motion Picture Production Code, 44
Motorola company, 60
Movie Movie (Donen, 1978), 102
Moving Picture World, 15, 16
Mr. T, 109
Muhammad, Herbert, 78
Muhammad Ali: The Greatest (Klein, 1974), 94, 95
Munteanu, Florian, 154
Murphy, Audie, 69
Murphy, George, 47
Murray, Jim, 77
Murray, Susan, 127
Muse, Clarence, 39
Musser, Charles, 11, 12
Mutual Broadcasting System, 90

NAACP, 37, 49, 153
Napper, Thomas Q., 155
National Amateur Wireless Association, 21
National Negro Industrial and Economic Union, 78
National Police Gazette, 9
Nation of Islam, 77, 78
Naval Cadet, A (play, 1896), 11
Navy Relief Society, 46
Nazi Germany, 37, 38, 42, 51, 56, 135, 168n63
NBA (National Basketball Association), 112, 123
NBC (National Broadcasting Company), 3, 24, 61, 70, 72–73, 131; Ali at Olympic Games (1984) and, 130; *The Contender*, 141; *Friday Night Fights*, 74; made-for-TV movies, 103
NCR-315 computer, boxing variables and, 82, 83, 85
Negro Soldier, The (Heisler, 1944), 47, 48, 49, 135
Neiman, LeRoy, 104
Nelson, Ralph, 71, 73, 74
Network (Lumet, 1976), 102
Neumann, Kurt, 54
Newfield, Jack, 103, 122
Newman, Paul, 69, 70
New Right (1970s), 92
newsreels, 84, 165n2

New York Clipper (newspaper), 9
New York State Athletic Commission, 74, 81
Next Great Champ, The (Fox, 2004), 179n14
NFL Today (CBS), 107
NHL (National Hockey League), 112
Nick Adams Stories (Hemingway), 70
Night Parade (St. Clair, 1929), 26, 27
Nixon, Marian, 25
noir films, 51, 52–53, 65, 69
Nolte, Nick, 140
Norris, James, 53, 74
Norton, Ken, 93
Notorious Elinor Lee, The (Micheaux, 1940), 41–43, *42*, 46, 49
Nova, Lou, 59

Oates, Joyce Carol, 2
Oates, Warren, 94
Obama, Barack, 156
O'Connor, Gavin, 140
Odets, Clifford, 44, 45
O'Hehir, Andrew, 150
Ohio State Bureau of Motion Pictures, 21
Olympic Games, 89, 130
O'Neal, Frederick, 70
O'Neal, Ryan, 102
O'Neil, Sally, 25
Only in America: The Life and Crimes of Don King (Newfield, 1995), 123
Onstott, Kyle, 93
On the Waterfront (Kazan, 1954), 67–68, 69, 99, 100, 105, 141
Opponent, The (Jarecki, 2000), 135
Opponent, The (Martino, 1988), 109

Pacquiano, Manny, 147
Page, Don, 87–88
Paget, Derek, 120
Palance, Jack, 71
Palmer, Lilli, 52
Papke, Billy, 31
Parks, Gordon, 92
Pathé, 20, 23
Patterson, Floyd, 77
Paymer, David, 135
pay-per-view feeds, 6, 115, 120
Peabody Award, 72
Penitentiary [three-part franchise] (Fanaka, 1979, 1987), 107, 114

Penn, Arthur, 70, 92
Pep, Willie, 60
Perenchio, Jerry, 89–90
Perroni, Patsy, 59
Philco, 60
Pittsburgh Kid, The (Townley, 1941), 46
Playhouse 90 (CBS), 71
Play It to the Bone (Shelton, 1999), 124–125
Plimpton, George, 131
Polonsky, Abraham, 108
Povich, Shirley, 77, 87
Preece, Michael, 102
Presley, Elvis, 44
Pride of the Yankees (Wood, 1942), 1
Prize Fighter, The (Preece, 1979), 102
Prizefighter and the Lady, The (Van Dyke, 1933), 29–32, 168n63
prizefighting, 6, 36, 57, 63, 69; cable television and, 111; closed-circuit exhibition and, 75; fame and wealth of boxing stars, 51; HBO and, 6, 112, 114, 115, 157; Hollywood takedown of, 65, 67; legal status of, 9, 12; masculinity and, 2; media relationship to, 5, 26, 27; MMA (mixed martial arts) and, 138; radio and, 29; shrinking fan base of, 7; teleplays and, 70; television and, 62. *See also* boxing
Pye, Brad, 79

Quarry, Jerry, 87–88, 90, 107
Quimby, Fred, 22
Quinn, Anthony, 73

race films, 20–21, 40
racism, 18, 35, 36; corruption and, 53; of German Nazis, 37; institutionalized, 56, 107, 133; legal conspiracies, 16, 17; mainstream sports establishment and, 119; persistence of, 134; White working-class, 101
Rader, Benjamin G., 19
radio, 3, 21, 24, 59, 158; Armed Forces Radio, 89; as primarily domestic medium, 29; Voice of America, 82
Raging Bull (Scorsese, 1980), 2, 73, 105, 119, 137, 143, 144, 176n23
Rahway State Prison (Woodbridge, N.J.), boxing in, 113–115, 177n9
Rall, Tommy, 69

Ramsaye, Terry, 9, 11
Rashad, Phylicia, 151
Ratner, Herbert, 54
RCA (Radio Corporation of America), 3, 21, 22, 24, 59, 60
Reagan, Ronald, 47, 105
reality TV, 6, 141
Rector, Enoch, 12
Redbelt (Mamet, 2008), 140
Remnick, David, 132
Requiem for a Heavyweight (Nelson, 1956), 71–73, 74, 103
Rhames, Ving, 122, 123, 139
Rice, Grantland, 19, 23–24, 31, 36
Rich, Frank, 98
Rickard, Tex, 18, 20, 22, 27, 35, 36, 167–168n55
Right Cross (Sturges, 1950), 54
Ring (boxing magazine), 19, 40, 63, 89, 124
Ring, The (Neumann, 1952), 54
Rivers, Joe, 31
Roberts, Leonard, 135
Roberts, Randy, 35, 75
Robichaux, Mark, 117
Robinson, Edward G., 44
RoboCop (Verhoeven, 1987), 102
Robson, Mark, 4, 65, 67, 68, 72
Rocky (Stallone/Avildsen, 1976), 91–92, 97–102, 111, 125, 144, 175n14; critics' responses to, 98, 137; evoked in *The Contender*, 141; evoked in *Girlfight*, 136; "Gonna Fly Now" theme song, 103; International Boxing Hall of Fame and, 2; as most popular film of bicentennial year, 97; popularity of, 6, 92, 97; reactionary politics and, 155; reboots of, 7, 102–109, 150–153, *152*, 155; romanticism of, 98
Rocky Balboa (Stallone, 2006), 141–144
Rocky II (Stallone, 1979), 103–105, 149
Rocky IV (Stallone, 1985), 109, 151, 153, 154
Rocky V (Stallone/Avildsen, 1990), 101, 109
Roddenbery, Seaborn A., 16–17
Rodriguez, Michelle, 135
Rodriguez, Sixto, 96
Rondinone, Troy, 54
Rooney, Mickey, 74
Roosevelt, Franklin Delano (FDR), 21, 64
Roosevelt, Theodore, 16

192 • Index

Rose, Norman, 81–82
Rosenstone, Robert, 120
Ross, Barney, 37
Rossen, Robert, 51, 107
Rowntree, Leslie, 79
Roxborough, John, 35
Runyon, Damon, 19
Rush, Barbara, 69
Ruskin, Shimen, 51
Russell, David O., 125
Ruth, Babe, 22
Ryan, Meg, 137
Ryan, Michael, 101, 104
Ryan, Robert, 53

Sackler, Howard, 82
Saint, Eva Marie, 67
St. Joe Louis, Surrounded by Snakes (Basquiat, 1982), 34
St. John, Howard, 69
Samaranch, Juan Antonio, 130
Sammons, Jeffrey T., 34, 64, 86
Sanders, Ed, 62
Sandomir, Richard, 127, 141
Sanello, Frank, 120
Santiago, Ray, 136
Saraceno, Jon, 131
Sarnoff, David, 21
Sarris, Andrew, 100
Savold, Lee, 60
Schaaf, Ernie, 66, 67
Schmeling, Max, 40, 42, 48, 54, 168n63; depicted in *Joe and Max*, 135; in *The Joe Louis Story*, 56
Schreiber, Liev, 126
Schulberg, Budd, 65, 67, 89
Schweiger, Til, 135
Scorsese, Martin, 1, 2, 73, 92, 102, 105, 176n23
Scott, George C., 120
Scott, James, 113–114, 115
Scott, Tony, 102
Seaton, Nikki Swasey, 107
Sedgwick, Josie, 20
Segal, Peter, 143
Seresin, Michael, 109
Serling, Rod, 71, 74
Set-Up, The (Wise, 1949), 52–53, 65, 71, 140, 150

Shaft (Parks, 1971), 92
Shannon, Vicellous Reon, 133
Shaw, George Bernard, 11
Shaw, Oscar, 27
Shaw, Stan, 101
Shelton, Ron, 124
Shire, Talia, 98
Showtime, 119, 122, 157, 158
Shroeder, Ricky, 102
Shumway, Lee, 26
Simon, Abe, 46
Simpson, O. J., 103
Sims, Thetus, 16
Sims Act (1912), 16–17, 18, 45
Sinatra, Frank, 89
Siskel, Gene, 108
Sizemore, Tom, 125
Smith, J. O., 21
Smith, Rainbeaux, 94
Smith, Red, 115
Smith, Will ("Fresh Prince"), 117, 131
Snipes, Wesley, 139
"social problem" films (1950s), 67
Somebody Up There Likes Me (Wise, 1956), 64, 69, 99
Sonenberg, David, 131
Sonnen, Chael, 144
Sonny Liston: The Mysterious Life and Death of a Champion (HBO Sports, 1995), 123
Southpaw (Fuqua, 2015), 7, 147–150, 153, 157
Spike TV, 138
Spinell, Joe, 99
Spirit of the Times (newspaper), 9
Spirit of Youth (Fraser, 1938), 39–41, 44, 49, 54
Split Decision (Drury, 1988), 109
sponsors, 24, 64; commercial breaks and, 60, 63, 82; female spectatorship and, 63; Gillette Company, 59, 60; Health Biscuit Corporation of America, 27; Pabst Blue Ribbon, 61
SportsBusiness Journal, 128
Sports Films Inc., 61
Sports Illustrated, 73, 82, 94, 116, 138–139
Sportsman of the Year, 94
sports media, 5, 10, 18–26
SportsVision, 77
Stallone, Ray, 128

Stallone, Sylvester, 2, 91, 98–99, 102, 151, 175n14; Ali's trash talk about, 106, 131; *The Contender* hosted by, 141, 179n16; in *Grudge Match*, 143; on the *Rocky* franchise, 141, 143; Trump and, 156

Star Wars (Lucas, 1977), 102

Starz cable channel, 135

Stehli, Edgar, 71

Steiger, Rod, 65, 67

Stein, Sammy, 28

Sterling, Jan, 65

Stewart, Alex, 118

Stewart, Anita, 27

Stewart, Paul, 54

Stone, Oliver, 1

Storm, Jerome, 18

Streible, Dan, 4, 5, 11; on Dempsey-Tunney, 24–25; on Johnson as first Black movie star, 14–15; on mixed-race fight pictures, 13

Streisand, Barbara, 102

Sturges, John, 54

Sugar, Bert, 1

Sugar Ray Robinson: The Bright Lights and Dark Shadows of a Champion (HBO Sports, 1998), 123

Sullivan, John L., 46

Sullivan, Russell, 64

Super Bowl football, 89

Super Fight (Woroner, 1970), 4, 76, 83–87, 142, 174n37, 174n43; put to test by Ali-Quarry match, 88; racial politics and, 6, 83, 95; revival of boxing films (1970s) and, 91; rise of closed-circuit TV and, 90; *Rocky* (1976) compared with, 101

Supreme Court, U.S., 73

Swank, Hilary, 138

Sweet Sweetback's Baadasssss Song (Van Peebles, 1971), 92

Sykes, Brenda, 93

Sylvania company, 60

syndicators/syndication, 61

Talbot, Lyle, 28

Tarver, Antonio, 141, 143

Taxi Driver (Scorsese, 1976), 102

Taylor, Estelle, 22, 23, *23*

Taylor, Jermain, 142

Taylor, Meldrick, 124

teleplays, 4, 70, 74

television, 3, 29, 59–61, 158; boxing films on television, 65–73; critique of boxing on TV, 62; fights and fighters on, 61–64; number of fight viewers, 61

Terrell, Ernie, 78, 81

Terrible Joe Moran (1984), 168n61

They Made Me a Criminal (Berkeley, 1939), 27, 44

They Never Come Back (Newmeyer, 1932), 27

30 for 30 series (ESPN), 124

This Is the Army (Curtiz, 1943), 46–47, 48, 169n25

Thomas, Reed, 20

Thompson, Bianca, 153

Thompson, Blanche, 21

Thorpe, Richard, 44

Thunderground (Mitchell, 1989), 109

Tirelli, Jaime, 136

Title Holder, The (1924), 22

TNT (Theater Network Television), 76, 77

Toback, James, 177n20

Tobey, Dan, 31

Toole, F. X., 136

Top Gun (Scott, 1986), 102

Torch Films, 45

Torres, José, 120

Toth, André de, 44

Tough Enough (Fleischer, 1983), 109

Townley, Jack, 46

Trevor, Hugh, 26

Trikonis, Gus, 109

Trump, Donald, 155–156, 180n8

Tunney, Gene, 3, 23–25, 26, 37, 168n55

Tunney-Dempsey Fight (Goodart Pictures, 1927), 25

Turah, Kenneth, 86

Turner, Mae, 40

Tuttle, Frank, 46

12 Round Gun (Younger, 2016), 155

Twentieth Century Sporting Club, 36, 37

24/7 (HBO Sports, 2007–), 126–128, 157

Tyson (Edel, 1995), 120–123, *121*

Tyson (Toback, 2008), 177n20

Tyson, "Iron" Mike, 4, 109, 116–120, 124, 131; dehumanizing tropes in depiction of, 120–121; rape conviction and prison term, 120, 122, 129; *Undisputed* (2002) based on biography of, 139

194 • Index

UFC (Ultimate Fighting Championship), 138

Ultimate Fighter (reality TV program), 138–139, 141

Undisputed (Hill, 2002), 139

Undisputed II: Last Man Standing (Florentine, 2006), 139

Undisputed III: Redemption (Florentine, 2010), 139

Undisputed Truth (Lee, 2013), 177n21

Unforgivable Blackness: The Rise and Fall of Jack Johnson (Burns, 2005), 133–134, 135

United Artists, 99, 103, 175n14

Universal Pictures, 22

Upton, Sam, 155

Van Dyke, W. S., 29

Van Every, Edward, 36

Van Peebles, Melvin, 92

Variety, 23, 38, 90, 141; on *Spirit of Youth*, 40; on TV versus boxing films, 64

Vejar, Chico, 69

Ventimiglia, Milo, 142

Verhoeven, Paul, 102

veriscope, 12

Veriscope Company, 11, 12

Versus (sports channel), 179n16

Vertinsky, Patricia, 137

video games, 6, 117, 126, 128, 152

Vidor, King, 1, 102

Vietnam War, 75, 78, 97

Viruet, Edwin, 103

Vitagraph, 15, 16

Voight, Jon, 102

Wahlberg, Mark, 125–126

Walcott, Joe "Jersey," 61, 66, 67, 85

Wallace, Coley, 54, 55

Walsh, Raoul, 46

Warner Brothers, 26

Warrior (O'Connor, 2011), 140

Washington, Denzel, 133

Washington, Jesse, 156–157

Weathers, Carl, 91

Weaver, Mike, 115

Wednesday Night Fights (TV show), 61, 64, 70

Welsh, Fredi, 43

Wepner, Chuck, 91

When We Were Kings (Gast, 1996), 130–131, 132

White, Chalky, 60

White, Dana, 138

White, J. Andrew, 21, 59

White, Michael Jai, 120, 139

White fighters, 5, 56, 125; boxing as path to success for White urban ethnics, 44, 51; Johnson's domination of, 13, 14–15; long shot, 6, 103; television and demand for, 64

White Hope narrative, 86, 95, 156, 157; Ali challengers, 88; Johnson challengers, 15, 16; Louis challengers, 36, 134; *Rocky* (1976) and, 100, 109; in *Southpaw* (2015), 147–150

White men, working-class, 97, 103, 104–105

Whiteness, 22, 51, 95, 107, 157

white supremacist attitudes/ideology, 14, 22, 122

Whittaker, Forrest, 149

Why We Can't Wait (King, 1964), 33

Why We Fight documentary series (Capra), 47

Wide World of Sports (ABC), 77, 78, 80, 88

Wiener, Frank, 62

Wilbur, George, 93

Willard, Jess ("the Pottawatomie Giant"), 17–20, 31, 46, 173n23

Williams, Cleveland, 80

Williams, Dootsie, 77, 79–80

Williams, Gladys, 41

Williams, Tony, 4

Williamson, Fred, 92

Wills, Harry, 22, 168n55

Wilson, Kristen, 120

Wilson, Woodrow, 18

Winfield, Paul, 120

Winkler, Charles, 134

Winkler, Irwin, 105

Winner Take All (Del Ruth, 1932), 25, 26, 30

Winning His Way (1924), 22

Wireless Age (journal), 21, 22

Wirtz, Arthur, 53

Wise, Robert, 52–53, 64, 71

women: in audience of boxing films, 12, 17, 19; films about women in boxing, 2, 135–138; Johnson's marriages to White women, 13, 17; reversal of "male gaze," 13;

TV coverage of women's sports, 64; as viewers of TV boxing, 63

Wood, Sam, 1

World Boxing Association, 116

World Boxing Historians Association, 84

World Boxing magazine, 84, 86

World Championship Boxing (HBO), 112, 113–115

World in My Corner (Hibbs, 1956), 68–69, 70, 71, 73, 93

World War I, 19, 47

World War II, 38, 46, 47, 48; Joe Louis's service in, 55; television broadcasting of boxing during, 59

Woroner, Murray, 82–85, 87, 88, 90, 174n37, 174n43

Woroner Productions, 4, 6, 76, 84

wrestling, 129

Wright, Michael, 155

Wynn, Ed, 72

Wynn, Keenan, 71

Young, Burt, 99

Young, John Sacret, 132

Young, Loretta, 28

Younger, Ben, 155

Young Man of Manhattan (1930), 25, 26

Zeffirelli, Franco, 102

Zieff, Howard, 102

Zouski, Steve, 116

About the Author

TRAVIS VOGAN is an associate professor in the School of Journalism and Mass Communication and the Department of American Studies at the University of Iowa. He is the author of *Keepers of the Flame: NFL Films and the Rise of Sports Media* (University of Illinois Press), *ESPN: The Making of a Sports Media Empire* (University of Illinois Press), and *ABC Sports: The Rise and Fall of Network Sports Television* (University of California Press).